FOREWORD

When I was asked to consider doing this project on British Leyland I wasn't sure I wanted to do it. My visions of BL at the time were I'm sure what most people would come up with – industrial unrest and some really poor quality vehicles. However, I did a bit of research and realised I'd fallen into the 'stereotype' trap.

This firm actually did make some very good products and at times was incredibly forward thinking. It must be said, however, that among the good ones some very bad vehicles were also made...

But what swung it for me was the fact that British Leyland played a part in so many people's lives in this country for so long – and I don't just mean those who worked there. I remember as a kid travelling to Skegness for my single day's holiday each year in my dad's Austin 1100 – and who cared that we had to stop and let it cool down half way there, it was all part of the adventure! When I left school I became a lorry mechanic and worked on various BL group lorries, particularly the T45 'Roadtrain'. In addition over the years I've owned loads of BL vehicles, as did my dad before me.

Writing this publication in such a small number of pages has been like trying to put an elephant into a carrier bag – there's bound to be loads left out. There is no way on earth it could ever include the complete histories of all the companies in the BL group and the products it made, but it will hopefully give you an idea of some of the firms and people involved, what they tried to achieve and perhaps give a few clues as to why it failed.

However, if you really want to read the complete history of British Leyland, its companies, people and products, I look forward to seeing your (very thick!) book in about 10 years' time. Good luck! ✦

Some of the British Leyland (and company predecessor/descendant) vehicles I've owned over the years.

CONTENTS

6 — LEYLAND MOTORS LTD
BLMC was formed in 1968 by the merger of Leyland Motors Ltd and British Motor Holdings. But what was its history?

14 — BRITISH MOTOR HOLDINGS
The other company that joined the Leyland Motor Corporation to form BL was British Motor Holdings.

22 — BRITISH LEYLAND
British Leyland came into being in 1968 and had high hopes for the future. However things just didn't turn out according to plan.

26 — THE RED TRIANGLE
BL company Alvis was once a well known car maker but moved on to manufacture military equipment.

30 — THE PRIDE OF LYONS
The luxury and sports tourer end of the BL car making empire was taken care of by an iconic make – Jaguar.

36 — TAXI!
Due to the creation of British Leyland the ubiquitous London black taxi, the FX4, now found itself being made by a massive multinational.

38 — VANDEN PLAS
For real luxury BL could call upon Vanden Plas, builder of cars for royalty.

40 — MOVING MOUNTAINS
Another product of the BL Group was construction, mining and road-making equipment, made by Aveling-Barford.

42 — THE BEST 4X4XFAR
Originally intended as a stop-gap vehicle the Land Rover went on to become a British motoring success story.

49 — FROM THE ARCHIVE
Here's how BL looked after your new car back in 1977.

50 — WOLSELEY
The Wolseley company may be said to be one of the founding fathers of the UK motor industry, in a round about sort of way.

54 — SHERPA
Often described as a 'parts bin special' the Leyland Sherpa van, and its successors, became good sellers for almost 40 years.

56 — TRIUMPH
Triumph was the first car maker purchased by Leyland Motors, which until then had concentrated on commercial vehicles.

64 — POWERING THE FUTURE
The formation of British Leyland wasn't just an amalgamation of two large vehicle manufacturers – there was far more to its products than that.

67 INNOVATIONS
The Dunlop Denovo run-flat tyre.

68 TILLING THE SOIL
BL produced tractors for several years, building on the work done by Nuffield.

72 ROVER'S ICON
The Rover V8 engine was conceived in America but became a British engineering success story.

76 OVERSEAS
As well as being a massive exporter of vehicles, BL also had overseas factories and licensed assemblers.

82 SCAMMELL
Scammell started in the early days of mechanised road haulage and became an international success.

86 A FEW ODDS AND ENDS
Here's a few things you may not have realised BL had anything to do with!

92 SAFETY FAST!
The MG marque became synonymous with the production of sports cars for the ordinary person – but what is its history?

98 FROM THE ARCHIVE
Here's a few pages showing the Leyland factory locations and some of the products made back in 1968.

104 LEYLAND NATIONAL
The Leyland National bus was designed in conjunction with a large bus user – a recipe for success you would think.

106 RILEY MOTORS LTD
Riley started in the 1890s and became one of the first marques to completely disappear under BL ownership.

108 FROM THE ARCHIVE
Here's what you would have paid for your new Leyland car back in 1978.

110 THE ASSOCIATED EQUIPMENT COMPANY
AEC was once one of, if not the, biggest competitor to Leyland Motors. So how did it come to be owned by its deadly rival?

116 SURE AS THE SUNRISE
One of the first companies to be taken over by Leyland Motors was the Scottish Albion concern.

120 ROVER
Rover became a minor part of Leyland Motors in 1967 but the name would eventually take the place of the British Leyland brand.

126 MINI
The Mini was a revolutionary design that changed small car design forever.

129 END OF EMPIRE
A quick look at the end of this once mighty industrial giant.

Author
Stephen Pullen

Design
Charlotte Pearson
Justin Blackamore
Anita Waters

Reprographics
Jonathan Schofield

Publisher
Steve O'Hara

Marketing manager:
Charlotte Park

Publishing director:
Dan Savage

Commercial director
Nigel Hole

Published by
Mortons Media Group Ltd,
Media Centre, Morton Way,
Horncastle, Lincs LN9 6JR
Tel: 01507 529529

ISBN
978-1-911703-68-6

© Mortons Media Group Ltd. All rights reserved. No part of this publication may be reproduced or transmitted in any form or by any means, electronic or mechanical, including photocopying, recording, or any information storage retrieval system without prior permission in writing from the publisher.

LEYLAND MOTORS LTD

The British Leyland Motor Corporation was formed in 1968 by the merger of Leyland Motors Ltd and British Motor Holdings. But what was the history of these two companies?

Leyland Motors could trace its roots back to 1896 when James Sumner and Henry Spurrier set up the Lancashire Steam Motor Company in a village just south of Preston. Initially the business made steam-powered lawn mowers but soon switched to the production of steam wagons, with its first being a 30cwt vehicle fitted with a 10-14hp two-cylinder compound engine and oil-fired boiler.

The business did well and soon several members of the Spurrier family became directors of the firm. Such was the demand for vehicles that by 1902 the business embarked on a large factory expansion plan. Even at this time exports were starting to play a part in sales, with the company's first overseas sale being a steam-powered mail van which went to Ceylon in 1901.

In 1904 the firm started experimenting with petrol engines and a year later managed to sell some petrol-powered buses for use in London.

In 1907 the company decided to change its name to Leyland Motors. This coincided with the takeover of rival steam wagon manufacturer Coulthard's of Preston. A new range of petrol lorries was also introduced, the 35hp 'X' and 50hp 'U' types.

The following year saw more expansion with the opening of a London office and a depot in Liverpool. In 1910 there was even more success with Leyland winning a large order to supply mail vans to the Post Office and the firm also produced its first fire engine, which went to the Dublin Fire Brigade. Petrol-electric railcars were another notable export order for that year, while trams were among vehicles sold on the home market.

By 1912 there was considerable military sales potential when two Leyland designs were the only vehicles to be awarded a Certificate of Success in the War Office Trials. Thus started production of the three-ton 'RAF' type lorry, which as we'll see was to become a very important vehicle for the firm.

The 'RAF' Type lorry was very popular with the Royal Flying Corps, Royal Naval Air Service and Royal Air Force. Here we see one together with a Bristol BE2 fighter. *Photo Richard Pullen Collection.*

A Leyland steam bus from 1900. *Photo National Motor Museum.*

At the outset of the First World War in 1914 Leyland had so far produced 1275 petrol and 415 steam vehicles, had 1,500 employees and its net profits were over £100,000. However, wartime was to be a period of even greater success.

INTO BATTLE

The First World War proved very lucrative for Leyland Motors (1914) Ltd as it was now named, mainly due to the 'RAF' type lorry. This had been designed as a 'subsidy scheme' vehicle, which appeared in 1912 and was built to a standard specification laid down by the War Office. These lorries were then sold to civilian users with a grant from the government to help with the purchase. This grant was paid only if the purchaser agreed to hand the vehicle over to the military should a war break out. Unfortunately the scheme was not that popular and only some 200 or so lorries were available for call-up at the start of the war.

The Leyland RAF type used a 34hp four-cylinder petrol engine and was built for military use in a variety of guises including mobile workshops. These were very popular with the Royal Flying Corps and Royal Naval Air Service, who in 1918 amalgamated to form the Royal Air Force. In fact they were so popular with these branches of the services that the majority of the 5,932 vehicles produced by Leyland during the war were used by them.

At the height of the war Leyland employed more than 3,000 people. In addition it had to open several new factories, including a steelworks.

However, as the conflict came to a close, Leyland's board considered what direction to take the company…and decided the future lay with luxury cars.

THE WORLD'S FINEST CAR

In 1917 Leyland charged its chief designer, J G Parry-Thomas, to come up with a car that would rival the one regarded as the best in the world at the time – the Rolls-Royce Silver Ghost.

Parry-Thomas was ably assisted by Reid Railton in the design of this luxury car, which was christened the Leyland Eight. It was launched at the 1920 Olympia Motor Show where it was hailed as 'The Lion of Olympia'. The car used a 6,967cc single overhead-cam, straight-eight engine (which was later enlarged to 7,266cc), which developed 90bhp, or 145bhp if using twin-carbs. It drove through a four-speed gearbox and was fitted with vacuum servo-assisted brakes, which like the Silver Ghost of the day were fitted to the rear wheels only.

The Eight could be bought as either an open two or four seater or just as a chassis for coachbuilt bodies. Two different wheelbase lengths were available of 126 or 150 inches. However, the car was not cheap – £2,500 for the rolling chassis made it the most expensive British car on the market at the time. Efforts were made to increase sales by reducing the price, which dropped to £1,825 in 1922. However, buyers were few and far between and production ceased in 1923 after just 18 cars had been made. It would appear that one of the main reasons for the lack of sales was Leyland was first and foremost known as a builder of commercial vehicles and this did not fit in well with the upper-class market it was aiming for.

As an aside, Parry-Thomas and Reid Railton went on to become very famous in the world of motor racing and record-breaking. Thomas actually made three racing cars based on the Leyland Eight, although it is not known if these were counted in the production total of 18 or not. ❯

As well as racing, Parry-Thomas also contested the World Land Speed Record and in 1924 successfully took the record in a Leyland Eight special by recording a speed of 129.73mph in June 1924. He later obtained the Brooklands racing car 'The Higham Special' (also known as 'Chitty 4') from the estate of the late Count Louis Zborowski. This was fitted with a 450hp, V12 Liberty aircraft engine of 27 litre capacity. The car was renamed 'Babs' and rebuilt for an attempt on the land speed record using different carbs and pistons. In April 1926 Parry-Thomas, who was born in Wales, decided to go for the record at Pendine Sands in Carmarthenshire, and succeeded in taking it to just over 170mph. This record was later broken by Malcolm Campbell and in 1927, while trying to reclaim it, Thomas driving Babs suffered a fatal accident. Parry-Thomas was laid to rest near Brooklands in Surrey, while 'Babs' was buried on Pendine Sands.

Reid Railton went on to great success in vehicle design. He was responsible for John Cobb's Napier-Railton which took the Brooklands outer circuit record in 1933, and also the design of the chassis of Malcolm Campbell's 'Bluebird' cars from 1931 until 1935. After the war he designed the 'Railton Mobil Special' which was used by John Cobb to set the Land Speed Record at 394.7 mph in 1947. He also worked for racing car maker ERA and designed Cobb's World Water Speed Record boat 'Crusader'.

BUSINESS PROBLEMS

In 1918 Henry Spurrier's son, also called Henry, was appointed company chairman and it was decided that Leyland should recruit some London-based board members in order to increase prestige and investment potential. To this end two 'City' figures were invited onto the board – and this may not have been a good idea. The first was Gerard Bevan who was chairman of the City Equitable Fire Insurance Group and the second was investor Clarence Hatry. To say that this was an unwise choice is perhaps putting it lightly – Bevan was bankrupt by 1922 while Hatry was imprisoned in 1930 for fraud and is 'credited' as one of the main contributors to the Wall Street Crash. However, that was all in the future – but it didn't stop them from damaging Leyland.

At the time the Treasury had to agree to new share issues and it was decided that Leyland Motors (1914) Ltd needed to raise £1 million in extra share capital. In order to do this without having to get the Treasury's sanction, Hatry suggested that the company should change its name to just Leyland Motors Ltd. This idea was accepted in principle but was postponed as Leyland was at the time considering merging with Daimler. These talks failed but in the meantime the government decided that Treasury consent was no longer required for share issues.

Despite this change of law Leyland went ahead with its name change and soon wished it hadn't. During the war the government had become aware that a lot of companies were profiting 'excessively' from producing

Top left: A Leyland 'RAF' Type tanker. *Photo Richard Pullen Collection.*

Top centre: The Leyland Eight was meant to rival the Rolls-Royce Silver Ghost. Only 18 were ever made. *Photo National Motor Museum.*

Top right: Sir Henry Spurrier (III). *Photo National Motor Museum.*

Opposite: J G Parry-Thomas pictured at the wheel of a Leyland Eight racing special. *Photo National Motor Museum.*

military vehicles and weapons. Therefore it increased the tax liability for these firms. However, after the war it was realised that this action could effectively destroy companies that were useful to the country and so it was decided to refund some of the tax to the chosen firms – and Leyland was very much in line for a refund. However, the change of name meant that as far as the government was concerned Leyland Motors Ltd was a totally different firm, and so no refund was due. This could have amounted to several hundred thousand pounds of badly needed capital.

The other decision made at the end of the war concerned the lorries supplied to the war effort over the previous few years. The board correctly assumed that these vehicles would be released from military service and sold onto the civilian market – and board members were afraid that worn-out and damaged ex-military Leylands flooding onto the market would ruin the firm's reputation for quality. With this in mind it started to repurchase the old 'RAF' type lorries and refurbish them before selling the vehicles to civilian customers.

To this end more than £400,000 was spent on a depot full of vehicles at St Omer in Northern France – and this was just one of its purchases.

However, the post-war slump of the early 1920s hit the firm hard. In 1922 Leyland was pleased if it could get £300 for a refurbished lorry, which could be less than half the price paid for the vehicle straight from the military, and by the following year its deficit was almost £1 million.

By now the company's bank was worried, as Leyland shares – which had cost 70 shillings each in 1918 – had dropped to just two shillings. And so things had to change quickly. Bevan had already been made bankrupt and Hatry was fired. Chairman Henry Spurrier also departed, to be replaced by shareholder John Toulmin.

During this period very few Leyland vehicles were actually made, and the money came in from selling reconditioned ex military lorries and also assembling the Trojan range of cars and vans. These were very basic vehicles, still using solid tyres, and Leyland paid a £5 royalty on every vehicle produced.

Leyland didn't actually turn a profit until 1924, and didn't pay off its deficit until 1928. The turnaround was helped by the 1925 introduction of specific designs for buses, which were not just modified lorries. These bus designs included the Lion, Lioness and Leviathan, and by the end of 1928 around 8,500 had been produced.

ONWARDS AND UPWARDS

In the summer of 1929 a merger between the Associated Equipment Company (AEC) and Leyland was considered. This was proposed by Lord Ashfield, who was the chairman of the Underground Railways Company which owned AEC. This proposed merged firm would be called British Vehicles, and Leyland was very interested as it would allow it to break into the London bus market, which by now had almost become solely AEC territory.

However, this idea came to nothing as Leyland considered the price too high. In 1931 however, the idea re-emerged – but this time the plan was for Leyland to buy AEC, which would guarantee the firm to be able to supply 90% of London's buses for the next 10 years at a price of cost plus 10%. However, talks broke down and were later abandoned. ›

Not that the failure of the talks were a problem for Leyland, as both production and profits for the next few years rose steadily, with the net profit in 1937 being over £613,000. Exports were also excellent with 20% of Leyland vehicles recorded as going for export in 1939.

A lot of this was due to the introduction of diesel engines by Leyland. The company had started experimenting with these engines in 1925 but it would be 1933 before the first appeared for sale. Within 12 months a diesel engine was available as an option on the entire Leyland range. Another 1930s success was the manufacture of fire appliances which were fitted with German made Metz turntable ladders.

The late 1920s also brought another addition to Leyland's history, but this wasn't anything to do with engineering. This was the start of what many call the Leyland 'Zoo' or 'Menagerie', when vehicles started to be named after animals – such as the Lion bus previously mentioned.

> THESE WAR MATERIALS INCLUDED ENGINES FOR THE MATILDA TANK, AND OVER 11 MILLION HIGH EXPLOSIVE AND INCENDIARY BOMBS.

THE SECOND WORLD WAR

At the start of the conflict commercial vehicle production continued but Leyland was soon ordered by the government to just go over to the production of war materials. This decision also meant opening a new factory at Farington. These war materials included engines for the Matilda tank, and over 11 million high explosive and incendiary bombs.

It also made the Covenanter tank – a cruiser tank named after a Scottish religious group from the period of the 17th century known as The Wars of the Three Kingdoms. It used a Meadows flat-12 engine that produced 340hp and had a top speed of around 30mph. However, the engine was fitted at the back of the vehicle and it was so wide the radiators had to be placed at the front, and this resulted in cooling problems. In addition the tank was soon declared to be too lightly armoured and gunned for use against German tanks and so they ended up being used as training vehicles, mine clearance tanks, mobile observation posts or as bridge-layers.

One interesting point to mention about Leyland's war contracts was actually the businesslike approach the firm took to them. Firstly it decided not to join with other companies to share out war-work between them, and insisted that it bid for all the contracts it was offered. Secondly it never accepted a 'cost plus fixed profit' price for work as the firm believed it might lead to poor quality from the workers.

POSTWAR PEACE

It would not be until the end of 1945 that Leyland was once again allowed to start civilian commercial vehicle production, and this was for double-decker bus chassis, as there was now a severe shortage throughout the country.

That year also saw an interesting business proposition emerge when it was proposed that Leyland, Albion, AEC, Dennis and Thornycroft should merge to produce one massive commercial vehicle maker. However, the idea was turned down by Leyland's board, whose members said it was against monopolies and in favour of competitive enterprise. It must be added that Leyland had unsuccessfully tried to take over Albion, AEC and

Above: A 1912 Leyland four ton lorry. *Photo National Motor Museum.*

Right: 1938 Leyland Cub fitted with a livestock body. *Photo Alan Barnes.*

Dennis in the past. Leyland and AEC did manage to come up with a different deal and formed British United Traction in 1946 to manufacture trolleybuses.

By now company founder Henry Spurrier's grandson, also confusingly called Henry, was general manager of Leyland, and towards the end of the war he asked one of the firm's employees Donald Stokes to write a report on what he thought should be Leyland's export strategy after the war.

This was the best news ever for the young Stokes and would change Leyland's future for ever.

Stokes' report suggested that the firm should first concentrate on the 'sterling area', and also those countries that had large sterling reserves such as Holland, Spain and France plus several Scandinavian countries. However, he also suggested that these would just be temporary markets, and that long term the best solution would be to go for sales in South America and the Middle East.

By 1946 Stokes was head of the new export department and he soon put his ideas into effect. These included the plan not to target industrialised countries as he knew that the competition would be harsh. This meant America and most of Europe were ignored and the major push would be into Empire and Commonwealth countries. Despite this decision, as Leyland grew, it did start exporting to some European countries such as Spain, but refused to try in Italy, France and Germany.

Under Stokes' leadership export orders were soon piling in. 250 buses went to Sweden, while another 620 were shipped to Cuba. By 1957 almost 15% of the entire Leyland business was being done with Africa. By 1957 Henry Spurrier (grandson of the founder) was also made chairman of the company.

As export orders flooded in, profits rose dramatically and reached £1 million in 1954. It was no surprise to find that Stokes was elected to the board in 1953.

EMPIRE BUILDING

In 1951 Leyland succeeded in acquiring the Scottish commercial vehicle builder Albion and in 1955 the Watford-based lorry maker Scammell was also taken over. Unfortunately Leyland then found itself in a price war with its main competitor, Associated Commercial Vehicles. This company had been founded when AEC took over two other goods vehicle makers, Crossley and Maudslay. Despite this Leyland was by now reporting profits in excess of £2 million per year. ›

Above: 1935 Leyland Hippo. *Photo Alan Barnes.*

Below: 1948 Leyland Beaver. *Photo Alan Barnes.*

ACV at this time was considered by many to be very badly run and organised. In addition AEC's monopoly of London buses had stifled innovation and therefore its exports were very small compared to Leyland. There seems to have been very little profit in its main market of London's buses at the time either.

In 1957 William 'Bill' Black was made managing director of ACV and he knew the firm was in trouble. In the previous financial year there had been a £1.3 million drop in income. In addition Crossley was losing money and many of the orders that it had accepted were actually costing far more to make than it was being paid.

To help this dire financial situation Crossley was shut down completely in 1958. Maudslay was also told to stop making its own vehicles around this time. In addition changes to ACV's pricing structure soon improved export sales, particularly in Africa.

In 1960 Leyland started thinking about expanding into car production and approached Standard Triumph. Initially this was said to be just an idea for the two firms to cooperate in certain export markets but Spurrier soon thought that buying Standard-Triumph would be a good idea. As for Standard-Triumph, the company was actually desperate to sell, as its financial situation was poor to say the least. Therefore later that year Leyland succeeded in purchasing its first car maker.

The Leyland takeover of Standard-Triumph temporarily diverted the board's attention away from its core business of commercial vehicle production and during this time BMC approached Associated Commercial Vehicles with a view to its purchase. There is no doubt that ACV knew that it would eventually be taken over, and the company really didn't want it to be by Leyland. BMC had a reputation for not interfering excessively with companies it purchased and so it seemed the best course of action. However, the deal, and another proposed three-way merger with luxury car maker Rolls-Royce, failed to come to anything.

Unsurprisingly Leyland then approached ACV with a view to merge the companies on a share exchange basis.

Right: 1952 Leyland Royal Tiger. *Photo Alan Barnes.*

Below: 1957 Leyland Comet. *Photo Alan Barnes.*

Opposite: 1964 Leyland PD3. *Photo Alan Barnes.*

It was pointed out that a merger would be good for both firms as they were so busy undercutting each other in various markets that it was helping neither of them. ACV really wasn't keen but soon had its hand forced. This happened because unexpectedly the American Chrysler company approached Leyland and offered to buy part of the firm. Spurrier didn't like the idea of foreign ownership but decided to look into it nonetheless.

Meanwhile, ACV became aware that an overseas company was in talks with Leyland and could see its chance of a deal with Leyland slipping away. And so, when Leyland offered a merger on a one-for-one share exchange, ACV reluctantly agreed. In 1962 ACV became part of Leyland, at a cost of £25 million.

A new company Leyland Motors (1962) Ltd was formed to take over the running of the company until the Leyland Motor Corporation could be formed. William Black, former managing director of ACV, was made chairman and Donald Stokes appointed deputy and managing director. This was due to the fact that Spurrier had become seriously ill.

Over the next few years the company went from strength to strength and profits shot up – in fact the only problem was being able to keep up with demand.

However, by 1966 things were starting to change. Although sales were continuing to rise profits were down and overheads rising. The main problem was that the management team had not grown at the same rate as the rest of the business so key people were spreading themselves too thin. In addition there were several engineering problems that raised warranty costs, such as the new Ergomatic lorry cab which was causing serious engine overheating on some models. In addition recent government tax increases on motoring had hit Triumph sales hard.

New people were appointed and several areas of the business were reorganised. Despite these changes 1967 also proved to be a difficult year for Leyland. However, the Leyland board was keen on growing the company as it did not want to lag behind the competitors. To this end it was decided a good buy would be Rover, with the main attraction being the Land Rover.

Rover too was thinking about what direction the firm should take. Its body maker, Pressed Steel, had recently been purchased by BMC and its range of vehicles (including Alvis) was at the fairly expensive end of the market. Developing a new car would cost more money than the company had, so taking this into consideration it is hardly surprising that when Leyland approached Rover the deal progressed very smoothly and Rover became part of Leyland in 1967.

Shortly afterwards came a very strange request from Labour MP and Minister of Technology Anthony Wedgwood Benn. He wanted to know if Leyland was prepared to be part of a scheme to help the Rootes Group, which consisted of Humber, Hillman, Sunbeam and Singer cars, together with Dodge and Commer lorries. The problem was that Rootes was in serious financial trouble and was about to be bought by Chrysler, thus making it an American firm – something the government did not want. It must be said, however, that many of Rootes' financial problems could be said to have stemmed from the government's recent policies...

The idea was looked at and a suggestion was made that BMC should be involved. It would then look after the Rootes car business and Leyland could run the commercial vehicle side. In the end the plan came to nothing and Rootes became American.

However, these discussions did resurrect an old idea – of Leyland and BMC at least working together. In the past it hadn't happened, but that's not to say it wouldn't in the future... ✦

BRITISH MOTOR HOLDINGS LTD

The other company that joined the Leyland Motor Corporation to form British Leyland was British Motor Holdings, owner of some of the best known car makers in the UK.

As the name suggests BMH was made up from several different companies, but the two major firms were the Austin and Morris Motor Companies.

Of these firms the Austin Motor Company Ltd was the oldest, having been set up in 1905 at Longbridge, Birmingham by Herbert Austin. He had previously worked for Wolseley and had left over a strange disagreement regarding engine design (see separate chapter).

The first Austin car was the chain-driven 24/30 which had a 5182cc four-cylinder 'T' head engine. This car was made until 1907 when the shaft-drive 18/24 appeared. Shortly afterwards two other models joined the range, one of 40hp while the other had 60hp.

In 1908 Austin entered motorsport when three 100hp 9657cc six-cylinder cars took part in that year's Grand Prix. Unfortunately only two finished, in 18th and 19th positions.

In the period between 1908 and the outbreak of the First World War Austin's firm grew quickly. This was due to not only producing in-house designs but also manufacturing other firm's vehicles, such as the 7hp single-cylinder car introduced in 1910 which was sold as an Austin but was in fact a Swift, and also making French Gladiator cars for the British market. Due to all this work production rose from around 200 vehicles in 1910 to approximately 1100 in 1912.

If the period up to the war was a good one for the firm, it was nothing compared to what would happen during the conflict. The company took on all kinds of war contracts including shells, artillery, lorries and aircraft. The factory was extended and the workforce grew from 2638 to around 22,000!

Herbert Austin received a Knighthood in 1917 for his contribution to the war effort and by the end of the war he had become a very wealthy man. However, on a personal note, none of this could make up for the fact that his only son Vernon, had been killed in January 1915 while serving with the Royal Field Artillery on the Western Front.

With the war over in 1918 Herbert Austin decided that a one-model policy would be best for the business and so selected a modified version of his Twenty car engine from 1914. This had its capacity raised from 3168cc to 3620cc and would form the basis of all the cars, commercials and tractors he planned to make.

Unfortunately the market didn't really take to the new Austins and in 1921 the firm went into receivership. However, the company's two major creditors, Midland Bank and Eagle Star Insurance, restructured the firm and put in new management. Austin was very unhappy about this and even tried to sell the firm to General Motors of America. However, when that fell through the restructured company was handed back to Austin.

In order to improve matters a new car was launched in 1922, the 1661cc Twelve. Unlike the Twenty this proved extremely popular due to its reliability and low price. It was in such demand that it was made until 1934.

The Austin Longbridge factory pictured in 1913. *Photo National Motor Museum.*

Herbert Austin, 1st Baron Austin KBE. *Photo National Motor Museum.*

However, if there is one car that can be said to have saved Austin in was the Seven. This was designed by Herbert Austin himself together with a draughtsman, Stanley Edge. This car was designed as a cheap small car able to be afforded by first time buyers. At first Austin thought of using a twin-cylinder engine but Edge argued that a four-cylinder unit would be smoother and far outclass the cyclecars that were on sale at the time.

The Seven was launched in July 1922 and was an instant success, virtually clearing the cyclecars off the roads at a stroke. Initially the Seven used a 696cc engine but that was increased in 1923 to 747cc.

The car remained in production for 17 years and was constantly improved including gaining an electric starter in 1924 and a four-speed gearbox in 1933. There were also a vast array of bodies on offer from both Austin and outside coachbuilders including two and four-seat tourers, saloons and even vans. Sevens were also raced and many were fitted with superchargers. In addition they were also built under licence abroad by BMW in Germany (as the Dixi), Rosengart in France and even in America where the vehicles were sold as the American Austin.

Altogether 375,000 Sevens were produced by Austin before production stopped in 1939.

Despite all this success it is interesting to go back to 1924 when Austin actually suggested a merger between Austin, Morris and his old firm, Wolseley. William Morris rejected the plan and to rub salt into the wounds made it his business to see that it was he who purchased Wolseley. This started the antagonism between the men of Austin and Morris that was to last for many years.

Throughout the 1930s Austin brought out all manner of new vehicles with the most popular being the Ten/Four which was introduced in 1932. This used a 1125cc engine giving 21bhp and could be specified with one of several bodies including a four-door saloon and later as a roadster or tourer. During the 1930s Austin also started naming the bodies after English towns such as the Cambridge saloon and Ripley sports tourer. The Ten/Four was actually made until 1947.

However, not everything was going well, and Herbert Austin himself was one of the main problems. By 1939 he was 73 years old and had really lost touch with modern car design, but still insisted on being involved. For example he would never let a windscreen be more than seven degrees from the vertical as he thought anything more would hurt the driver's eyes. This sort of thing had seen the firm's share of the British car market slump from 37% in 1929 to 22% in 1938. ›

> **THE CAR WAS LAUNCHED AS THE MINOR IN 1948 AND WAS AN INSTANT SUCCESS – EXCEPT WITH LORD NUFFIELD WHO HATED IT AND SAID IT LOOKED LIKE A POACHED EGG!**

In addition the feud between Morris and Austin was not helped by the 'defection' of one Leonard Lord to Austin in 1938. He had been the Managing Director of Morris for six years and as you'll see had totally turned the firm round. However an argument with William Morris saw him move to Longbridge.

Ever since the death of his son in 1915 Herbert Austin had been looking for somebody he could trust to direct his company and decided Lord would be the man, and so he was elected to the board.

Herbert Austin, by then Baron Austin KBE, died in 1941 and was immediately succeeded as chairman of the company by Earnest Payton, who had been his deputy. When Payton died in 1946 Lord took his place.

WAR PRODUCTION

Austin Motors were one of the fortunate few who actually continued vehicle production throughout the Second World War. These included cars and lorries for the military, although the company also made aircraft including Avro Lancaster bombers.

The firm actually announced its postwar range of cars, including a new 16hp overhead valve model, in 1944 and production started as soon as the conflict was over. This quick start back into car production really annoyed the men from Morris, who hadn't made cars during the war so had to restructure the factories.

As Austin production got underway in 1945 the government launched its 'export or die' phase. Basically the country was in severe financial straights and earning foreign currency was the way out. Steel was in extremely short supply at the time and so was rationed, with the lion's share going to those firms who could export. Fortunately for Austin its cars were popular abroad, particularly the new Sixteen, and so of the entire 5394 cars exported from Britain from June to December 1945, 3197 were Austins.

Morris made motorcycles from 1902 until 1905. This shows his 2.75hp De Dion engined machine. *Photo Mortons Media Archive.*

Opposite top: An Austin Seven Chummy of 1928. *Photo National Motor Museum.*

Opposite: William Morris, Lord Nuffield. *Photo National Motor Museum.*

Below: The Morris paintshop pictured in 1925. *Photo National Motor Museum.*

The Sixteen was dropped in 1949 although its petrol engine survived for many years in Austin's FX3 & FX4 taxis (see separate chapter).

Next came the Princess (see separate chapter) and Sheerline luxury cars, which both used the 3993cc ohc six-cylinder engine.

In 1947 the popular 1200cc A40 appeared, which was available as the two-door 'Dorset' or four-door 'Devon'. These also became big export sellers, even to America. Due to this, Austin became so keen to increase sales in the US that in 1948 the firm used the Earls Court Motor Show to launch the A90 Atlantic. This could be bought as either a two-door coupe or convertible and was styled to appeal to the American buyer. However the car was a flop in the States and only 350 were sold. Despite its decent performance (92mph top speed) the Americans simply preferred the V8 engines to the Austin 2660cc four.

In 1951 Austin launched the A30, a new integral-bodied small car fitted with an 803cc engine. However, things were about to change for the Austin company in a big way.

MORRIS

Unlike Herbert Austin, William Morris had not worked for a car maker before designing his own. He was born in 1877 in Worcester but the family soon moved to Oxfordshire where they lived for a while on his grandfather's farm. He left school at the age of 14 and took an apprenticeship with a bicycle repairer. However, Will Morris, as he was known, was an ambitious sort of chap and he soon scraped together the sum of £4, around £240 in today's money, in order to set up his own repair business. This business was run from the shed at the back of his parents' home and did very well. Soon he was actually also building bikes to order as well as doing repairs and he set up a 'showroom' in his parents' front room. He also started racing bicycles and won several local races.

The first Morris bicycle was sold in 1892 and by 1901 he had moved to large premises on Oxford High Street. That year he also assembled a prototype motorcycle but a proposed partnership with one John Cooper fell through and production was put back. However, the first Morris motorcycle appeared the following year and production lasted for three years.

By then Morris had obtained financial support from an investor called Launcelot Creyke and set up the Oxford Automobile & Cycle Agency. Here he expanded his premises into Oxford's Longwall Street and entered the motor trade as an agent for several car and motorcycle makes. However the arrangement didn't last long, as due to Creyke's alleged extravagance the firm was placed in liquidation. Morris decided never to share control of his business again.

By 1910, with Morris in sole control, the firm had stopped repairing bicycles and gone completely over to the motor vehicle. His firm then became WRM Motors Ltd in 1913 and he registered the name Morris Garages the same year.

The reason for the change of name was that in 1912 Morris had designed his first car, the Oxford. This two-seater only existed on paper at the time but a London car dealer called Gordon Stewart was impressed enough to place an order for 400 cars, after driving the prototype first of course. Stewart's deposit allowed Morris to set up a factory in Cowley in a derelict school/military academy.

Production started in 1913 and by the end of the year 393 Oxford's had been produced.

The same year Morris showed his entrepreneurial flair by purchasing six Daimler double-deckers and starting the first motorbus service in Oxford. The council favoured horse-drawn vehicles and tried to stop Morris but because he sold the tickets from shops along the bus routes and not from the vehicles he got around the law. In the end the council gave in and started operating motorbuses themselves, and even bought the ones owned by Morris.

The Oxford car followed a similar pattern to the Morris bicycles produced before – just assemble other people's components. However, the Oxford had used components from just British manufacturers but his next car, the Cowley, would use parts from around the world. These included Continental engines from America. Gearboxes, steering components and axles were also sourced from the States. The reason for this was cost. For example a 1496cc Continental engine cost around £18 while a British White & Poppe of 1018cc cost almost £50. ›

Despite this good business sense the timing could have been better, as the First World War broke out before the negotiations with the US suppliers had been completed. However, Morris didn't cancel his orders and despite his factory also taking on war contracts, such as the production of trench mortars, hand grenades and mine sinkers, Morris launched the Cowley in 1915. The car was made until 1918, but numbers were limited due to the amount of war work Morris took on and also the sinking of British and, three years after war started, American merchant ships bringing the engines to Britain. In fact around half the engines Morris ordered went to the bottom of the Atlantic.

William Morris received the OBE in 1918 for his war work, but more importantly the war had also shown him the principles of mass production. It also made him very wealthy and so he set about expanding and modernising production. The firm was also renamed as Morris Motors Ltd.

This restructuring was quite fortunate as Continental had decided to cease production of the engine Morris needed. In addition new import duties increased the cost of materials from America so it was time for a change.

In the end the British arm of the French Hotchkiss company agreed to make a licenced copy of the Continental engine, so production of the Cowley could continue.

Morris went on a bit of a buying spree at this point and purchased several companies including the vehicle body builders Holland & Pratt, Osberton Radiators and in 1923, the British side of Hotchkiss, who had been making car engines for him for four years.

In buying Hotchkiss, Morris also gained a key member of staff who would go on to play a big part in the future of not just Morris Motors, but also Austin and ultimately BMC, Leonard Lord.

Lord was an engineer who had started out as a draughtsman at Courtaulds before moving to Vickers. During the First World War he worked at the Coventry Ordnance Factory and had been at Hotchkiss since 1920. He hadn't been there long when the order was received to make the Continental engines for Morris. However he realised that the French Hotchkiss machinery would have to be modified, as it cut metric threads and the Continental used imperial. Lord suggested it would be quicker and cheaper to cut the threads in metric but put Whitworth heads on the bolts to fit British spanners.

Upon purchasing Hotchkiss, which became the Morris Motors Engine Branch, Lord moved to Cowley and became a manager at the age of 27. One year later Morris purchased the car components maker EG Wrigley & Co of Birmingham and reorganised the works to set up Morris Commercial Cars Ltd, in order to make commercial vehicles. The assistant managing director of Wrigley's, Frank Woollard, was kept on and moved to Morris Motors Engine Branch in order to modernise production. He recognised Lord's potential and when Morris purchased Wolseley in 1927 Lord was sent over to reorganise and modernise the factory.

He did such a good job that in 1932 Lord found himself back at Cowley as Managing Director. From 1932 until 1936 Lord totally reorganised the Cowley plant including the introduction of 'flow line' production.

However the run up to 1936 things had not always been going well at Morris. Morris himself, who became Lord Nuffield in 1934, seemed to lose interest in his firm as it got larger. From the late 1920s he stopped attending the weekly board meetings and often spent three or more

1924 Morris 'Bullnose' Cowley. *Photo National Motor Museum.*

1957 Austin 701 FE lorry. *Photo Gyles Carpenter.*

months away on holiday each year. Despite all this he would often return and reject car designs and over-rule business plans, particularly for modernisation, for no real good reason. In addition he hated anybody from his firm who he thought was stealing his limelight.

In the early/mid 1920s the Cowley had been a very popular car, and had helped Morris to take 41% of the British car market by 1925. Other cars had followed and been successful, particularly the Minor that was launched in 1928 to compete with the Austin Seven. This was mechanically more advanced than the Seven as it had an 847cc engine with an overhead camshaft. Initially it could be bought as a tourer for £125 or a saloon for £135. However, in 1931 in the aftermath of the Wall Street Crash Morris offered an economy version of the Minor with a side valve engine for just £100. However this did not sell well at all as it was incredibly basic.

In should come as no surprise then, when you add up

Here's your new...
AUSTIN 1100
SALOON AND COUNTRYMAN

all the above problems, to find that the share of the UK market taken by Morris in 1933 had dropped to just 27%.

By then of course Lord was in charge and things soon started to improve. In 1933 he commissioned the Morris Eight which replaced the Minor the following year and became an excellent seller. Other new vehicles were also offered and by 1935 the Morris share of the market had risen to 33%. This increase in sales combined with the lower costs caused by Lord's new production methods meant profits improved dramatically.

Things continued to improve and in 1938 Lord asked Nuffield for a larger share of the profits. This caused a vicious argument. Both men had short tempers and things got out of hand which resulted in Lord resigning and joining Austin.

Before moving on I must add something about William Morris, as the above does make him appear to be some sort of ruthless dictator. Perhaps in business he was at times, but outside the company he was actually a philanthropist. For example he donated large sums of money to hospitals all over the country and also to Oxford University. In 1943 he founded the Nuffield Foundation for the advancement of education and social welfare. Altogether it is estimated that he gave around £30 million to good causes during his lifetime.

In 1939 Morris Motors launched the Series 'E' version of the Eight. This had a 'waterfall' grille, a 918cc engine and fared-in headlights. However, it was to be the last new Morris car for a while due to the Second World War.

The previous year the firm had taken on a 'shadow factory' at Castle Bromwich to built Supermarine Spitfires. Throughout the war the firm also repaired damaged aircraft and churned out thousands of jerry cans. Morris also made the C8 Field Artillery Tractor, better known as the 'Quad'. This was built at the Morris-Commercial plant and was a four-wheel-drive 3.3ton vehicle designed to tow field guns. ›

Below: Over three million Morris Minors were made from 1948 until 1971. This example dates from 1957. *Photo National Motor Museum.*

Modern cars need modern brakes! The full hydraulic system on the footbrake includes 8 in. (0·20 m.) diameter front discs. Safety spot for dead-in-line *stopping* is a pressure limiting valve introduced in the line between the master cylinder and the rear brakes to direct a correct balance of braking effort between front and rear wheels, reducing the possibility of wheels locking under extreme pedal pressure.

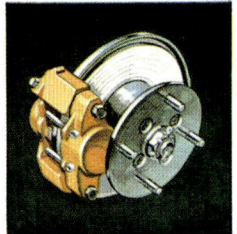

From your very first glimpse of the Austin 1100 there will be a lasting impression of British designing ingenuity and constructional craftsmanship at its sparkling best. Its clean, functional lines are styled to please and yet are completely unostentatious. Because of this, it can be cleaned—and kept clean—in minutes with very little effort. The advanced engineering features you will find beneath its compact exterior are numerous—like the 'Hydrolastic' suspension system which irons out the road to velvet smoothness. Only by trying the Austin 1100 will you be convinced of the amazing contribution this system has made to the general handling and the fascinatingly level riding qualities you would only expect to find in much larger luxury limousines.

'Hydrolastic' suspension... for perfect road adhesion

The most advanced system of its time, 'Hydrolastic' suspension employs inter-coupled units, front to rear, which automatically control fluid displacement, giving a sensationally smooth, controlled ride. It does away with metal springs and shock absorbers, its anti-rust, anti-freeze fluid is sealed in for the life of the car and because it has no moving parts, no glands to leak or wear, it is absolutely maintenance free.

'Hydrolastic' is a registered Trade Mark.

AUTOMATIC TRANSMISSION NOW AVAILABLE !

Designed within the Automotive Products Group and developed mutually with B.M.C. the new AP automatic transmission is manufactured in conjunction with the British Motor Corporation exclusively for their use.

Control of the system is by a centrally mounted floor lever giving seven positions: reverse, neutral, and automatic, plus first, second, third and top for manual operation. This allows the system to be used in three different ways:

(1) As a fully automatic four-speed transmission giving smooth progression from rest to maximum speed. 'Kick-down' to a lower gear for greater acceleration, and engine braking on hills is provided.

(2) Use of the selector lever giving full manual control of all four gears. For the sporting driver very rapid changes at full throttle are possible utilizing maximum speeds in each gear. There is no clutch pedal.

(3) For leisurely driving it is possible to engage any gear and use the very smooth take-up of the torque converter for starting from rest.

No transmission in the world gives so much choice of control, to all types of driver, from the inexperienced to the expert—and you can enjoy it in your new Austin 1100 Saloon.

Why not try the new Austin 1100 Countryman? Capable of carrying up to five people in de-luxe comfort, it can be converted into a spacious load carrier in a matter of seconds.

Mechanically, the 1100 Countryman is identical to the Saloon which has already proved itself the world over as a new concept in four- to five-person transport.

Inside, the Countryman is designed for hard wear and maximum luggage capacity—yet at the same time retaining all the luxury of the De Luxe Saloon. The rear seat squab is hinged and, by lifting the rear seat cushion, the squab can be folded forward to give a large rubber covered floor area for load carrying purposes. Alternatively, the 1100 Countryman can become your mobile, private sleeping accommodation for two, by having the optional reclining front seats at extra cost. When fully reclined, in conjunction with the rear seat which can also be fully reclined, they form a really comfortable full-length bed.

To enable the last inch of space—floor to roof—to be used, the Countryman is fitted with two wing-mounted rear view mirrors.

Both front seats are fully adjustable fore and aft, and also fold forward to give easy access into the rear passenger compartment.

The single-piece, top-hinged load compartment door makes loading possible with a minimum of effort, at the same time affording a measure of protection from rain.

For holidaying couples with an eye to economy, this comfortable double bed can be had simply by specifying the optional reclining front seats when ordering the vehicle.

the AUSTIN 1100 countryman doubles up on space!

- Four to five persons can travel in comfort—and still leave 14 cubic feet (0·40 m³) for luggage, in the new 1100 Countryman.
- With the rear seat folded two people have no less than 37·7 cubic feet (1·07 m³), with rubber protected floor, to use for luggage or other goods.
- The optional extra reclining front seats, in conjunction with the folding rear one, provides comfortable sleeping accommodation for two and perhaps a little one !

In 1943 Morris Motors started to look at what sort of cars it could make after the war was over. To this end work began on the design of a new car codenamed 'Mosquito'. Its designer was Alec Issigonis who had worked at Morris since 1936, having previously worked at Rootes. In the run up to the war Issigonis had worked on suspension designs and when the conflict started he designed all manner of military equipment including an amphibious motorised wheelbarrow!

Issigonis wanted the new car to be fitted with a horizontally opposed flat-four engine driving the front wheels but in the end it used the 918cc side valve unit from the Series E Morris Eight and was rear wheel drive.

The body styling was the responsibility of draughtsman Jack Daniels and he was very influenced by American designs at the time, with flared wings etc.

The car was launched as the Minor in 1948 and was an instant success – except with Lord Nuffield who hated it and said it looked like a poached egg! Altogether 1.3 million Minors would be made before production ceased in 1971. There were two restyles during this period and the vehicle could be bought as a saloon (two- or four-door), convertible, van, pick-up or the Traveller estate which had a structural external wooden frame.

Between 1948 and 1950 Morris's profits rose from £1.5 million to £8 million. But again there was a problem, and it stemmed from the antagonism between Morris and Austin. They always wanted to have competing models within £10 of each other, and would sometimes just drop the price of cars just to be a few quid less. You'd think that being competitive is what business is all about. However, neither really paid that much attention to other manufacturers, even the likes of Ford who were rapidly taking market share.

Some vehicles still carried the BMC badge even after the formation of British Leyland. *Photo G Carpenter*

The ideal situation was a merger between Austin and Morris particularly as both firms had taken considerable losses in the US after the war. It is even on record that Nuffield agreed that it was stupid that Britain's two largest vehicle makers were acting in such a way, but he wouldn't tell Austin's boss Leonard Lord.

However, Nuffield's personal secretary, one Charles Kingerlee, was also friends with Lord and after speaking to him managed to get Nuffield to agree to see Lord. Surprisingly after all the years of feuding a deal was soon struck whereby the firms would merge. After initial objections from the Morris board the deal finally went through in February 1952. Nuffield retired six months later and Lord became chairman of the newly formed British Motor Corporation.

Unfortunately there was a lot of resentment from Morris towards Austin due to the way Lord had taken over. Therefore although there was a fairly quick rationalisation of mechanical components used throughout the group, the merger never achieved its full potential. You would have thought the BMC would have had more to worry about, such as Ford who by 1953 had captured some 27% of the UK car market to its 35%.

Of course this period was a seller's market which didn't help encourage reform. For example the Morris and Austin dealerships remained separate and BMC actually encouraged competition between the two even though the vehicles were becoming increasingly the same. Austin and Morris also had separate boards of directors and even kept separate books.

Despite this BMC did bring out some innovative cars, notably the 1100 of 1962 and the Morris Mini Minor/Austin Seven of 1959. Both were the work of Issigonis and such is the importance of the Mini that it will be covered elsewhere.

Despite the problems BMC did well and in 1963 purchased the vehicle body maker Fisher & Ludlow of Castle Bromwich. This was followed two years later by the acquisition of another body maker, Pressed Steel. This Cowley based firm had been set up in 1926 by William Morris and the Budd Corporation of America. In 1966 Jaguar Cars was purchased (see separate chapter) and a new company was set up, British Motor Holdings. Despite this, many vehicles, particularly commercials, continued to be sold under the BMC brand for several years.

However, British manufacturing in the 1960s as a whole was declining and the remedy of the day was merger and expansion. Size meant strength – so BMH had to get bigger. ✦

Opposite: The 1100 was for a long time Britain's best selling car. It could be bought as a saloon or estate.

Left: Leonard Lord, later Lord Lambury, became chairman of BMC in 1952. *Photo National Motor Museum.*

British Leyland MOTOR CORPORATION

British Leyland came into being in 1968 and had high hopes for the future. However things just didn't turn out according to plan.

Official talks aimed at a merger between the Leyland Motor Corporation and British Motor Holdings (or BMC) had actually started in 1964 but would be a long drawn-out process. However, as the years went by this was seen as increasingly important as neither firm considered itself big enough to compete with foreign competition. This situation was going on with small companies around the world at the time. For example, in 1964 Volkswagen had taken over Auto Union, a firm made up of Audi, DKW, Horch and Wanderer (the four ring badge on Audis still represents these firms).

Despite this, merger talks didn't seem to get anywhere until the government stepped in, in the shape of the newly formed Industrial Reorganisation Committee. Again various schemes were thought up including joint operations in various countries. The Prime Minister, Harold Wilson, was particularly keen to see both merge and actually met with the MDs of both firms, Donald Stokes and George Harriman.

The deal was finally done in 1968 and BL came into being and Stokes became chairman. Unfortunately, the problems soon started and on the whole came from the BMH side. The main problem was that many of the cars produced were very dated, such as the Minor which first went into production 20 years before. It is true, there were some successful models such as the Mini and 1100, but both were getting on now and each made very little profit. In addition there was nothing much in the pipeline except the Maxi. However, the blame can't just be levelled at BMH as a lot of Leyland's car offerings in the shape of Rover and Triumph were hardly cutting edge.

The first new car to appear after the formation of British Leyland was the Maxi.

In addition to the lack of new vehicles, it had long been recognised that BMH was incredibly overmanned. Even Labour PM Harold Wilson had commented on it and made himself very unpopular with the unions as a result.

The first new car to go on sale was the Austin Maxi. Work had started on this design in 1966 and it was intended to fit into the range between the 1100 and 1800. However, the designers weren't given a free rein with the car – doors from the larger 1800 saloon had to be used. The design was almost finished by the time BL was formed and Stokes hated it. He knew it wouldn't sell well and thought was given to scrapping the project. However in the end the design was tidied up and the car was launched in 1969.

The Maxi used a transverse mounted 'E' series engine of 1485cc and a five-speed gearbox mounted in the sump like in the Mini. The gear-change was initially by cables and was quite vague, particularly when the cables had stretched a bit. One motoring magazine at the time likened it to stirring a bag of marbles with a knitting needle.

The first ever completely British Leyland car appeared two years after the Maxi in 1971. This was the Morris Marina, and was intended as a stop-gap design, and had been developed in a bit of a hurry. This was shown up in one particular area – its front suspension. This used lever-arm shock absorbers and trunnion joints like on the 1948 Morris Minor, and gave the Marina terrible roadholding. Despite this BL kept the car in production until 1980 and it was available as a saloon, coupe, van, estate or pick-up. In 1980 it was given a facelift to become the Ital. Some think this is because it was penned by Ital Design of Italy – actually it was designed by Harris Mann.

If the Marina had received a bad reception it was nothing compared to that received by the Allegro. This was the replacement for the 1100/1300 and much was expected. However, the car that appeared in 1973 just didn't do it. The main thing the designers had missed on cars of this class at the time was it had to be a hatchback – the Allegro had a boot. This was due to an odd idea that BL management had come up with – only the Maxi would have a hatchback so it could have a unique selling point.

Above left: The Marina was the first car designed by British Leyland.

Above right: The Allegro could have done far better if it had just had a hatchback.

Below: Baron Donald Stokes. *Photo National Motor Museum.*

However, the Allegro did have a unique selling point – its 'square' steering wheel. Actually this was the 'Quartic' steering wheel and was a square with rounded corners. It lasted for one year before it was dropped. Despite its faults Allegro production lasted until 1983, although this is more due to lack of money to develop something else than how good the car was. In fact that statement could be true for many of the cars BL produced over the years.

The replacement for the 1800 arrived in 1975 in the (wedge) shape of the Wolseley 18/22 (see separate section) which was dropped after six months and redesigned as the Austin Princess. The car was striking to say the least and was designed by Harris Mann. However, its wedge styling was crying out to be a hatchback but due to the 'Maxi rule' it had to have a boot. It did eventually get one in 1981 when it was restyled and re-launched as the Ambassador, but it was a bit late then. ❯

> **MANY OF THE CARS PRODUCED WERE VERY DATED SUCH AS THE MINOR WHICH FIRST WENT INTO PRODUCTION 20 YEARS BEFORE**

In 1975 the Labour government appointed Sir Donald Ryder as head of the National Enterprise board and asked him to report on the state of British Leyland. The report entitled: British Leyland: The Next Decade soon appeared and stated that BL was in a very poor state. It went on to say that there were too many competing models and unions were a problem in some areas. It recommended a radical management restructure and £1264 million expenditure from the government plus £260 million working capital. If this wasn't done the firm would collapse putting hundreds of thousands people out of work. This was acted upon by the government, and effectively nationalised the British Leyland Motor Corporation.

The company was renamed as just British Leyland Ltd and split into four divisions. These were Leyland Cars, Leyland Truck & Bus, Leyland Special Products (for construction equipment, refrigeration etc) and Leyland International which not only looked after exports but also overseas plants.

The first fruit of the new firm was the Rover SD1 (see separate chapter) which was a step towards rationalising the range of vehicles offered, by replacing both the Rover P6 and Triumph 2000/2500.

Unfortunately the SD1 was plagued with problems and many stemmed from the terrible workforce relations that were so common in the 1970s. It would take a publication far bigger than this one to go through all the problems and reasons, so instead I'll just detail a few that befell the Rover SD1, as I feel it could have been a real world-beater given a bit of a chance. I have taken for reference the book by Karen Pender, 'Rover SD1: The complete story published in 1998 by Crowood.

To design and develop the SD1 cost British Leyland (i.e. the British taxpayer) £95 million, which included £31 million for a new factory and £6.2 million for a state-of-the-art paintshop. However, it soon became apparent that the cars were very badly made. Several magazines had these cars on long term test and the list of faults seem endless including water leaking into the cabin from round the windscreen to the fusebox lid constantly falling off. The trim in the boot (which was usually damp due to water leaks) was described by one journalist as looking like a 'DIY job' and the paint was far too easy to chip off. Early body corrosion was also noted, and the six-cylinder engines gained a terrible reputation for leaks and general unreliability.

But who was to blame? Well, both unions and management certainly didn't help. Unions were very powerful and caused serious overmanning, and problems caused by job demarcation were rife. If a car was found to have a minor problem at the quality control stage it often meant several people had to fix it, sometimes taking days. The workforce on the other hand

Top: The wedge shaped Princess was another car that would have done better as a hatchback. It finally got one when it was restyled as the Ambassador in 1982.

Above: The Mini received a front end restyle in 1969 to make the Clubman.

Left: 1986 Maestro 1.6L. *Photo National Motor Museum.*

Right: The T45 lorry range included the Freighter four-wheeled rigid.

said that the management often speeded up the production lines to get more cars out of the door. This in turn created more problems with the unions.

One of the big SD1 problem areas was with its electrics, mainly central locking and electric window faults. However, these were supplied by Lucas, which at the time was also having labour problems. Even so, British Leyland constantly put pressure on Lucas to reduce its prices, so are you surprised the company didn't get a top quality product?

There were also reports of management overruling quality inspectors and shipping defective cars to dealers for them to sort out. All that mattered to them was getting cars out of the gate.

So who was to blame? I think it's six of one and half a dozen of the other.

In 1977 Sir Michael Edwards became chief executive and he set about more reorganisation. This included splitting Leyland Cars into Austin Morris, which would produce the bread and butter cars, and Jaguar Rover Triumph which would look after the luxury end. The following year British Leyland Commercial Vehicles was formed which would look after not just trucks and buses but also military equipment, forklifts etc. The whole group became just BL Ltd in 1979.

In 1980 the 'saviour' of BL was announced – the new Austin Mini-Metro. Originally this car was intended to replace the Mini but Mini fans the world over decried such a move. Besides it was selling too well, so the Metro became a sister vehicle to the Mini and so was renamed the Austin Metro.

The Metro had a very modern looking three-door hatchback body, although a five-door saloon, two-door convertible and three-door van became available later. However, beneath the modern shell lurked either the 998cc or 1275cc 'A+' engine from the Mini. It even had the same four-speed gearbox. As the Metro was meant to compete with the likes of the Ford Fiesta and Volkswagen Polo it was a bit penny-pinching. Despite this the car was developed over the years and became the Rover 100, with production finally ceasing in 1997 when over two million had been made. There were of course the MG versions (see separate section) including the fire-breathing Metro 6R4 rally car, but to be honest this last car has probably about as much in common with a normal Metro as a herring does with a pair of pliers.

Above: The Marina could also be purchased as a van or pick-up.

Right: The Metro appeared in 1980 and could be bought as a saloon, convertible or van.

1984 Austin Montego. *Photo National Motor Museum.*

By now BL had a tie-up with Honda and produced two different versions of the Ballade, firstly as the Triumph Acclaim and then the Rover 213/216. However, BL did produce two other cars on its own at this time, the Maestro and Montego. The Maestro took the place of the Allegro in 1983, and was a five-door hatchback initially available with either a 1275cc 'A+' engine or a 1598cc 'O' series lump. The Montego arrived in 1984 and was basically a four-door saloon version. These cars actually sold quite well, and more importantly were very profitable. In later years other engines became available including the two-litre Perkins Prima diesel engine, which was turbocharged in the Montego. In addition an estate version of the Montego was also offered, and there were also MG versions. The Maestro could also be bought as a van.

In 1986 Graham Day took over control of British Leyland, and immediately decided to change the name to the Rover Group, with the cars to be made by the Austin Rover Division. Three years later all cars were badged as Rovers, except the Mini which was by now a separate make. But was this a new beginning? ✦

THE RED TRIANGLE

Some of the lesser known products from British Leyland were armed military vehicles, which usually came from a firm in the group that was once far better known for producing luxury and sports cars – Alvis.

In 1919 naval architect and engineer Thomas George John set up TG John Ltd in Coventry to manufacture the 'Electra' range of stationary and marine engines, the rights for which John had just purchased from Hillman. In addition the firm also started assembling 'Stafford Mobile Pup' motor scooters and later the 'Buckingham' cyclecar.

Late in 1919 John received a visit from engineer Geoffrey PH de Freville, who had just designed a 1498cc side valve four cylinder engine and hoped John's firm could build it. In addition, de Freville also brought with him the name 'Alvis' which displayed in a red triangle was the trademark of his company, Aluminium Alloy Pistons Ltd. It has been suggested that the name Alvis was made up from the words 'aluminium' and the Latin word for strength/force 'vis'. However, de Freville always said it was just made up as it would be easy to say in most languages.

John liked the engine design and an agreement was signed where John would manufacture it under the Alvis name and pay a royalty to de Freville for each one produced. It was also decided that instead of just selling the engine the firm should produce an entire car.

The first post Second World War Alvis car was the 1892cc TA14. *Photo Stephen Pullen Collection.*

CAR PRODUCTION

The first Alvis was completed in March 1920 and was launched at the Scottish Motor Show. The first production models followed soon after. This was sold as the Alvis 10/30 and by the end of 1920 two cars were leaving the factory per week.

In 1921 John decided to cease production of the Electra engines, cyclecars and motor scooters and concentrate just on car production. The company name was also changed to the Alvis Car & Engineering Co Ltd.

Production continued and new models were introduced and in 1924 Alvis produced over 900 chassis'.

In 1926 the firm started experimenting with front-wheel-drive and even made some racing cars. However, it would be 1928 before any were available for sale. These were the FD roadster and FE tourer, and could be bought in naturally aspirated or supercharged forms.

In 1935 Alvis decided to start producing aircraft engines as well as cars, and a licence was purchased to allow them to produce engines designed by the French manufacturer, Gnome et Rhone.

The following year Alvis set up a subsidiary company called Alvis-Straussler Mechanisation Ltd in order to start producing armoured cars designed by Hungarian Nicholas Straussler. Other military products soon followed, including the production of aircraft propellers.

Due to the increase in military work the company changed its name again in 1937, this time to Alvis Ltd.

By 1938 Alvis decided to start designing its own aircraft engines and armoured cars. Straussler left the firm and the military subsidiary was renamed Alvis Mechanisation Ltd. The first aero-engine, the 'Leonides', was soon on the drawing board and was first test flown fitted in a Bristol Bulldog fighter in January 1939.

Despite the need for military equipment, car production continued until July 1940. During the conflict the Alvis factories were damaged several times by the bombing, with the car factory being severely hit.

During the war Alvis was involved in all kinds of work including producing over 10,000 complete Rolls-Royce aircraft engines. In fact at the height of production the firm was delivering 50 Merlins per day! In addition Alvis made all manner of aircraft parts and also overhauled damaged military road vehicles.

PEACETIME PRODUCTION

With the war over Alvis looked to restart car production, and its first new model, the TA14, was unveiled in 1946. Unfortunately the same year saw the passing of Thomas John, the founder of the company, at the age of 66. He had retired three years previously due to ill health.

The following year the company received an enquiry from the Ministry of Supply for an engine for use in helicopters. This went on to be a big market for Alvis with its Leonides engines ending up in helicopters made by Westland, Bristol, and Fairey. Incidentally, another more unusual job at the time included building printing presses. ›

The TE21 and TF21 were externally identical. Only around 350 TEs and 100 TFs were ever built.
Photo Stephen Pullen Collection.

The TA14 car was very similar to the prewar 12/70, and used some of its components. It was fitted with a slightly bored-out version of the 12/70 engine, which increased it to 1892cc capacity as opposed to 1842cc for the 1940 version. The standard body was a four-door saloon that was built by Mulliners, but coachbuilt versions soon appeared.

The next car, the TA21, appeared in 1950. This was the first 'all-new' postwar Alvis version and was marketed as the '3-Litre'. The engine was a 2993cc straight-six which developed 83bhp in its standard tune. This engine, in various forms, would be the power unit that Alvis used in its cars until the firm went over to just military vehicle production in 1967.

During this period however, it was the sales of military vehicles that kept the company profitable. This started in 1947 when Alvis was asked by the government to design a six-wheeled, high mobility armoured car. The design it came up with was the 'Saladin' (FV601). This used an eight-cylinder Rolls-Royce petrol engine, five-speed Wilson pre-selector gearbox and a Daimler fluid flywheel. This was a good selling product for Alvis who not only sold them to the British Army but also to Australia, Germany, Portugal and Jordan among other countries.

The Saladin spawned a series of military vehicles based on the same chassis and mechanicals. These were the 'Saracen' armoured personnel carrier, which appeared in 1952 and the 'Salamander' airfield crash tender in 1956. This could produce 7500 gallons of foam per minute and as well as RAF service was also used by the Royal Canadian Air Force.

The other variant was the Stalwart amphibious truck. This entered service with the British Army in 1966 and could carry five tons. The vehicle could travel at six knots through the water or about 40mph on the road. The water speed was increased to nine knots with further work.

However, despite all this success Alvis needed further investment and in July 1965 it was taken over by Rover.

In March 1966 the TF21 car appeared which used a triple-carb version of the three-litre engine. However this was to be the last Alvis car, as the decision was taken to concentrate on the production of military vehicles. The last one was produced on September 29, 1967.

The Alvis Stalwart amphibious truck could carry five tons, and could travel at six knots in the water or about 40mph on the road. Photo National Motor Museum.

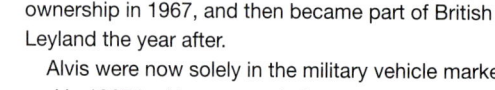

A late version of the aluminium-hulled Alvis Scorpion.

As part of Rover, Alvis passed into Leyland Motors ownership in 1967, and then became part of British Leyland the year after.

Alvis were now solely in the military vehicle market, and in 1967 had been awarded a contract to design and build what was designated a 'Combat Vehicle Reconnaissance (Tracked)' by the Ministry of Defence. The first prototypes appeared in 1969 and after testing, a production order soon arrived. The vehicle Alvis produced was the 'Scorpion', and was the world's first series produced aluminium bodied tank. This seems very apt given the beginnings of Alvis and the possible meaning of its name.

The Scorpion was designed to be air portable and could be dropped by parachute. In addition it was capable of operating in a nuclear warfare environment.

The new tank had its hull and turret made from aluminium-zinc-magnesium alloy. Due to its low weight (8.074 tonnes) it had a top speed of 50mph and had a range of 400 miles. The engine for the first version of the tank was a 4.2-litre Jaguar unit driving through a seven-speed gearbox. The main armament was a 76mm L23A1 gun that could fire six rounds per minute and had an effective range of 2.2km. A 7.62mm coaxial machine gun was also fitted as were smoke grenade dischargers.

The first versions entered service with the British Army in 1973 and were given to the 'Blues and Royals' regiments of the Household Cavalry. In 1981 the RAF Regiment also took delivery of some 184 Scorpions.

The Mk2 version that came out after a few years was fitted with a 90mm Cockerill gun and a Perkins turbocharged diesel engine that produced 155bhp.

The Scorpion saw service with British forces in the Falklands and also in the first Gulf War. In addition it was purchased by many other countries including Ireland, Spain, Belgium, Thailand and Brunei. It was withdrawn from British service in 1994.

The Scorpion also formed the basis of several other military vehicles including the Scimitar light reconnaissance vehicle, Spartan personnel carrier, Striker anti-tank missile launcher, Sultan command vehicle, Samson recovery vehicle, Stormer personnel carrier, Samaritan ambulance and the Streaker load carrier.

In 1981 BL sold Alvis to United Scientific Holdings for £27million. The company is now part of BAE Systems but the name Alvis has sadly been dropped. ✦

Subscribe to

SPECIAL OFFER!
Expires 31/12/25

6 issues from £27.95

Best of British is the UK's premier nostalgia magazine, covering every aspect of life from the 1930s to today. Packed with features that celebrate classic entertainment, transport, food and drink, and more, not to mention Postbag and the Yesterday Remembered memoir section, it really is a walk down memory lane.

GET YOURS TODAY

Visit: www.classicmagazines.co.uk/bob018

Call: 01507 529529 and quote **BOB018**

The pride of LYONS

The luxury and sports tourer end of the BL car making empire was taken care of by an iconic make that's still with us today – Jaguar.

The origins of Jaguar go back to September 4, 1922 when William Lyons and William Walmsley set up in business as the Swallow Sidecar Company in Blackpool in order to make motorcycle sidecars. The formation of the business was apparently delayed as Lyons was not 21 years old until that date and therefore a minor. To set up the firm both partners obtained a £500 guarantee from their respective fathers, which is worth almost £11,000 each in today's money. This business grew and in 1927 they started to build bodies on Austin Seven chassis' which were sold as Swallows. Other car bodies soon followed on various chassis including Morris, Swift, Fiat and Standard. By this time the firm had changed its name to The Swallow Sidecar and Coachbuilding Company. Such was the success of the enterprise that in 1928 the firm relocated to much larger premises in Coventry.

In 1931, with the move completed, a sleek saloon body was built by Swallow on to a chassis made to Lyons design by Standard and was named the S.S.1. This car used the Standard 2054cc straight-six engine. Similar bodies were also fitted to Wolseley Hornet chassis and a 2552cc engine was also made available.

In 1933 came the S.S.2 which was built on the chassis from a Standard Nine which used a 1054cc engine. The year 1933 also saw the introduction of the firm's first open car, the S.S.1 Tourer.

By the end of the following year the company recorded sales of some 1800 cars for the previous 12 months, but this still wasn't enough for Lyons. However, Walmsley wasn't keen on further expansion and so sold his half of the firm to Lyons. Walmsley then went into the caravan business.

Lyons was now free to expand the firm as he saw fit and in 1935 launched the company's first sports car, the S.S.90. The '90' apparently showed the car's top speed. This car used a 2.6-litre twin-carb engine which developed 75bhp.

Two Jaguars from the BL era – the XJ6 and XJS.

THE LAUNCH OF THE CAT

Shortly after this the name 'Jaguar' was chosen as the model name for a new four-door sports saloon, designed by William Heynes, with Harry Weslake responsible for modifying the engine. The car they came up with was powered by a 104bhp Standard engine of 2663cc capacity, although it was always referred to as a '2.5'. A smaller engine of 1608cc was also an option from 1936, which rose to 1775cc in 1938.

Additionally 1935 also saw the firm split, with the cars being made by SS Cars Ltd and the rest of the business becoming Swallow Coachbuilding Co (1935) Ltd. These business changes saw the firm drop the full stops in their initials and the cars were then sold as the SS Jaguar.

Later that year also saw the introduction of one of the best known of the firm's cars, the SS100. This was a short-chassis two seater which used an almost identical chassis and body to the SS90 but fitted with the engine and other mechanicals from the new Jaguar saloon.

In 1938 more power was added to the range when a 3485cc overhead-valve engine was made available for the sports and saloon cars.

For 1939 SS recorded sales of over 5000 cars, but with the outbreak of war production ceased and the company took on war contracts. These included the manufacture of military trailers and parts for fighter and bomber aircraft.

Towards the end of the war Lyons realised that the initials 'SS' were no longer acceptable as he certainly didn't want his cars to invoke memories of the Nazi SS, and so in March 1945 the company name was changed to Jaguar Cars Ltd.

As an aside the Swallow Coachbuilding Company was sold by Lyons to Tube Investments just after the war. ❯

Above right: The SS100 is one of the firm's best known prewar cars. *Photo National Motor Museum.*

Above: The XK120 appeared in 1948 and with a top speed of 120mph was the world's fastest production road car at the time. *Photo National Motor Museum.*

A 1960s icon – the E-Type. *Photo National Motor Museum.*

> **EVEN ENZO FERRARI DECLARED IT THE MOST BEAUTIFUL CAR EVER MADE.**

The Mark 2 wasn't just a competent road car – many were also used for racing. *Photo National Motor Museum.*

However, by the early 1950s income was dropping and so a sports car was designed that used a Reynolds tubular chassis and Triumph TR2 running gear. This car was the Swallow Doretti and soon some 10 cars per week were being made. A coupe version named the Sabre soon followed but in 1955 production ceased even though sales were good. The reason was that Tube Investments had taken a call from William Lyons who didn't like them producing a rival car. At the time Jaguar was buying all manner of components from TI and Lyons made it clear that if they continued to produce sports cars he would take his business elsewhere. Hence the end of the Swallow.

A LEGENDARY ENGINE

After the war car production soon got underway again. For the first three years the cars were produced to the prewar designs, and still used Standard engines. However, 1948 saw the first new postwar car, the Mark V. This was available as a saloon or drop-head coupe and either a 2664cc or 3485cc engine. This car was launched at that year's Motor Show but it was somewhat overshadowed by the other Jaguar on show – the XK120 sports car. This was capable of 120mph which made it the world's fastest production car at the time. It was powered by a new engine that was to become an engineering legend, and would be produced in various forms until the 1990s – the XK.

The origins of this engine go back to the war years when William Lyons and two of his engineers, Bill Heynes and Claude Baily, were on fire-watch on the roof of the Jaguar factory one night and had a discussion as to what sort of engine they should develop for use after the war.

Development of these ideas soon got underway and prototypes were being tested by 1943. The first two prototype engines were the XG and XF, of approximately 1.8- and 1.4-litres respectively. Both were four-cylinder units, but the XF used a double overhead cam configuration and after testing was considered by far the best design.

Therefore the XG was dropped and the XF developed into the XJ, which was again a four-cylinder dohc unit but had grown to 1996cc. In 1947 a prototype 3.2-litre six-cylinder version of the XJ was tried, which in turn was developed into the six-cylinder 160bhp 3442cc XK, which finally went into production. Incidentally, a four-

cylinder version of the XK engine was also developed but never went into production.

The XK120 sports car proved a sensation, far beyond anything Lyons had hoped for. In fact he envisaged the car to be nothing more than a test-bed for the engine and components that were to be used on the Mark VII saloon that finally came onto the market in 1950. In addition he thought Jaguar would only sell around 200 XK120s but demand was so great that the car stayed in production until 1954. By then some 12,000 cars had been made with over 90% being exported.

In 1951 a competition version was made available, the XK120C, which was designed by Malcolm Sayer. This car used disc brakes all-round, a tuned XK120 engine and a lightweight aluminium alloy body built over a tubular frame. It became known as just the C-Type and an example driven by Peter Walker and Peter Whitehead won the Le Mans 24 hour Endurance Race on the first attempt. A C-Type also won in 1953.

The competition success of the C-Type was followed by the D-Type, which again used the XK engine but the body was a monocoque construction with no separate chassis or framework. Jaguar D-Types won at Le Mans in 1955, 56 and 57.

ON THE ROAD

A new generation of smaller road cars of unitary construction was launched in 1955 with the arrival of the 2.4, which eventually became known as the Mark 1. The engine was a short-stroke version of the XK which developed 112bhp. In 1957 the 3.4-litre engine was also offered as an option.

The Mark 1 proved very popular and was also raced by Stirling Moss, Mike Hawthorn and others. Over 37,000 cars had been produced by the time production ceased in 1959 to make way for the Mark 2.

The new car was available with the same engines as the Mark 1, but there was an additional option in the shape of the 3.8-litre variant. The Mark 2 became a real 1960s icon and was so fast it became known as a bit of a 'villains car', particularly, it seems, if you wanted to rob a bank. However, they were also used extensively by the police and in later years one even became a television star as the car of choice for Inspector Morse.

Production ran until 1969, although the car was re-branded as the 240 and 340 in 1967, when it also lost the 3.8-litre engine. Altogether around 90,000 were made, with approximately the last 7000 being the 240/340 models. ›

Above left: An engineering work-of-art – the straight-six XK engine. *Photo National Motor Museum.*

Above right: The Series 3 E-Type didn't have the flowing lines of the earlier cars, but it didn't stop almost 15,000 cars being sold before production stopped. *Photo National Motor Museum.*

Below: The XJS replaced the E-Type in 1975. This is a later HE model.

60S ICON

Despite the success of the Mark 1 and 2, the real 'star' of the 1960s was something altogether different that first appeared in 1961 – the E-Type, another car designed by Malcolm Sayer.

The first E-Types, which replaced the XK150, were fitted with the 3781cc XK engine that was tuned to produce 265bhp. The car also had disc brakes and independent suspension all round and was available as a coupe or open two-seater.

The moment it was launched it was greeted as a sensation – even Enzo Ferrari declared it "the most beautiful car ever made." And there was no wonder that it was so highly praised. Here was a car capable of 150mph for £2100, which is approximately £40,000 in today's money. Comparable performance only came from the likes of the Aston-Martin DB4, but that cost £3755, or around £71,500 today.

In 1966 Jaguar put a 2+2 coupe version onto the market. They also started selling E-Types with automatic gearboxes, mainly for the American market, which was the company's major export market.

In 1967 came what is now known unofficially as the Series 1 1/2 models. These featured items to comply with US regulations such as un-fared headlamps and some de-tuning of the engine.

The Series 2 appeared in 1969 when the company was under the control of BL. This would be produced until 1971 and could be bought as an open two-seater, coupe or 2+2. The engine was the 4.2-litre version of the XK. Air conditioning and power steering were available as special order.

Unfortunately all these extras and less power, mainly due to US emission laws, greatly eroded the performance of the E-Type and so in 1971 came the Series 3 – and this had real power in the shape of the 5.3-litre Jaguar V12 engine.

This car, which had many mechanical upgrades over the Series 2, was available as either an open two-seater or a 2+2 coupe. Incidentally a very small number of 4.2-litre Series 3 cars were also made and are now incredibly rare.

The V12 engine was a design based on an experimental engine for the XJ13 Le Mans racing car that was only produced in prototype form. Strangely it was only the second Jaguar designed engine to go into full production.

The new engine in the E-Type restored the car's performance while also meeting the new US emission rules. However there was a problem. The Series 3 just didn't have the beautiful lines of the earlier models.

Despite this some 15,287 Series 3 cars were produced before an even more controversial car was to replace it in 1975. This was the XJS, but more of that in a moment.

GRACE, PACE AND SPACE

Let's rewind now to 1969, when Jaguar had only recently become part of the BL empire, as that year saw a very important car being launched onto the market. This was the first XJ6 saloon, a car that epitomised William Lyons' motto for the firm of 'Grace, Space and Pace'.

The first XJ6 cars were available with either the 4.2-litre straight-six or a new version of the engine with a capacity of 2790cc. This smaller engine proved a bit unreliable, and was prone to overheating and so was dropped in 1973. The V12 also found its way into the car and was named the XJ12. Daimler versions were also offered, with the V12 being sold as the 'Double Six'.

Daimler had been acquired by Lyons in 1960 and he marketed many of Jaguar's car designs as Daimlers over the years. Some were quite different to the Jaguar's on

Opposite top: Jaguars have always been used in motorsport – a tradition that continues to this day. *Photo Stephen Pullen.*

Opposite bottom: The interior of a 4.2 XJ6.

Below: The XJ6 was launched in 1968. This is an early 70s XJ6C two-door coupe.

offer, such as the 1960s Daimler 250, which used a Mark 2 body but was fitted with a 2.5-litre V8 engine designed by Edward Turner. This engine had first been used in the SP250 'Dart' sports car which was produced by Daimler from 1959 until 1964. Other firms acquired by Jaguar were bus and lorry builder Guy Motors in 1961 and engine and forklift manufacturer Coventry Climax in 1963.

As previously mentioned, 1975 saw the last E-Type roll off the production line. Whatever followed it had to be very good, as it really had a lot to live up to. The replacement was the 5.3-litre V12 XJS, and many were disappointed. Although it was more aerodynamic than the E-Type it didn't look it. Gone were the flowing lines and sporting looks – the XJS was definitely more of a 'grand tourer' than a sports car.

Despite this almost 15,000 cars were produced by 1981 when the car was improved with the new High Efficiency (HE) engines, which took the car to 155mph.

However, all was not well, and the 1970s were not a good time for Jaguar. The company had become part of the British Motor Corporation in 1966 and therefore became part of British Leyland in 1968. Lyons remained in charge until he retired in 1972, when Jaguar's former competition department manager FRW 'Lofty' England took over. He retired in 1974 and the firm was then headed by Geoffrey Robinson, who found himself so unhappy at the way BL were running Jaguar he resigned in protest. The quality of the cars also suffered badly during this period and sales also slipped, particularly in the key export market of North America.

However, things were soon to change. Sir Michael Edwards took over control of BL in 1977 and in 1980 reinstated the post of chairman at Jaguar. In addition the company was separated from Jaguar-Rover-Triumph Ltd where they had been placed by BL and the firm renamed Jaguar Cars Ltd.

The new chairman of Jaguar was John Egan, and it can be said that he saved the company. At the time sales were very poor and the firm was losing £2million per month.

After settling a strike Egan arranged for the firm to take over the former Pressed Steel Fisher plant in Castle Bromwich which was converted into a highly automated engine manufacturing facility. He also looked into the company's quality problems and found that 60% of reported defects came from cheap parts from outside manufacturers. In 1980 when he took over, productivity ran at just 1.2 cars per worker. Within three years this was raised to 3.5 cars.

However, his greatest achievement came in 1984 when he managed to organise Jaguar's 'escape' from British Leyland and become a private company once more. As an idea of how highly confident people were now becoming in the company the share issue was eight times oversubscribed, which put its value at £300million.

Since its separation Jaguar has continued to have its ups and downs. In 1989 the company was taken over by Ford. This provided a massive cash injection for new models and better quality. In 2008 the company was bought by Tata Motors and in 2013 became Jaguar Land Rover. Sales in 2013 amounted to 76,668 units – an increase of 42% on 2012 and a definite high point. However, some difficult sales years followed and plans to downsize were announced in 2023. In November 2024, a new logo was unveiled for Jaguar ahead of a relaunch as an electric-only brand in 2026. ✦

TAXI!

Due to the creation of British Leyland, the ubiquitous London black taxi, the FX4, now found itself being made by a massive multinational. But was this for better or worse?

> *IN 1956 THE REPLACEMENT FOR THE FX3 STARTED TO BE DESIGNED. THIS WOULD BE THE VEHICLE REGARDED BY MOST AS THE LONDON TAXI, THE FX4*

In August 1897 London saw its first horseless motor cabs. These were the Hummingbirds, so called because they were electrically powered. By the end of the following year there were around 75 of these vehicles plying for trade around the capital, but they proved quite unreliable and so by 1900 had disappeared.

By 1903 petrol-powered cabs started to be seen on the roads and by 1906 there were 100 such vehicles in service. 1906 also saw the introduction of the 'Conditions of Fitness' regulations which basically dictated the design of vehicles that could be used as Hackney carriages. These included the famous requirement that cabs had to have a 25ft turning circle. By the way, the word Hackney actually comes from a Norman French word 'Hacquenee' which meant horse for hire.

The following year a law was passed that made it compulsory for cabs to be fitted with 'taximeters'. This was shortened and cabs then became known as taxis.

One of the main vehicles used in London at the time was the French Unic, which was sold by Mann & Overton. This firm continued importing Unic taxis into Britain until the late 1920s when the rates of duty imposed on imported vehicles made them too expensive. The firm then looked to find a suitable British vehicle which they could modify to satisfy the Conditions of Fitness.

A BRITISH DESIGN

It soon settled on the Austin Heavy 12/4, an example of which was successfully modified and tested. Mann & Overton then approached Austin who agreed to supply 500 modified chassis. Mann & Overton had the new Austin cab on sale by 1930. This cab soon went on to dominate the London taxi market due to its competitive price and ease of maintenance.

However, the war changed everything. Firstly Austin stopped making the Heavy 12/4 chassis. In addition Austin's rivals Morris, made a prototype cab called the Oxford which ran on test throughout the war. This meant that the new cab was ready to be passed for use straight after the war and it was soon picked up and sold by Beardmore.

Mann & Overton however had to start from scratch and needed to do so in a hurry. London was crying out for new taxis to replace those destroyed by enemy bombing or those that were just worn out after six years on the road during this very difficult time, and the new offering from Morris was rapidly taking market share.

Austin started the process by sending Mann & Overton a modified version of their current 12hp chassis, fitted with a 1792cc side valve engine and modified steering to comply with the turning circle rule. This was fitted with an old taxi body for testing purposes and given the designation 'FX'.

However, this taxi was just not up to the job so Austin went back to the drawing board and came up with the FX2. This had a much stronger chassis and used an 1800cc 14hp engine.

NEW METHODS

Prior to the war taxi bodies had all been built by traditional coachbuilders, but that would make the FX2 far too expensive when compared to the Oxford, which had a pressed steel body. Austin at that time did not have the facilities to produce such bodies so a Coventry-based company called Carbodies was contracted to build them.

In fact the project ended up jointly financed, with Mann & Overton paying 50% and Carbodies and Austin 25% each.

The body was designed and received its type approval in June 1947. However, before it could go on to the market there was a problem with the supply of the 1800cc engines and Austin suggested fitting its 2.2-litre petrol unit in its place. This was successfully tested and the vehicle therefore became the FX3 and was launched in 1948.

Over the next few years, in order to improve fuel economy, several FX3 users had fitted diesel engines in place of the thirsty petrol unit. This encouraged Austin to come up with a diesel of its own which was based on the 2.2 petrol. Its diesel appeared in 1954 and not only gave around 30mpg, compared to the petrol's 18mpg, but the fuel was about half the price. By 1955 over 90% of new FX3 cabs sold were fitted with the new diesel engine.

In 1956 the replacement for the FX3 started to be designed. This would be the vehicle regarded by most as THE London taxi, the FX4.

This cab was to use an uprated version of the FX3 chassis with Austin Westminster independent front suspension and rear axle. It was decided that only the diesel engine would be offered and it would drive through an automatic gearbox.

LAUNCH

The FX4 was finally launched at the 1958 Commercial Motor Show, but there were a few problems. One notable problem was that the cabbies didn't like the idea of just having an automatic gearbox, despite the fact that previous trials on converted FX3 cabs had received a favourable reaction. In the end Austin had to offer a manual gearbox from the Austin Gipsy 4x4 as an option. In 1962 another option appeared (or reappeared!) as the 2.2 petrol engine from the FX3 returned.

In 1968 the FX4 got a bit of a facelift receiving new indicators and other detail changes. However, this was nothing compared to what could have been, as Austin had been looking into replacing the FX4 with an entirely new design. However, British Leyland was now in charge and the project was scrapped before it really began.

The next major change therefore didn't happen until 1971 when the engine capacity for the diesel was increased to 2.5 litres. However, the bigger news for that year was that BL had decided to stop producing FX4 chassis and a deal was done where all the tooling was purchased by Carbodies and shipped to its Coventry factory. It now made the whole vehicle, although it still carried the Austin badge.

BL INDIFFERENCE

BL became increasingly less interested in the FX4 and eventually decided to cease production of the 2.2-litre diesel engine. Carbodies approached another BL company Land Rover and eventually adopted the four-cylinder 2286cc unit made for the Series 3. Another possible tie-up with Land Rover was also tried when a new taxi design, the CR6, was looked into that was to use panels from the Range Rover. Unfortunately it came to nothing.

In 1981 a new set of regulations governing taxi design and use was expected, and Carbodies was worried. BL wasn't interested and these new laws could have spelled the end for the FX4 and possibly Carbodies as well. Therefore the company started negotiations with BL and in 1982 successfully purchased all the rights.

Carbodies and Mann & Overton were owned at the time by Manganese Bronze Ltd and in 1984 they set up London Taxis International to manufacture the cabs. They also improved the FX4 by fitting the larger 2.5-litre Land Rover engine, which was designated the FX4S. A wheelchair accessible version appeared in 1986, the FX4W, while the 1987 FX4S Plus featured improved suspension and better instruments.

The last FX4 was the Fairway with a 2.7-litre Nissan diesel engine, from 1989 to 1997. LTI became the London Taxi Company in 2010 and was placed in administration in 2012. Some assets were bought by Chinese firm Greely to form what is now the London EV Company, making TX model electric black cabs. ✦

Top: The taxi was 'facelifted' in 1968 receiving new indicators and other detail changes. The rear lights are from the Austin 1100.

Above: The 2.5-litre BMC diesel engine developed 60bhp at 3500rpm.

VANDEN Plas

Many traditional coachbuilders flourished in the early part of the 20th century only for their fortunes to decline from the 50s on, as manufacturers started to make their own unitary bodies. Vanden Plas however survived and managed to become a car maker in its own right.

Opposite top: The Daimler DS420 replaced the A135 Princess in 1968. It was still trimmed and finished by Vanden Plas.

Opposite bottom: The Daimler Double Six Vanden Plas used a 5.3-litre V12 engine. Jaguar can still use the name in certain markets to this day.

Below: The first cars Vanden Plas produced for Austin included the A135 Princess. These were made until 1968. *Photo National Motor Museum.*

The Vanden Plas company (pronounced Van Der Plass) was started in Belgium in 1870 in order to make components for horse-drawn carriages. In 1884 it started to make complete carriages and became one of the top makers in Belgium. So when the 'horseless carriage' appeared it didn't take long for the firm to find itself building bodies for them.

Vanden Plas vehicle bodies were first seen in Britain in 1906 when Metallurgique cars started to be imported. These vehicles were very highly thought of and in 1913 motor dealer Warwick Wright managed to purchase the British rights to the Vanden Plas name, setting up Vanden Plas (England) Ltd.

During the First World War the firm made parts for aircraft and in 1917 were bought by The Aircraft Manufacturing Company of Hendon.

With the war over car body construction recommenced although things didn't go so well for the new firm of Vanden Plas England (1917) Ltd. Strangely it also seemed to have lost the exclusive British rights to the name as the original Belgian company was also selling its products over here.

In 1922 Vanden Plas England was placed into receivership and the rights were purchased by one Edwin Fox and his brothers who moved the firm from Hendon to Kingsbury and started trading as Vanden Plas (England) 1923 Ltd.

The Fox brothers had good contacts throughout the industry and concentrated on building bodies for Bentleys although many other cars also received Vanden Plas designs, notably Rolls-Royce, Alvis, Daimler, Lagonda and Delage.

In 1938 it looked as if war was inevitable and so Vanden Plas took on aircraft work once again. It continued in this field until 1945 when the conflict ended and the company looked to return to car body production. However, instead of enquiries from the established luxury makers, it was surprised when it was approached by Austin, looking for a firm to manufacture a new luxury car on its six-cylinder chassis. Vanden Plas was ideal for the job and so in 1946 the company became part of the Austin Motor Company.

The car it initially made the body for was the A120 but when the design was fitted with the 4-litre engine it was renamed the A135 Princess. In 1952 a long-wheelbase limousine was also produced, which at less than half the price of a Rolls-Royce, but offering similar levels of comfort, proved very popular in the class. The first two were bought by the Queen, while many others were exported for foreign dignitaries.

Production continued and from 1958 Vanden Plas also took on the manufacture of the chassis as well as the body. In 1960 BMC realised that Vanden Plas was now a car manufacturer in its own right and so the Austin name went and the car was then sold as the Vanden Plas Princess. Production of this car ended in 1968 when BL replaced it with the Daimler DS420.

Other cars sold under the Vanden Plas name in the 60s included the Princess 3-litre, which was an upmarket version of the Austin Westminster and the Princess R saloon which was fitted with a 175bhp 3.9-litre Rolls-Royce straight-six engine.

BMC's smaller cars also got the Vanden Plas wood and leather treatment, these being the 1100 from 1963 until 1968 and the 1300 which was produced from 1967 until 1974. In 1974 a luxury version of the 1500 Allegro was made, which continued in production until 1980.

Some regarded these smaller cars as a bit of a joke but the same couldn't be said of the Daimler Double Six Vanden Plas which was launched in 1972. With its V12 5.3-litre engine it really was the sort of car Vanden Plas had always been about. A 4.2-litre version became available in 1975.

Also in 1975 BL decided to take the Princess name from Vanden Plas and put it on the replacement for the Wolseley 18/22 'Wedge'. The firm was asked however to produce a prototype Vanden Plas Princess 'Wedge' but it never went into production. This mock-up did survive though, and is currently on display at the Heritage Motor Centre at Gaydon. A proposed Marina conversion also never came to anything.

1979 saw BL close the Vanden Plas factory. The last of the 1500 models was then made at the MG works in Abingdon. From then on the name was just used as a badge attached to various top of the range cars produced by BL including Austin's Ambassador, Metro, Maestro & Montego and Rover's SD1 & 213/216.

Jaguar's Vanden Plas Daimler had to be renamed as just the Double Six when the company managed to escape from BL, but this was for certain markets only, Jaguar can still use the name to this day in some countries, notably in North America.

The last Rover product to carry the Vanden Plas name was a batch of high-spec Rover 75 saloons, some of which ended up as limousines.

Like many other ex British Leyland company names and trademarks, the Vanden Plas brand is now owned by the Chinese Nanjing Automobile Group since it bought the assets of MG-Rover. ✦

Above: The Vanden Plas 1500 was based on the Austin Allegro. It was made from 1974 until 1980.

Left: The wood and leather interior of the Vanden Plas 1500. Note the picnic tables on the seat backs.

MOVING MOUNTAINS

Another product of the BL Group was construction, mining and road-making equipment, most of which was made under the name of Aveling-Barford.

Aveling-Barford Ltd was formed in 1933 from the ruins of Agricultural and General Engineers Ltd, better known as AGE. This company had been formed in 1919 to combat the huge expansionist plans of the American agricultural machinery companies of the day. The idea was to amalgamate several small British machinery manufacturing companies into a force to be reckoned with. The companies included Charles Burrell & Sons Ltd, Aveling & Porter Ltd, Richard Garratt & Co Ltd and Barford & Perkins Ltd. Unfortunately the company hit financial troubles in 1932 and the receiver was brought in. One of the Barford family, Edward, not wishing to see his family firm disappear, managed to rescue it from the ruins, together with Aveling & Porter, and the company of Aveling-Barford Ltd was born. After the merger it was set up just outside Grantham in Lincolnshire, in a factory provided by the famous engineering concern of Ruston & Hornsby.

The new company did however keep the rearing horse symbol from the Aveling & Porter days, together with the motto 'Invicta' which basically means 'unconquered'.

Initially just concentrating on what it knew best, road rollers, the company soon began diversifying into other areas of earthmoving and construction equipment. It also continued in the manufacture of steam engines and equipment all the way through until the late 1950s.

During the Second World War, in common with most other engineering works in Britain, the company went over to war work, which included the production of Bren Gun Carriers. In 1946 a sister company, Barford's of Belton Ltd, was set up to take over the production of Barford's agricultural equipment, such as dairy machinery. This was followed by acquiring a company involved in the manufacture of quarrying and asphalt making machinery and another involved with structural steelwork.

The year 1947 saw the company make its first large dump truck. This six-wheeled lorry had a 12 ton capacity and was fitted with a six-cylinder Dorman diesel engine giving 128bhp.

By 1958 the range of dump trucks had increased and the company introduced its largest truck to date, the bonneted 'SN' series. This 30 ton machine was available with either a Rolls-Royce V8 diesel giving 450bhp or a Cummins six-cylinder diesel of 335bhp. A six-speed gearbox was fitted in both cases. A 35 ton vehicle was introduced shortly after which was available with either the Rolls-Royce V8 or a Detroit Diesel two-stroke engine.

In 1968 the company became part of the Special Products Division of the British Leyland Motor Corporation. That year it was recorded that the Grantham works covered an area of 70 acres. It was also noted that, apart from a few special order fitments of propriety power and transmission units, everything except castings, was made on site. Aveling-Barford also had a factory in Newcastle upon Tyne, where some machinery fabrication was carried out. Barford's of Belton had ceased the manufacture of agricultural equipment, and was producing the 'shuttle' building site dumper, which by now had a payload of two-ton. The company also had overseas subsidiaries in places as far flung as Canada, Australia, France and Rhodesia.

Below left: The TS 185 Loading shovel had a capacity of 6500lb.

Below right: The Centaur was launched in 1970. This is the 50 ton model, the largest in the range.

Upon becoming part of the Leyland Group, Aveling Barford took over the manufacture of the six-wheeled 690 'Dumptruk' which had previously been made by another Leyland company, AEC. This road legal lorry was fitted with a 187bhp six-cylinder Leyland diesel engine and had a payload of 13.8 ton.

Other machinery made at this time included motor-graders, loading shovels and road rollers. The range of road rollers made at the time included the 'Master Pavior' series that went from 7.5 to 12 ton in weight, the 'PneumaVicta' pneumatic tyred roller and the 'VibraVicta' towed vibratory roller.

In 1970 the 'SN' series trucks were replaced by the five model 'Centaur' range, which had capacities of 25 to 50 ton. The largest model, the Centaur 50, was powered by a General Motors supplied V16 two-stroke diesel engine giving 635bhp and had a fluid/nitrogen suspension system. The Centaur range was updated in the late 1970s and was re-designated the RDO series.

Early in the 1970s Aveling-Barford was transferred within the British Leyland group to its Truck and Bus Division, and in 1975 BL purchased the well known maker of crawler tractors, Marshall-Fowler Ltd. At this point the tractor firm was renamed Aveling-Marshall.

In the early 1980s BL decided to sell off all non-core businesses and this included Aveling-Marshall and Aveling-Barford. The tractor firm was sold in 1982 to Lincolnshire businessman and farmer, Charles Nickerson. New offices and a showroom were built, and the business re-structured. Nickerson also bought the ailing British Leyland tractor division.

After leaving British Leyland Aveling-Barford went through a very tough period, particularly when foreign investors were involved, and in 1988 the company was placed into receivership, where it was bought by Duncan Wordsworth, of the Wordsworth group. The company continued, for a while, to make rigid four-wheeled dump trucks of up to 65 tonnes payload and six-wheeled articulated vehicles of up to 28 tonnes, all to special order only.

Today the Bardford name is still in business with Barford Equipment, based in Northern Ireland, which makes screening and materials handling equipment such as loaders, trailers and conveyors. ✦

Above: The MT motor grader was one of several such machines to be offered by Aveling-Barford during BL's ownership.

Below: The TDC range of tandem rollers went from six to 11 tonnes.

The best 4x4xFAR

Originally intended as a stop-gap vehicle to help overseas sales during Britain's 'export or die' period after the war, the Land Rover went on to become a British motoring success story that continues to this day.

The Stage One V8 had the grille placed further forward in order to accommodate the larger engine. *Photo National Motor Museum.*

The story of the Land Rover starts almost by accident, just after the Second World War. At the time Rover were looking to increase its export market and decided some sort of agricultural vehicle was the way to go. Rover's chief designer, Maurice Wilks, was using an old American Jeep on his farm in Anglesey and he suggested that something along those lines that could be used as both a tractor and road vehicle were the way to go.

There was very little money available for tooling and Rover never envisaged the new vehicle having anything but a very short production run, to tide the firm over until economic situation picked up, so it would be a very simple design. The first prototype appeared in the summer of 1947 and used a Jeep chassis and a Rover 10 engine of 1389cc capacity. The gearbox was also from a 10 and it had a high-low range transfer box to provide four-wheel-drive. In order to simplify production for both home and export markets the driving position and instruments were placed in the middle of the car, with a seat on each side of the driver.

Maurice's brother, Spencer Wilks, was general manager of Rover and he inspected the prototype and gave the go ahead for 25 development vehicles to be built, an order that was later increased to 50. These differed somewhat from the prototype. Firstly the central steering position was dropped, and the instruments moved to the centre. The engine too had been changed to the 1595cc unit from the Rover 60. The Jeep chassis had also now gone to be replaced with a Rover designed one, while the body was a simple design made from an aluminium alloy called 'Birmabrite', as although steel was in short supply at the time wartime aircraft production had left a surplus of aluminium. Altogether 48 of the 50 development vehicles were built and surprisingly 16 are known to have survived.

The Land Rover was launched at the 1948 Amsterdam Motor Show, and had a price tag of £450. The car, which at this time was only available with an 80in wheelbase, was an instant hit and orders poured in. Within three months of production starting in July 1948 the Rover handbook listed dealers in 68 countries. Production had to be increased dramatically to keep up with demand and Rover suddenly realised it had a real winner on its books. In fact it just got better and Land Rovers continually outsold Rover's ordinary cars all the way through until 1963!

Above right: Land Rover's soon ended up in military service such as this 1952 Series I. *Photo Stephen Pullen.*

Above: Although envisaged as an agricultural vehicle Land Rovers were soon to be found doing all kinds of jobs in all kinds of industries. *Photo Stephen Pullen.*

NEW MARKETS

The appeal of the Land Rover quickly moved outside the world of agriculture and soon Rover were offering such variants as mobile compressors, fire appliances and mobile welders. The company also listed a 'station wagon' which had a body built by the coachbuilder Tickford. This even had the luxury of leather seats, wind-up windows and a heater!

1950 saw the first Land Rovers enter military service when a batch of 100 was ordered by the RAF. Several Land Rovers had previously been successfully tested by the government's Fighting Vehicles Research & Development Establishment at Chertsey.

The 1950s saw more development work, including the fitment of a larger 1997cc petrol engine in 1952. Two years later the 80in wheelbase also disappeared to be replaced by a choice of two new lengths, one of 86in and the long wheelbase 107in. The Tickford station wagon by now had been dropped and Land Rover started production of its own version, which although far less luxurious was cheaper and quicker to make.

1956 saw the wheelbase lengths increase again to 88in and 109in respectively and these would be the standard sizes until 1983 when the new coil-sprung 90 and 110 models were introduced.

The 1956 chassis extensions were actually in the engine bay as the following year a 2052cc diesel engine was offered as an option and needed the extra room.

In 1958 came the Series II – and to some this is the archetypal Land Rover. Initially the short wheelbase models were available fitted with the old two-litre inlet-over-exhaust petrol engine from the Series I or the 2057cc diesel. However the long wheelbase models got the new 2286cc petrol engine, as well as the diesel option. In the autumn of 1959 the station wagon models were introduced and this coincided with the two-litre engine being dropped and the 2286cc petrol unit becoming the standard power unit across the whole range, with the 2057cc diesel still being the option. The Series II also started to be assembled abroad including Australia, Spain, South Africa and Zambia. ›

> IN FACT IT JUST GOT BETTER AND LAND ROVERS CONTINUALLY OUTSOLD ROVER'S ORDINARY CARS ALL THE WAY THROUGH UNTIL 1963!

The Series IIA was launched in 1961. *Photo Stephen Pullen.*

The success of the Land Rover models over the years astounded Rover. In the autumn of 1954 the 100,000th vehicle had been produced, while the 500,000th rolled off the production line in April 1966.

1961 saw the introduction of the IIA, and with it the introduction of the 2286cc diesel engine. The following year however saw a very different model join the range – the Forward-Control.

BIGGER AND SMALLER

In answer to calls for more payload Land Rover came up with the Forward-Control. This still kept the basic overall dimensions of the long-wheelbase Land Rover, but the cab had been moved forward so the driver now sat at the side of the engine instead of behind it, thus giving a longer load bed. The chassis was also reinforced to give a payload of 30cwt on road or 25cwt off road. The first of these models was designated the Forward-Control IIA and were all fitted with the 2286cc petrol engine and all were for export. The IIB appeared in 1963 and had lower gear ratios and lighter steering than the IIA FC – and this time it was also available in Britain.

The next major change came via a strange route. In the early 1960s the Royal Marines had just started using the Westland Wessex helicopter, which could carry a slung payload of 2500lb. The Land Rover in use with them at the time weighed 3146lb and was just too heavy to lift and so development work started on making a lighter version – the first time Rover would ever design a specific Land Rover for military use. Other design considerations were that it had to have a width of no more that 60in so that two could fit side-by-side in the Armstrong Whitworth Argosy cargo aircraft then in use with the RAF. The new Land Rover also had to able to carry a payload of 1000lb including the driver for a range of 300 miles.

The first prototype was completed in 1965 and sent to the FVRDE for evaluation, although a 'Scheme A Airportable' version of the Land Rover had been shown at an exhibition some three years earlier, together with 'Scheme B' which used glass fibre bodywork. This second vehicle was also intended to be amphibious.

Production of the Lightweight (or more correctly the 'Military Half-ton' or 'Rover 1') started on November 11, 1968 and entered service with the Royal Marines later that year. Use soon spread to the other services, with the Army taking the majority of Lightweight's produced. Almost 11,000 vehicles were produced for UK forces until production finished in 1984. Incidentally it is worth mentioning that by the time the Lightweight went into production it actually weighed some 150lb more than the standard Series IIA Land Rover and in order to reach its target it had to be stripped of its doors, tailgate etc! However, advances in helicopter design by that time actually made the original target weight less important and so the vehicle was accepted.

A criticism often leveled at British Leyland is that they took good companies and ruined them. However, in the case of Land Rover it could be said that the opposite is true and that BL actually set the firm up to be the success it is today. We must accept that there were a few 'quality issues' with the vehicles during their ownership as well...

That having been said one of the first all-new Land Rover vehicles to appear under BL rule really has become a real icon – the Range Rover.

OFF-ROAD LUXURY

Ever since the launch of the Land Rover there were calls for a version that was a bit more civilised and less Spartan. Rover responded in the early days with the Tickford, but having this vehicle built by a traditional British coachbuilder meant it was very expensive, especially as it was classed as a car and therefore attracted purchase tax. Therefore only some 641 were sold, mostly for export, before the plug was pulled on production.

The next try was the 'Road Rover' of the early 1950s, which was designed by Maurice Wilks and Gordon Bashford. This was a very angular design based on a Rover P4 but came to nothing. However by the mid 50s the idea appeared again. This time it had very American styling but again the project got nowhere as Rover's bosses decided to concentrate its efforts on the Rover P6 2000 car. ›

Above: The Range Rover appeared in 1970 and became an instant classic. *Photo National Motor Museum.*

Left: A IIB Forward Control. *Photo Stephen Pullen.*

Right: The 'Military Half-ton' or Lightweight was introduced in 1968. *Photo National Motor Museum.*

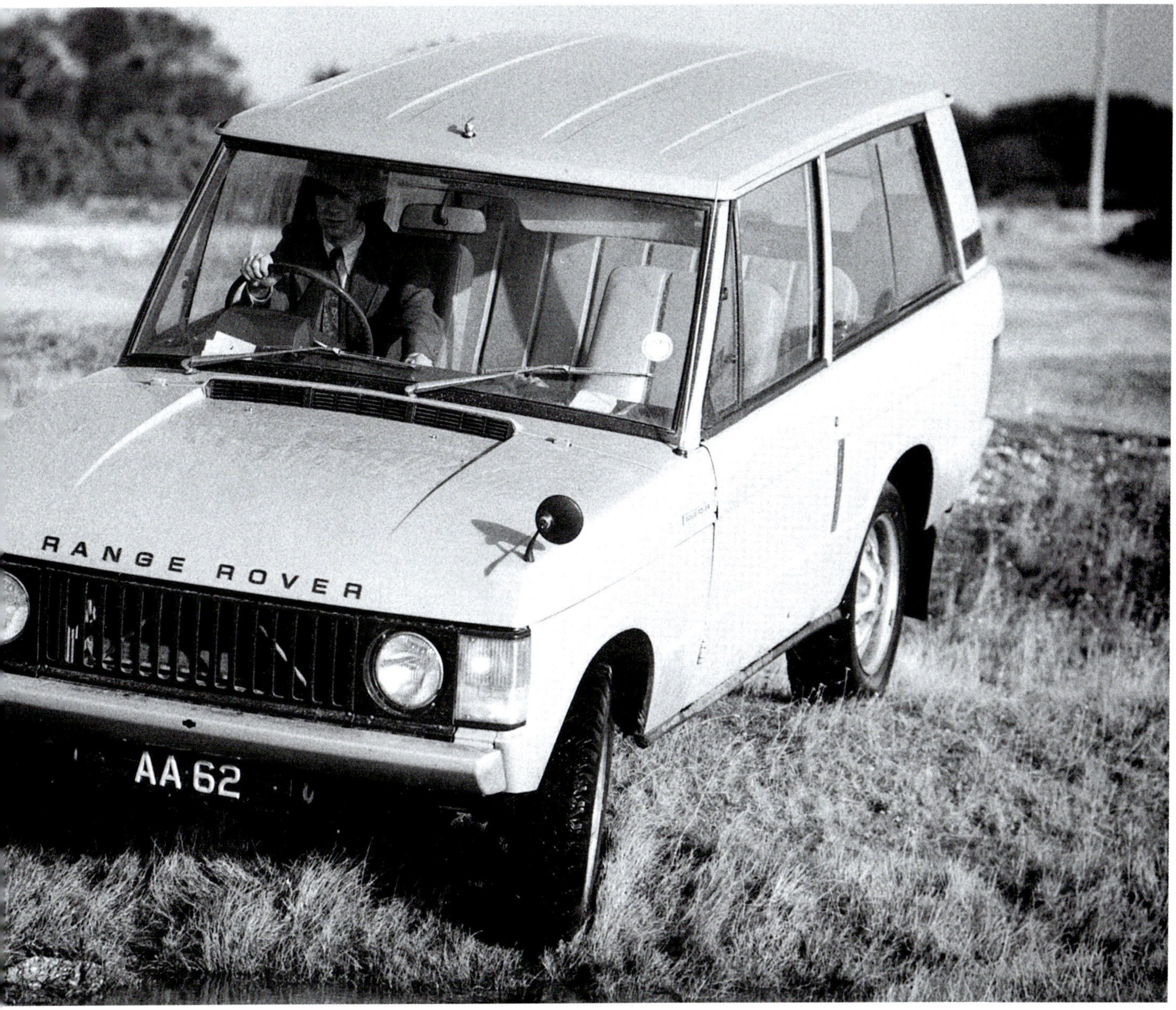
RANGE ROVER
AA 62

LAND-
- ROVER

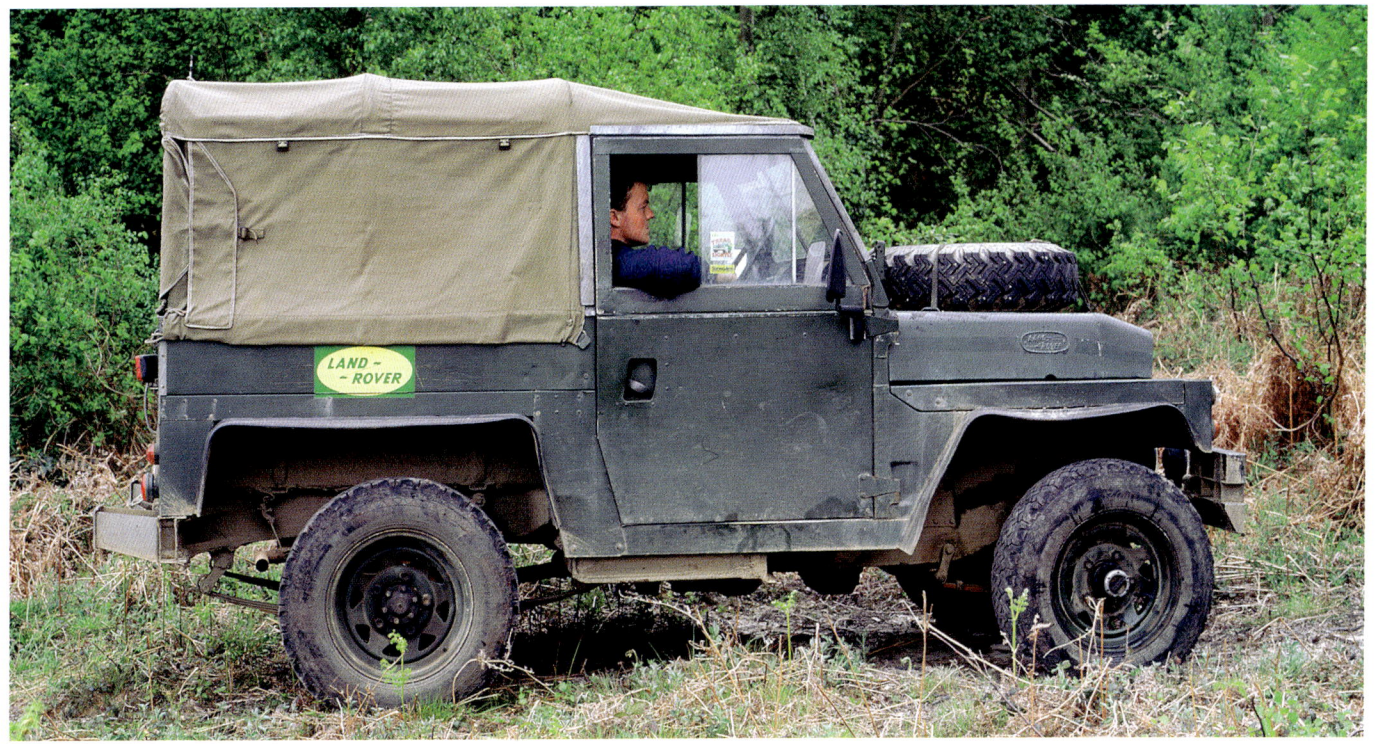

The Series III was launched in 1971 and became the best selling of all the Series Land Rovers. *Photo Stephen Pullen.*

> "THE RANGE ROVER WAS FINALLY UNVEILED TO THE WORLD IN JUNE 1970 AND BECAME A SENSATION – DESPITE ITS £1999 PRICE TAG!"

However, the idea did not die. In the mid 1960s Rover became aware of the trend in America for four-wheel-drive vehicles aimed less at farmers and the military and more towards leisure users who also needed a working vehicle. These people wanted a vehicle that could do almost every job imaginable from towing large trailers and horseboxes, to taking them camping in the forest, doing the shopping and then wafting them off to the opera!

The first Range Rover (or '100in Station Wagon' as it was then known) prototype was ready for road testing in 1967. This was designed by a team led by Charles Spencer King. The original idea had been to fit it with the three-litre straight-six engine from the P5, but luckily the new V8 unit was now available and so was specified from the start. Also, unlike the Land Rover, that used part-time four-wheel-drive, the Range Rover had such a powerful engine in the V8 that it had to use permanent four-wheel-drive.

As well as the engine and permanent four-wheel-drive the other thing that really made the Range Rover was its long-travel coil sprung suspension. This gave superb off-road ability together with excellent comfort on-road.

Several prototypes were tested and all were given the badge 'Velar'. This apparently was a name used on many Alvis prototypes and was made up from letters from 'Alvis' and 'Rover', and was particularly apt as 'Velar' in Spanish means 'veiled', 'covered' or 'under wraps' – perfect for a secret prototype vehicle on test! Another suggestion of the word is actually V Eight LAnd Rover.

The Range Rover was finally unveiled to the world in June 1970 and became a sensation – despite its £1999 price tag. The design, which was done by Charles Spencer King and stylist David Bache, was so popular that it hardly changed in 18 years of production. Initially it was available as an aluminium bodied three-door V8, with a four-door version coming to the market in 1981. It must be added that this variant was long overdue and had been offered by many coachbuilders, including Monteverdi of Switzerland whose conversion was actually approved by Land Rover. As well as four doors the Range Rover gained an automatic gearbox option in the early 1980s and in '83 the standard manual gearbox went up to five-speeds.

MORE SUCCESS

The Range Rover wasn't the only new vehicle to appear in the early 1970s, as September 1971 saw the launch of the Land Rover Series III. Basically this was a makeover of the IIA and the most obvious difference was the interior which had a completely new dashboard with the instruments in front of the driver. In addition the gearbox now had synchromesh on all forward gears and the four-cylinder petrol engine's compression ratio was raised to 8:1. It should be mentioned that there was now also the option of a 2.6-litre straight-six engine on the long wheelbase models, an engine that had been introduced in 1967 on the IIA.

Outwardly the Series III was very similar to the late IIA models where the headlights had been moved from the grille and into the wings. The Series III became the most popular of all the Series models, and the millionth Land Rover rolled off the production line in 1976.

The mid 1970s also saw the introduction of another vehicle designed specifically for the military – the Forward Control '101'.

The idea for this vehicle goes back to 1968 when the Army specified a vehicle to tow its new 105mm light gun and also be capable of towing a trailer of up to four tonnes. In addition it would have to form the basis of many other specialised vehicles such as command post, signals vehicle and ambulance.

Ten prototype vehicles were ready for testing in 1970. These were fitted with the 3.5 litre Rover V8 engine and permanent four-wheel-drive. Six were sent to the FVRDE and were extensively tested including in tropical and arctic environments. The other four went to the military for user testing. These trials were scheduled to end in 1972 – but don't think it was a forgone conclusion that the Land Rover would go into production, as a competitor in the shape of the Volvo 4140 Laplander was also being trialled at the same time.

In the end the Land Rover was the clear winner and the vehicle was displayed at the 1972 Commercial Motor Show to announce the fact.

Production actually started in 1975 with the General Service/Artillery Tractor being the first to see service. Altogether 2129 vehicles were made for the British Army, with 520 of them being bodied as ambulances. Another 127 were purchased by the RAF and 413 others were exported to Australia, Egypt, Luxembourg and Iran. Production ceased in 1978.

MORE POWER

One thing that had often been said of the Series Land Rover was that it was underpowered but this changed in 1979 when the 3.5-litr V8 engine was finally available in the new Land Rover Stage One V8. This vehicle was available until 1985 and had a detuned version of the Range Rover V8, which produced 91bhp as opposed to 135bhp. The Stage One was also the first Series Land Rover to have permanent four-wheel-drive.

The Stage One was only a taste of things to come as in 1983 Land Rover launched the 90 and 110. As well as an increase in wheelbase lengths (strangely the 90 is actually 92.9in) the new models featured permanent four-wheel-drive and coil springs all round. It was initially available with the 2286cc four-cylinder petrol or diesel engines from the Series III or the 3.5-litre V8, but the following year the four-cylinder units were upped to 2.5-litres. The diesel also received a turbocharger in 1986. From 1985 a third wheelbase length of 127in was added to the range. The 90/110/127 range were eventually given the name Defender in 1991.

While all this had been happening don't think the firm's other models were neglected. In 1986 the Range Rover received a boost when it could finally be specified with a diesel engine in the shape of a 2393cc unit from the Italian firm of VM. Also that year saw the last right-hand-drive three door as sales had dropped to virtually nothing in the UK. ›

Above: The Discovery was launched in 1989 and was designed to compete in the market for leisure 4x4s. *Photo National Motor Museum.*

Below: Production of the 90/110 started in 1983. They were given the name Defender in 1991. *Photo National Motor Museum.*

The interior of the Discovery was designed by the Terance Conran Design Group. *Photo National Motor Museum.*

The P38A Range Rover was launched in 1994. *Photo National Motor Museum.*

By then it was realised that there was a market for four-wheel-drive vehicles that fitted between the utilitarian 90/110 and the luxurious Range Rover, and that the market was being quickly taken up by imports, particularly from Japan.

PROJECT JAY

The answer to the problem was 'Project Jay' which would eventually deliver one of the best selling Land Rovers of all time – the Discovery. This finally went on sale in 1989 as a three-door V8 petrol, however there soon followed a brand new engine that was to make the Disco's fortunes – the direct-injection 2.5-ltr '200TDi'. This engine, codenamed 'Gemini' used the same block and crank as the previous Land Rover diesels but had an aluminium cylinder head and a new Bosch fuel injection system. It was far more economical and powerful than the old engines and proved an instant success. In 1990 it was also made available in the 90/110/127 and in 1992 it also found its way into the Range Rover.

The Discovery also had other features to attract buyers including an interior designed by the Terance Conran Design Group. The chassis and running gear were actually Range Rover based so despite its 'leisure' market design it had true off-road performance. It even ended up being used in the punishing Camel Trophy events.

In 1990 a five-door version came onto the market and helped sales further. As an example of how highly thought of it was, in 1993 they were even exported to Japan, where they were re-badged as the Honda Crossroad.

In 1994 the 200TDi engine was replaced by the all-new 300TDi. This was a much more refined unit and gave reduced emissions. The 3.5-ltr V8 petrol also went to be replaced by 3.9-ltr fuel injected V8 that was then being used in the new Range Rover.

The new Range Rover was designated the P38A and had an entirely new body and uprated engines. These included BMW units as there had just been a big change at the firm – a foreign takeover. Since the early 1980s parts of the nationalised British Leyland had been closed or sold off. Rover Group, including Land Rover had been acquired by British Aerospace in 1988, and in 1994 the firm changed hands again to BMW. This appears to be because BMW realised that Rover produced two vehicles that it didn't – very small saloons, such as the Mini, and four-wheel-drives.

Over the next six years BMW did much to improve the Land Rover brand, including launching the popular Freelander model. However, in 2000 the Rover Group broke up, and Land Rover was sold on to Ford. Here it became part of the Premier Automotive Group alongside another ex-BL car maker Jaguar, who had been owned by Ford since 1989. In 2008 both companies were sold by Ford to the Indian based Tata Motors for US $2.3billion.

Despite the change of ownership Land Rover continues to prosper. Recent new models have included the Range Rover Velar in 2017 and the range-topping Defender Octa. Hopefully the company will continue to enjoy success in the future – but much is owed to its British Leyland past. ✦

FROM THE ARCHIVE

Here's how Leyland looked after your new (or second-hand) car back in 1977.

OUTSTANDING SERVICE AT AN UNDERSTANDING PRICE

Leycare is the recommended systematic approach to servicing for Leyland Cars, featuring:

- Comprehensive Check Lists
- Qualified Operators
- 3,000 mile/3 month guarantee
- Specialised Tools and Equipment

It is a carefully organised modern and efficient way of keeping your car in top condition at a reasonable price, and with more than 2500 outlets nationwide:

Leycare is closer than you think

The Unipart Sign. You'll see it wherever you are in the UK, in cities, towns and along the road. Always near at hand, always at your service. Not just for a fine selection of top flight accessories, but a complete range of quality parts from a nut and bolt to an exhaust system, rigorously tested by Leyland engineers and chemists to ensure that your car runs efficiently, safely—longer. So for all parts and accessories, call in at your nearest Unipart stockist today—you'll be welcome, wherever you see this sign.

P.E.D.

Leyland Cars, in conjunction with Leyland International, operate a Personal Exports Scheme under which entitled purchasers can buy vehicles free of Car Tax and Value Added Tax. You may be eligible if you are a UK Resident intending to spend at least 12 months abroad, or an Overseas Visitor returning to your own or another country.

Advice is available on delivery times, insurance, specifications, British and Overseas Customs requirements, and overseas servicing facilities on request and without obligation. You can use the vehicle in the UK if time permits, in which case we can advise on return shipping, or alternatively it can be shipped directly overseas from the factory.

You should note, however, that not all of the vehicles described in this brochure may necessarily be available for export to all countries. In particular, export prices, specifications and delivery availability may differ from information generally published in the UK.

Full details may be obtained from any Leyland Cars Distributor or Dealer, from the Personal Exports Department, Leyland Cars, PO Box 41, Longbridge, Birmingham B31 2TB—Telephone 021-475 2101 or the London Tax Free Sales Centre, 41-46 Piccadilly, London W1V 0BD—Telephone 01-734 6080.

GAUNTLET—LEYLAND'S WAY OF TELLING YOU WHERE TO BUY BRITAIN'S BEST USED CARS

Buying a used car can be a chancy business. For many, the prospect of handing over hard earned cash to someone they may never have seen before, for something they may know very little about, can be quite unnerving to say the least.

This is where GAUNTLET comes in. The Scheme is specifically designed to take the worry out of buying a used car and give used cars a good name.

The advantages of buying a used car from a GAUNTLET Dealer can be summed up in one word—CONFIDENCE.

The confidence of knowing that every Gauntlet Dealer has been checked and approved by Leyland Cars. The confidence of knowing that every Gauntlet car carries a full parts and labour Warranty for a minimum period of 3 months and in many cases a lot longer.

And choice as well. Not every Gauntlet car is a Leyland car—all makes and models are sold under the Scheme.

The Gauntlet scheme is operated by many Leyland Cars' Distributors and Dealers throughout the country—so if you feel a new car is beyond your reach and are thinking of buying a used car call into your local Gauntlet Dealer—we think you will find it worthwhile.

Even if you never need it, it's good to know you've got it.
Applicable only to vehicles used within the United Kingdom.

Every new vehicle detailed in this brochure has Supercover. It's one of the most comprehensive service schemes ever offered in the United Kingdom by any motor vehicle manufacturer.

At each and every stage in their production, vehicles are thoroughly examined by our experts and engineers. In addition, the dealer puts each vehicle through a long and extensive check.

So when you buy your new vehicle from Leyland Cars you can be confident that everything possible has been done to ensure that it is in perfect condition.

Supercover is a very comprehensive package. But if you have any trouble whatsoever, no matter how small, you just contact your dealer. He'll do his best to keep your vehicle in perfect condition.

If you're not 100% satisfied with the service you get, then we provide a special card with every vehicle, which should be sent direct to the Managing Director of Leyland Cars, and he'll make sure the problem is solved quickly and efficiently.

Supercover is a permanent charter for the British motorist. It gives you one more reason for buying from the Leyland Cars range.

WOLSELEY

The Wolseley company may be said to be one of the founding fathers of the UK motor industry, in a round about sort of way. However, the man who gave his name to the firm had nothing at all to do with the cars they produced.

Frederick York Wolseley was born in 1837 at Kingstown, County Dublin in Ireland. He was the second son of Major Garnet Joseph Wolseley, of the King's Own Scottish Borderers. His elder brother, also named Garnet, rose through the ranks of the British Army to become Field Marshall Viscount Wolseley.

However, a military life wasn't for young Frederick, who in 1854 arrived in Australia to work for his brother-in-law Ralston Caldwell at a sheep station on the Murray River. After a few years Frederick had financial interests in several sheep stations and in the 1860s began experimenting with machines to shear sheep. By the late 1880s the use of Wolseley's sheep shearing machines had spread throughout Australia and New Zealand and in 1888 he went to England and set up the Wolseley Sheep Shearing Machine Co Ltd in Birmingham.

Back in Australia the works were being run by one Herbert Austin, who had gone to Australia in 1884 at the age of 18. In 1893 he returned to England to become Wolseley's production manager.

In 1895/6 Austin built the first Wolseley car based on a design by Frenchman Leon Bollee. This was a three-wheeler, with two wheels at the front. A year later Austin came up with a design of its own. Again it was a three-wheeler, but this time it had two wheels at the back.

The first four-wheeled Wolseley, the Voiturette, appeared in 1899 but sales did not start for another two years, as Frederick Wolseley died in 1899, and in 1901 the company was taken over by Vickers, Sons & Maxim Ltd, and renamed the Wolseley Tool & Machinery Co Ltd.

The 'new' firm moved to a factory at Adderley Park in Birmingham and soon had two models ready for sale. These were basically the same as the 1899 Voiturette although they did use chain drive as opposed to the belts that had been used on the original car. One version was fitted with a 10hp 2.6-litre twin-cylinder engine while the other had a 1.3-litre 5hp single. In 1902 a four-cylinder engine also joined the range. This produced 20hp and had a capacity of 5.2 litres.

Initially these cars sold well but after 1903 the company started to make a loss. The cars all had horizontal engines and Austin believed that was the only way to go. Unfortunately the company directors (and customers) didn't agree and so Vickers took over a firm that used vertical engines, the Siddeley Autocar Company Ltd. Austin was not happy and so resigned and started his own company. Ironically, Austin only ever used vertical engines in the cars his own firm made.

Shortly afterwards John Siddeley was appointed as Wolseley's general manager and by the end of 1906 all the horizontal engined cars had gone, replaced by a 12hp twin and four different four-cylinder models of between 15 and 32hp.

By 1911 production had risen to around 1600 cars per year. The company also made other products such as marine and aircraft engines, and had also made the motor-tractors used by Captain Scott on his ill-fated expedition to the Antarctic from 1910-12.

WARTIME CONTRACTS

As with most other engineering works, Wolseley soon stopped production of cars at the outbreak of the First World War and took on war contracts. These included gun mountings and the production of Viper V8 aircraft engines, which were based on a design by Hispano-Suiza. From 1917 the company also started making Royal Aircraft Factory SE5 biplane fighters.

The last car to carry the Wolseley name was the 18/22 of 1975. It was restyled after six months and relaunched as the Austin Princess.

The car that's got it all together in styling.

The new Wolseley is nothing if not elegant.

Its tinted windows, vinyl roof and stylish, aerodynamic wedge-shaped body with that long, raking bonnet are guaranteed to make a few heads turn.

The car that's got it all together in luxury.

Without doubt, the new Wolseley is a very luxurious motor car.

The spacious interior has fitted carpeting (including the large boot) and great care has been taken to ensure that interior soundproofing keeps noise levels to a minimum.

The push-button radio is fitted as standard, and there's a long centre console.

Even the ventilation system has a superb, in-built 3-speed fan heating system.

With the war over in 1918, car production soon restarted. As with most other makers, the designs were almost identical to their prewar designs but in 1920 a new single overhead-camshaft engine was launched which improved performance across the range. There is no doubt that these engines were influenced by the wartime Hispano-Suiza aircraft engine designs, particularly their overhead camshafts and detachable cylinder heads. Some of these cars actually ended up racing and there were even sports car versions such as the Sports Ten.

Light commercial vehicles were also produced and one was to strangely help kick-start the Japanese motor industry. In 1918 the Tokyo based Ishikawajima Shipbuilding & Engineering Company purchased a licence to produce Wolseley's 1.5-ton 'CP' lorry. Production ran from 1919 until 1923 when the company started selling vehicles of its own design under the name of 'Sumida'. In 1933 a new firm was formed to take on the production of these vehicles called Kyodo Kokusan Jidosha Kabushiki-Kaisha, and the vehicles were sold under the brand name 'Isuzu' which translates as '50 bells' and was named after the Japanese river Isuzu. Although the company has since changed its name, Isuzu commercials are still sold throughout the world, although many have been rebadged over the years, such as the Isuzu KB pick-up, which was sold in the UK as the Bedford KB and in the US as the Chevrolet LUV.

Anyway, back to Wolseley in the 1920s, as all its recent success was not to last. In 1923 it sold some 4427 vehicles but by 1926 this had dropped to around 2000. In addition the company had borrowed heavily to extend the factory and build a prestigious new showroom in London. Therefore late in 1926 Wolseley was declared bankrupt with debts of around £2 million.

In 1927 Vickers placed Wolseley up for sale, and there were three major bidders – General Motors, Herbert Austin and William Morris. At the end of the day the prize went to Morris who paid some £730,000 for the firm, which is around £22 million in today's money. It was quickly renamed Wolseley Motors (1927) Ltd and for several years remained the personal property of Morris as he didn't know whether it would be a success or not and didn't want to cause problems for his company of Morris Motors Ltd. It would be 1935 before he was sure enough to sell Wolseley to his company, making himself a very tidy profit in the process. ›

Above left: The car was nicknamed the 'Wedge'.

Above right: Typical 1970s luxury.

Below: The Hornet name appeared in 1930. The car used a 1271cc straight-six engine which went on to be the basis of the six-cylinder ohc engines made by sports car maker MG.

Upon buying Wolseley, Morris quickly started reorganising things. Part of the Adderley Park plant was turned over to the production of Morris Commercial vehicles, while the rest was sold. Wolseley cars were then made just at their other factory at Ward End in Birmingham.

COMMON ENGINEERING

For several years Wolseley continued to make cars of its own design. These included the 16/45 'Silent Six' and the 21/60 which used a straight-eight engine of 2680cc. There was even a four-litre straight-eight called the 32/80 but it didn't sell well – in fact there were only five ever made!

The year 1930 saw a very well known name appear, the Hornet, which was given to a car with a 1271cc straight-six engine and virtually the same body as the Morris Minor of the period. Incidentally, this engine went on to form the basis of the six-cylinder ohc engines made by sports car maker MG.

In 1936 Wolseley announced a new range of models, the Series II range, with engine capacities from 1292cc up to 3485cc. All these cars however shared their styling with Morris, although they did differ mechanically in that they had overhead valve engines and four-speed gearboxes.

Although some 'commonality' was creeping in, Wolseley did still make some individual designs such as the Salon de Ville and a long wheelbase limousine.

1938 saw the introduction of the Series III models which featured new, more upright, all-steel bodies made by Birmingham based Fisher & Ludlow.

It must be mentioned that the 1930s also started the tradition of the Wolseley being the iconic British police car. Apparently this began in 1932 when the London Metropolitan Police bought a second-hand Wolseley saloon for the princely sum of £40. This was to mark the beginning of an association between Wolseley and the police that lasted until the 1960s.

The 1930s also saw the first of a very famous piece of marketing on Wolseley's part – the illuminated radiator grille badge, something that would tell you a Wolseley was travelling towards you even on the blackest night.

LUCK – BAD AND GOOD

A Wolseley version of the very successful Morris Eight Series E was due for launch on September 11, 1939. However, the start of the Second World War quickly put paid to that and Wolseley soon turned over to war contracts.

However, Wolseley was fortunate as it became one of the first British motor vehicle companies to get back into civilian production after the war, as it received an order for a batch of cars from the British government in September 1945.

1946 saw the introduction of the Wolseley Eight that had been delayed due to the war. This used the Morris Eight body and chassis fitted with an ohv 918cc engine and a Wolseley styled radiator grille. William Morris, who became Lord Nuffield in 1934, actually used one as his everyday car until 1955.

The Earls Court Motor Show of 1948 saw the introduction of the 4/50 and 6/80 models. These were basically just Wolseley versions of the Morris Oxford and Six cars. The 6/80 and Morris Six were virtually identical except that the 6/80 had twin-carbs, a more luxurious interior and the trademark Wolseley grille. The 4/50 however had an ohc version of the four-cylinder Morris MO engine as well as the usual Wolseley differences.

In 1949 all Wolseley production was switched from Ward End to the Morris factory at Cowley. It is interesting to note that by the time the 6/80 finished production in 1954 it had sold more than twice as many as the Morris version...

1957 saw the first 1500, which was basically a stretched four-door Morris Minor fitted with a 1489cc 'B' Series engine. If you wanted a bit more poke you could buy the almost identical Riley 1.5 that had twin-carbs but less wood and leather. Over 100,000 1500s would be made before production stopped in 1965.

The 16/60 shared its styling with the Farina-styled Morris Oxford, Austin Cambridge, Riley 4/68 and MG Magnette.

Wolseley versions of the Austin/Morris Farina saloons soon followed. These included the 15/60 and 16/60 which shared their basic body styling with the Morris Oxford, Austin Cambridge, Riley 4/68 and MG Magnette. There was even a version of the Vanden Plas Princess designated the 6/99.

By the 1960s 'badge engineering' really had taken hold. The Hornet name was used for a version of the Mini that used the same modified front and rear ends as the Riley Elf. Similarly, the Wolseley Six was basically the same as the Morris 2200, which in turn could be said to be a six-cylinder version of the Austin 1800.

The last car to use the Wolseley badge was also the first of a new range. This was launched in 1975 as the 18/22 and featured a transverse 2.2-litre straight-six engine driving the front wheels. However production of this car only lasted for six months before it was restyled due to costs and relaunched as the Austin Princess. Some 3800 Wolseley 18/22 cars were made.

There have been no more Wolseley cars produced since then and the brand is now owned by the Chinese Nanjing Automobile Group since it bought the assets of MG-Rover. ✦

Above: The 1800cc transverse engine in the 18/85 MkII. This is the 'S' version with twin-carbs.

Below: The 18/85 MkII range used the Austin 1800 'Landcrab' body. Note the trademark illuminated grille badge.

SHERPA

Despite often being described as a 'parts bin special' designed on the cheap, the Leyland Sherpa van, and its successors, became good sellers for almost 40 years.

Above left: The interior of the 1974 van.

Above right: The integral pick-up was offered for several years before being replaced by drop-side versions.

By the late 1960s British Leyland light commercial vehicle models were becoming increasingly long in the tooth and a new design was needed to compete with the likes of the Ford Transit. The task of designing the new model was given to Stan Dews who had been an engineer at Longbridge before moving to Ford where he had actually been involved in the development of the Transit. He therefore seemed an obvious choice to develop a van that would seriously threaten the popularity of the new Ford offering. However, BL was very 'cost conscious' to say the least, and his first design ideas, using front wheel drive, were rejected because they were considered far too expensive.

By now BL were rapidly losing market share to Ford and also Bedford who had begun producing its CF range. Dew decided that to keep costs down and also reduce development time he would look to use existing components from other BL vehicles for his new design.

Using this approach Dew's new van was soon ready. This used the chassis frame and axles from the JU van, the 1.8 litre petrol engine from the Morris Marina and the Austin 'C' Series gearbox from the 3-litre car. The roof and side panels were from the J4 van and items such as the steering wheel, door handles, heater etc were also taken from existing BL vehicles. Obviously some new body pressings and parts would be required but using so many components from the BL 'parts bin' certainly kept costs down, although it definitely did nothing for the van's style. However, as the money men were happy the project, designated CV306, was given the go-ahead.

Despite the fact that the name 'Sherpa' had been thought of prior to launch, when the van did go on sale in 1974 it was called 'The New Leyland Van from Austin Morris'. However after a few months it was replaced by the originally proposed name – Sherpa.

There was no way the Sherpa could compete head on with the Transit so the van was marketed as a value for money option. In addition much was made of how narrow it was (due to the J4 roof) which made it more agile in cities.

By this time Ford was struggling to meet the demand for the Transit which was selling faster than the company could build it and that created opportunities for BL, and the Sherpa starting selling well.

The van was available with 12 different door options, including sliding cab doors and side loading doors. In addition the Sherpa flat topped chassis frame meant it was easy to build special bodies on, such as tippers, ambulances, Luton bodies etc. The design allowed so many different bodies to be fitted that BL set up a 'Special Advisory Service' to assist customers with bespoke requirements and to recommend bodybuilders able to carry out the work that would not invalidate the factory warranty.

As well as a petrol engine, the Sherpa was also available with a 1.8 litre diesel engine which was an up-rated version of the existing 1.5 litre 'B' Series unit. Initially the models in the range were designated by gross vehicle weight. The vans were the 185 (1.85 tons) the 220 (2.2 tons), and 240 (2.4tons). There were also the 215 and 240 pick-ups, a 240 minibus and there were several chassis cab options based on the 220 and 240.

In 1978 the original petrol engines were replaced with the new overhead-cam 'O' Series units, which could be ordered as either a 1.7 litre or a 2-litre. The existing B

The Sherpa. It can take it.

Series diesel unit was retained. A change of name was also made – from 1978 until 1981 the range was sold as the Morris Sherpa.

By 1981 sales were starting to fall and so BL set up the Freight Rover division as part of the Land Rover Group, and the Sherpa was re-badged as the Freight Rover Sherpa. In 1982 the range got the 'K2' facelift with a re-styled grille among other improvements. The side access to the loading bay was also altered allowing a full-width pallet to be loaded. By now the range comprised the 200, 230, 250 and 280. A larger bodied 'high capacity' variant also appeared which used the 255 or 280 chassis and increased the load space to 330 cu ft from 190. A four-wheel-drive Sherpa van was also introduced, but it was never a popular seller and was soon dropped.

The range was further re-styled in the mid 1980s and a wide bodied version designated the 300 series was also introduced. This was available in two wheelbase lengths and could be ordered with twin rear wheels. The Land Rover 2.5 litre diesel engine was also now available as an option.

In 1984 London's Metropolitan Police contacted BL requesting the development of a 'Rapid Intervention Personnel Carrier.' The basis of this vehicle was a high roof 300 minibus which was fitted with the 3.5-litre V8 petrol engine from the Range Rover. The chassis was also modified to be able to fit a ZF automatic gearbox. Other modifications included a stronger roof and bulletproof glass. The first of these new vans was in service by August 1985. The design was later used as the basis for an ambulance version and the V8 also became an option for the 300 goods vehicles.

In 1987 Leyland Trucks (of which Freight Rover was now a part) was merged with Dutch truck maker DAF. The new company was called DAF NV and was owned 60% by DAF and 40% by Rover Group. This also marked the end of the Sherpa name, with the vans now being called the 200 and 400.

In 1993 DAF NV went bankrupt and Leyland DAF Vans as they were then known were the subject of a management buyout. The 200 series was renamed the Pilot and the larger van the Convoy. LDV unfortunately failed late in 2008 due to the recession. ✦

Below: Sherpas have always been a good base for special bodies – as demonstrated by this 1983 Freight Rover 280 fire appliance. *Photo Stephen Pullen.*

TRIUMPH

Triumph was the first car maker purchased by Leyland Motors, which until then had concentrated on commercial vehicles. Famous for mass market sports cars, Triumph survived until well into the BL era, but ended up as just a shadow of its former self as a name on badge-engineered Honda saloons.

A Triumph Super Seven of 1932. *Photo National Motor Museum.*

Triumph produced around 30,000 motorcycles for the British and Allied armies in the First World War. *Photo Richard Pullen Collection.*

In 1885 one Siegfried Bettmann emigrated from Nuremberg in Germany to Coventry. After a few jobs he started his own import and export agency, S Bettmann & Co. This firm specialised in selling bicycles and sewing machines, many of which were sold under the Bettmann brand name. In 1886 Bettmann decided to rename his company as the Triumph Cycle Co. A year later, the company was registered as the New Triumph Co Ltd as it had received funding from Dunlop. During that year, Bettmann took on a business partner, Moritz Schulte, who also came from Nuremberg.

In 1888 Triumph actually started manufacturing bicycles instead of just selling those made by others, and a new factory was set up. The business prospered and in 1896 a Nuremberg factory was opened to make bicycles for the German market.

In 1902 Triumph made its first motorcycle, which was fitted with a Belgian-made Minerva engine. The following year the German factory also started making motorbikes.

These early motorcycles were based on other people's designs and it would be 1905 before a completely Triumph-designed machine went on sale. However, it was definitely the right way to go as by 1907 the firm had to expand to keep up with demand and a new factory was opened. The firm also introduced an economy brand motorbike called the Gloria which was made in the original factory.

By this time many British Triumph machines were being exported and this caused a bit of confusion when German Triumphs were also on offer. Therefore the German machines were renamed TWN which stood for Triumph Werke Nurnberg.

The First World War was good for Triumph, which supplied over 30,000 motorcycles to the British and allied armies. Among them was the famous 550cc Model H Roadster which was nicknamed the 'Trusty Triumph'.

After the war Schulte left the company and in 1921 Triumph purchased the factory of the bankrupt Dawson Car Company. Two years later the first Triumph car was launched onto the market. This was the 10/20 which had a 1393cc four-cylinder engine and four-speed gearbox. This was designed by an employee of Lea-Francis, Arthur Alderson, and as such Triumph had to pay a royalty on each car made. This made the price a little on the high side but it was still listed for sale until late in 1925.

By this time Triumph had become one of Britain's largest motorcycle and car makers, with a 500,000sq ft of factory space capable of producing as many as 30,000 motorcycles and cars per year. Triumph was also still a large bicycle manufacturer and this side of the business contributed to a high proportion of the company's income, particularly through exports.

The 10/20 car was followed by the 1872cc 13/35, which was incidentally the first British car to have Lockheed hydraulic brakes fitted to all four wheels, and the 2169cc 15/50 which became known as the Fifteen.

However, the breakthrough car did not appear until 1928 in the shape of the Super Seven. This car was designed by Stanley Edge, who had played a big part in the design of the Austin Seven. The new car was fitted with a 832cc four-cylinder side-valve engine which developed 21bhp. It also shared the hydraulic brakes fitted to the larger Triumphs which gave it quite an advantage over other cars of this size, including the popular Austin Seven. The price was competitive as well at just £149 for the tourer-bodied version while the equivalent Austin went for £135.

Over the next few years many bodies became available for the Super Seven chassis, some made by Triumph while others came from outside coachbuilders. A sports car with a supercharged engine was also offered that could top 80mph, over 20mph up on a standard Super Seven tourer. Altogether some 17,000 Super Sevens were made before the model was replaced in 1932.

By now, however, the Depression was really being felt at Triumph. At the start of the economic problems Triumph had sold its German operation, TWN. This was followed by the sale of the Triumph bicycle business to Raleigh in 1932. However, a bigger change was to come.

In 1933 Bettmann, the company's founder, stepped down as chairman and was replaced by Claude Holbrook. He had joined Triumph in 1919 after military service with the Army Service Corps and then as head of a military procurement section at the War Office. One of his jobs at Whitehall had been to organise the supply of military vehicles, including motorcycles, which is how he came to know Bettmann and the Triumph company. However, Holbrook's interest was in cars not motorcycles. And so once in charge he began the process of splitting the company up and in 1936 succeeded in selling the Triumph motorcycle business to Jack Sangster, who also owned the motorcycle maker Ariel.

With Holbrook in command things soon started to change on the car front as well. He decided that it wasn't worth continuing trying to compete with the likes of Austin and Morris in the small car market, as both could simply produce far more cars, and so the Super Seven was dropped. Instead Triumph started to produce larger cars fitted with Coventry Climax engines, such as the Super Nine. A sports version of this car was also made available which was called the Southern Cross.

In 1934 a completely new range of cars was introduced, the Glorias. These used Coventry Climax engines with four cylinders (1087cc) or six cylinders (1476cc). In 1935 these sizes increased to 1232cc for the four and 1991cc for the six.

Also in 1934 came the first Triumph to carry the 'Dolomite' name. This was fitted with a 1991cc double-overhead-cam, eight-cylinder engine and a Roots type supercharger. Its power output was 120bhp at 5500rpm which gave the car a top speed of 110mph. However, the project was cancelled after just three chassis had been made. Many say this was due to an argument with Alfa Romeo, which produced a very similar looking engine, but the most probable reason was simply lack of money.

Triumph started to make its own engines again in 1937. These were designed by Donald Healey, and were produced as 1496cc four-cylinder, 1767cc four-cylinder or a 1991cc six. All were overhead valve. However, a Coventry Climax unit of 1232cc was kept on for the 'economy' model Gloria. The range was also redesigned and now consisted firstly of the 1232cc and 1496cc Glorias. The 1767cc and 1991cc six-cylinder engines were fitted to the Vitesse and the new Dolomite. This new Dolomite was totally different from the previous car and featured a very distinctive radiator grille, often referred to as the 'waterfall grille'. ›

Above left: The first Triumphs to bear the 'Dolomite name used a straight-eight double overhead-cam sports racer. *Photo National Motor Museum.*

Above right: A Standard Nine Sports pictured in 1928. *Photo National Motor Museum.*

1946 Triumph 1800 Roadster. *Photo National Motor Museum.*

The first of the postwar Triumph sports cars, the TR2. *Photo National Motor Museum.*

However, money was still tight at Triumph. In 1939 a low-priced 1496cc four-door saloon was launched, but it was too late. In June of that year Triumph went into receivership.

Shortly afterwards the company was purchased by Thomas Ward & Co. At the time Triumph had two car-making plants and one was immediately sold to the Government for war work, while the other was let to the Armstrong Whitworth Aircraft Company. This factory was badly damaged in the Coventry Blitz and so in 1944 it, together with the rights to Triumph's designs and name, were sold to the Standard Motor Company.

STANDARD

Standard had been founded in 1903 by civil engineer Reginald Maudslay, who was the great grandson of the famous engineer Henry Maudslay, the inventor of the screw-cutting lathe. It must be noted that Reginald's brother, Cyril, had set up a separate car building company some two years previously, the Maudslay Motor Co, which went on to make commercial vehicles until 1960. Indirectly it also ended up as part of BL. It is also interesting to note that one of Reginald's financial backers at the start was Sir John Wolfe-Barry, the designer of Tower Bridge.

The first Standard used a single-cylinder horizontal engine and a three-speed gearbox, while the second had two horizontal cylinders and was the first Standard to be sold. Soon, however, vertical engines were being made and in 1905 a six-cylinder 18/20hp unit was put on the market which could be supplied for fitment to other vehicles if required.

One of Standard's greatest strokes of luck in this period came from appointing a London car dealer named Charles Friswell as chairman, a position he held until 1911, and from 1906 until 1911 he took the entire output of the Standard works. However, his biggest coup came in 1911 when he managed to arrange for every vehicle used in the Coronation of George V as Emperor of India to be Standards. This was held in Delhi and altogether there were some 70 vehicles shipped out including lorries to carry beaters on tiger hunts.

Unfortunately Friswell left the company that year due to a disagreement and his shares were purchased by a solicitor named C J Band and, ironically, Siegfried Bettmann, the founder of Triumph!

Car production continued until 1914 when the company went over to war work, including producing shells, mortars and, later on, aircraft including the Sopwith Pup and Bristol FE2-B. In order to make these aircraft Standard acquired a larger factory at Canley near Coventry.

In 1919 car production resumed with the prewar 1087cc Model S. Larger cars soon followed including the four-seater SLO which used a 1597cc ohv four-cylinder engine. The SLO was developed over the years, increasing in size to 1944cc in 1922, when it became known as the SLO-4, and the inclusion of front wheel brakes from 1926. By the time production ended in 1928 some 20,000 had been manufactured.

It was replaced with a smaller model, the Nine, which was a fabric-bodied saloon. This used a 1155cc side-valve engine and sold for less than £200. Over the next few years other engines and bodies were also offered including a supercharged sports car.

However, the big event of this period was the arrival of one Captain John Black in 1929. Born in 1895, Black had studied law before volunteering for military service in 1914. After time in the Royal Navy he transferred to the Army to serve in the Tank Corps. After the war he went to

1951 Standard Vanguard Phase 1. *Photo National Motor Museum.*

– 58 –

Left: The TR3A appeared in September 1957. It had a redesigned exterior and a 100bhp engine. *Photo National Motor Museum.*

Below: A 1938 Triumph Dolomite with 'waterfall' grille. *Photo National Motor Museum.*

Bottom: The TR4 of 1961 used a completely new Michelotti-styled body. *Photo National Motor Museum.*

work for Hillman and ended up marrying into the Hillman family in 1921. He then became joint managing director of the firm, eventually leaving to join Standard.

His arrival marked a period of reorganisation at Standard. He also brought a much needed injection of capital. In 1933 he became managing director and in 1934 production had risen to over 34,000 vehicles per year.

New models continued to be launched during the 1930s, and engines and chassis were also sold to other manufacturers, most notably SS, the forerunners of Jaguar.

During the Second World War, Standard was one of the few firms which did still make some road vehicles, which were fitted with 'utility' bodies. However, they also set up two 'shadow factories' and produced de Havilland Mosquito and Airspeed Oxford aircraft, various aircraft engines and the 'Beaverette' armoured car.

And it is here that we return to Triumph, as in 1944 the company was purchased by Standard for £75,000.

STANDARD-TRIUMPH

After the war Standard got back into the car market with three models, the Eight, 12 and 14. These were produced until 1948, and could also be purchased as wooden-bodied estates, which were classed as commercial vehicles and could therefore get round the 33% purchase tax that new cars attracted at this time. These were followed in 1947 by the Vanguard. Although this sold well, particularly overseas, not everybody appreciated its styling. It's interesting to note that when the Phase Two Vanguard appeared in 1954 it was available with a two-litre diesel engine and was therefore the first British diesel-engined, mass-produced car. The engine used was the 20C which was being made by Standard for the Ferguson tractor that the firm was assembling at the time. More of that later.

Triumph on the other hand brought out something much different in style in 1946, although it did share most of its mechanical components with the Standard models. This was the 1800, which could be bought as a saloon or roadster. These used a tubular steel chassis and an aluminium and steel body made by the coachbuilder Mulliners. These were made until 1948

when they were replaced by the 2000 models, which used the 2088cc engine from the Standard Vanguard. After a short while the roadster was dropped. However, the saloon was re-engineered with a new chassis and front suspension and relaunched as the Renown, which was produced until 1954 with a few modifications along the way. Incidentally the roadster version did achieve a small amount of fame in the 1980s when one was chosen as the car used by the Jersey TV detective Bergerac. ›

Another new Triumph car from this period was the Mayflower saloon launched in 1949. This sold well, particularly in export markets, but in 1953 something altogether much more exciting appeared. This was the TR2 sports car. An attempt had been made previously at producing a postwar Triumph sports car, using a left-over prewar Standard Flying Nine chassis, but it proved totally unsuitable. The TR2, however, was a much different animal and was developed by Ken Richardson, who had been hired from the Lincolnshire-based racing car manufacturer BRM.

Five TR2 prototypes were built and were fitted with Vanguard engines reduced to 1991cc and fitted with twin-carbs to give 90bhp. One was tested on a Belgian motorway where it topped 115mph in touring trim and 125mph in stripped trim. However, when put into production, the TR2 with overdrive could do 102.5mph.

The TR2 remained in production until 1955 when it was replaced with the TR3. This had front disc brakes and its power was increased to 95bhp. This was eventually superseded by the TR3A in September 1957, which had a redesigned exterior and a 100bhp engine. Over 58,000 would be made before the TR4 appeared in August 1961.

Over this period the Triumph TR sports cars notched up considerable success in motor racing including a win in the 1954 RAC Rally for Johnny Wallwork and John Cooper's TR2, and a Coupe des Alpes for Dutchman Maurice Gatsonides (inventor of the speed camera) in the 1954 Alpine Rally.

While Triumph was going for the sports market, Standard was looking after the 'bread and butter' end, although it must be said that some of the 1950s Standards did do quite well in international rallying. As well as the Vanguard in its various forms the company was producing the Eight, launched in 1953 specifically designed to compete with the Morris Minor and Austin A30. This was a monocoque saloon fitted with an 803cc overhead valve engine. There was also the Ten which used a 948cc version of the engine, while the Phase 2 Ten launched in 1957 had the option of automatic transmission. The Ten was also the basis of the Pennant which had slightly restyled bodywork and two-tone paint. These cars were made until 1960, while the Vanguard, which had by now been completely restyled by Italian designer Michelotti and made practical by the coachbuilder Vignale, continued in production until 1963. Standard also introduced the Atlas van in 1958. This used the 948cc engine from the Ten so was very underpowered, so the Atlas Major was brought out in 1961 which used a 1670cc engine.

Above: The Herald van version, the Courier, was only available for just over two years.

Right: The Standard Atlas van was rebadged as a Leyland after it was taken over.

Below: The Triumph Herald was introduced in 1959 and used a separate chassis.

THE FERGUSON TRACTOR

Despite all these new vehicles, Standard-Triumph did have a major problem; it was too small to compete with the major manufacturers. In addition money was tight and this caused problems when developing new vehicles. In fact during the 1950s the only thing that really kept the company afloat was the profit earned from assembling tractors for Ferguson.

Production of these tractors had started in 1946 in one of Standard's old wartime shadow factories. By 1948 tractor production overtook Standard-Triumph car production and by 1953 accounted for 70% of the company's net profit. Unsurprisingly then, talks began in that year to merge the two interests, but instead Harry Ferguson decided to sell the business to the Canadian manufacturer of agricultural equipment, Massey Harris. Despite this bad news Standard did manage to get a 12-year deal from Massey Harris to continue making tractors.

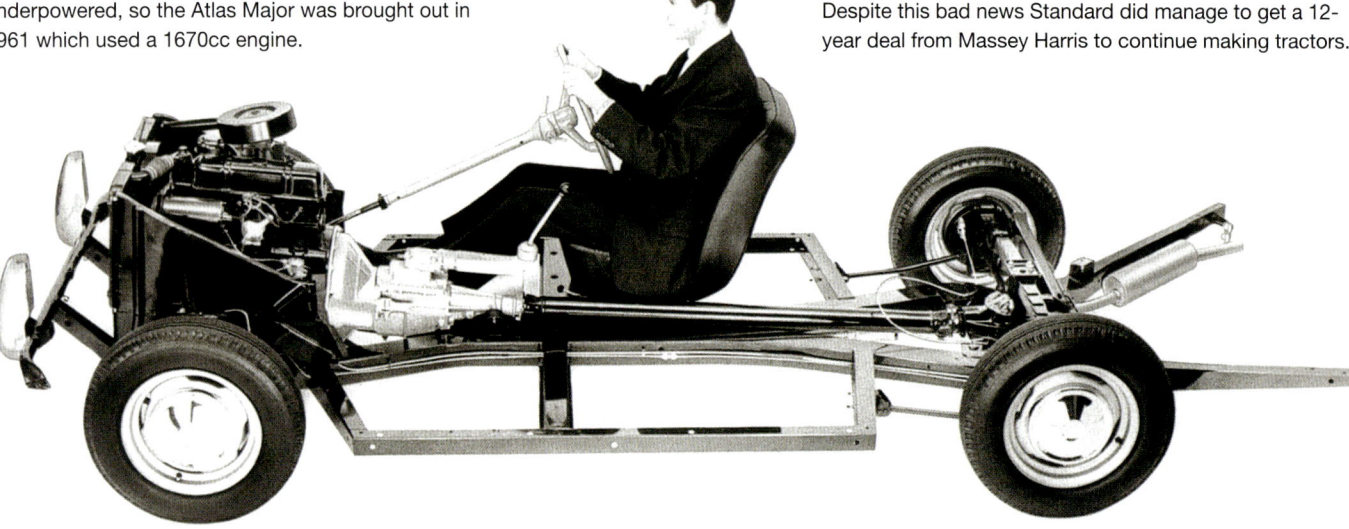

In 1954 John Black was replaced as head of the company by Alick Dick, who immediately started to look for ways to improve the company. Merger talks were held with both Rover and Rootes but both came to nothing. A takeover by Massey Ferguson was also considered but failed. However, it did cause a few problems between the two firms, which resulted in Massey Ferguson buying the tractor plant from Standard in 1958.

Despite the loss of the lucrative tractor contract, at least the firm now had money to invest in new vehicles, the first of which would be Project Zobo. This was the codename for the Michelotti-designed Triumph Herald, which would replace the smaller Standard models.

However, there were a few more problems. Firstly another attempt was made to merge with Rover. All this seemed to do was take up valuable time, as again the idea failed. However, the next problem proved far more serious – finding a supplier for the Herald body. Standard had traditionally used Fisher & Ludlow but that firm had now been bought by BMC and the company was not keen on helping a competitor with a new vehicle. The other major supplier was Pressed Steel but it did not have the capacity.

Therefore it was decided to have the major body components made by different companies which would then be assembled at Canley in a newly built hall. In addition the firm also managed to buy the Fisher & Ludlow Tile Hill plant. A Liverpool engineering works was also purchased with a view to turning it into a body plant. Other factories were also purchased including one in Belgium.

The Herald finally went on sale in 1959, but there were a few problems, notably the fact that as all the bits of body had been made in different factories the panel fit often left a lot to be desired (I should know, I've got one! SP)

The first Heralds were fitted with the 948cc Standard Ten engine that gave 38bhp, and could be bought as a coupe, two-door saloon or convertible. It had independent suspension all round and swing axles at the rear. In 1961 the engine size increased to 1147cc and an estate and van version (the Triumph Courier) were added to the range. A stronger chassis came later in 1961 and the following year a lengthened Herald was fitted with a six-cylinder 1596cc engine to make the Vitesse. Herald production continued until 1971 by which time over 525,000 had been made making it the best selling Triumph of all time.

Despite the long-term success of the Herald, Standard-Triumph's fortunes in 1960 were very bleak. This was caused by the Government tightening domestic credit followed by a global recession. Car sales were obviously very badly hit, and the firm's buying spree with the tractor money really hadn't helped. Standard-Triumph was now deeply in the red.

Leyland at this time was looking to expand and despite the financial situation at Standard-Triumph, bought the entire firm late in 1960 (see chapter one).

Leyland then set about improving Standard's fortunes. These included 800 redundancies, axing the Atlas Minor van, putting the remaining workers on a 2.5-day week and improving the quality of the Herald. Standard's plan to design its own tractor was also scrapped.

All this helped but a real boost came in 1962 when the Government cut car purchase tax. The demand for cars soon increased and so did the financial situation at Standard-Triumph. Therefore it was decided that a new car would be developed – the 2000 saloon.

This new car appeared in 1963 and used the Standard Vanguard six-cylinder engine of 1991cc. It also had ❯

The Triumph 2000 Mk1 was introduced in 1963.

The 2000's engine was a straight-six 1991cc until previously used in the Vanguard.

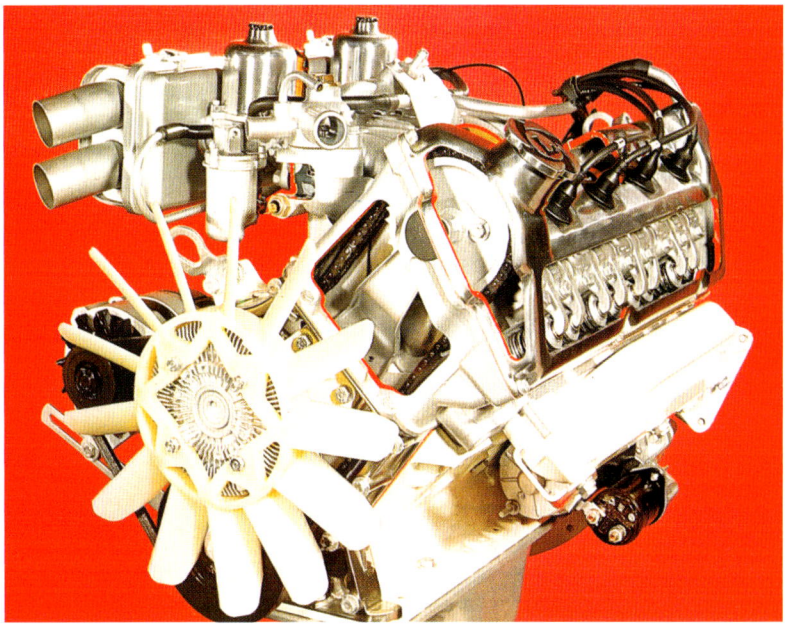

The Dolomite Sprint used an ohc 1998cc slant four-cylinder engine.

independent suspension all round, front disc brakes and could be bought as a saloon or estate.

However, 1963 also saw another announcement by Leyland – the end of the Standard name. As of then all cars produced by the firm would carry the Triumph badge, except the Atlas vans, with the Atlas Major becoming the Leyland 15 and a new long wheelbase model with a 2138cc engine becoming the Leyland 20.

MORE SPORTS CARS

The Triumph Spitfire appeared in 1962 and was basically a sports version of the Herald, sharing its engine, suspension and also having virtually the same chassis. Altogether there were five different versions of this car made over the years. The Mark 1 remained in production until 1965 when the Mark 2 appeared which had more power and an increased top speed of 92mph.

The Mark 3 ran from 1967 until 1970 and had a larger capacity 1296cc 76bhp engine. This in turn was replaced by the Mark 4 which had a restyled body. The final version appeared in 1974 as the 1500. This used the 1493cc 71bhp engine and was made until 1980. Almost 96,000 of the 1500 were made making it the most popular of the Spitfire models.

A close relative of the Spitfire was the coupe bodied GT6. This appeared in 1966 to rival the MGB GT and used a straight-six 1998cc Triumph Vitesse engine. The car was updated twice before production ended in 1973 due to poor sales.

The TR4 of 1961 used a completely new Michelotti-styled body which was built at Speke near Liverpool. Over 40,000 were made before the TR4A took over in 1965. This looked very similar to the previous model but had independent rear suspension using coil springs and trailing arms.

The TR5 used a new fuel-injected straight-six engine of 2498cc. This produced 150bhp and could propel the car to 118mph. Production ran from 1967 until 1968.

The TR6 was the first new Triumph sports car under British Leyland rule. This appeared in November 1968 and used a new Karman-styled body. This was the longest running TR as production didn't stop until July 1976 by which time over 94,000 had been made.

All the previously mentioned sports cars could be considered to be traditional Triumphs, but the same could not be said of the next such vehicle, the TR7.

The TR7 was designed by Harris Mann who had become chief stylist at BL in 1970. He had started his career at bus builder Duple before working for Commer and then Ford. Here he was persuaded by his boss Roy Haynes, designer of the Cortina Mk2, to leave Ford and

Above left: The Spitfire was basically the sports version of the Herald.

Above right: The TR6 was made from 1968 to 1976.

The Stag used a specially designed V8 engine. Unfortunately this proved quite unreliable.

join him at BL in 1967. When Haynes left, Mann took over the Austin Allegro project and also the Diablo, which became the Wolseley 18/22, later renamed the Princess. However, it is the TR7 which he is most remembered for.

The first TR7 appeared in 1974 and had a striking 'wedge' shape and pop-up headlights. However, the rear end was much more reminiscent of a saloon car. The engine fitted was a four-cylinder 1998cc single overhead cam unit that had to be inclined to fit under the low bonnet. This gave 105bhp (but only 92bhp in the US due to the emissions controls required over there at the time). Initially the car was only available as a two-seat coupe with a four-speed gearbox. However, five-speed manuals and an automatic box became available in 1976 and a convertible in 1979.

The car was first made at the Speke factory but when that factory was shut in 1978 production was transferred to Canley. In 1980 production moved again, this time to the Rover plant at Solihull.

Production continued until 1981 by which time over 112,000 had been made. However, the TR7 had never done that well in America so from September 1979 there was also a TR8 version, which used the 3.5-litre Rover V8 engine. Only 18 of these were made for the UK market with the rest going for export. Unfortunately poor build quality combined with a strong pound meant it didn't sell well either. In the end just 2722 were made.

MORE SALOONS

The Triumph Herald was supplemented in 1965 by the introduction of the front-wheel drive 1300. This was an integral four-door saloon (unlike the Herald with its separate chassis) and used a 1296cc four-cylinder engine. A twin-carb version was available from 1967 that could do 90mph, some 12mph quicker than the standard model. A 1493cc single-carb version was also available at this time.

The 1300 was dropped in 1970 and replaced with the Toledo. This used the same engine and basic body shell as the 1300 but this had rear wheel drive. For the first two years it could only be purchased as a two-door saloon. Similarly, when front wheel drive 1500 was discontinued it was replaced with a rear wheel drive version called the 1500TC.

1973 saw the reintroduction of a familiar Triumph name – the Dolomite. This was the name given to the re-branded 1300 and 1500TC, which became the Dolomite 1300, Dolomite 1500 and the new 1500HL which could be instantly recognised by its four round headlights. There were also much sportier versions, the 1850 and the 16-valve 1998cc Sprint. The latter car was much used in racing and rallying.

The other Triumph saloon was of course the 2000. This car had been designed by Michelotti and was introduced in 1963. Available as a four-door saloon or estate, it was powered by the Vanguard six-cylinder engine. However, from 1968 it was also available fitted with the 2.5-litre fuel-injected six-cylinder unit from the TR5, these being designated the 2.5PI (Petrol Injection). The following year the body was restyled, becoming the MkII. These cars were made until 1975 when the PI was dropped. It was replaced with the 2500S and the less well equipped 2500TC. Production stopped in 1977 as BL had decided that the executive car it wanted to concentrate on was the Rover SD1.

Another car closely related to the 2000/2500 was the Stag. This was a short-chassis version of the 2000 and looked very similar to the MkII. However, the Stag was a two-door, four-seat convertible coupe that had been designed to compete with the likes of the Mercedes Benz SL. Introduced in 1970 the Stag was fitted with a specially built Triumph V8 overhead cam engine of 2997cc. In the design stages the engine was to have used fuel injection, but this proved troublesome and made it virtually impossible to meet American emissions target. Therefore the production engine used twin Stromberg carburettors. In this form the engine gave 145bhp and could power the Stag to 115mph. However, the engine proved very unreliable and was prone to overheating. This led to massive warranty claims. However, the Stag was offered

The wedge shaped TR7 was designed by Harris Mann. Production ran from 1974 until 1981.

The Acclaim was a badge-engineered Honda Ballade. It wasn't even made in a Triumph factory.

until 1977 when almost 26,000 cars had been made. Many have suggested that a better choice of engine would have been the Rover V8 and that it was internal rivalries within BL that stopped it being fitted. However, it must also be remembered that Rover was having trouble producing the amount of V8s needed so maybe that is just a myth.

As the 1970s were coming to a close, the death knell for Triumph was sounding. Sir Michael Edwards was now in charge of BL and he was very much in favour of Rover, and he certainly didn't like sports cars. The Dolomite was axed in 1980 as was the Spitfire, while the TR7 and TR8 lasted for just one more year.

Although at the time no new Triumph cars were planned, the Triumph name did get a short stay of execution by being used on a badge-engineered Honda Ballade saloon that would be sold in Britain as the Triumph Acclaim. However, this wasn't even made at a Triumph factory, as the engine, gearbox etc. were shipped from Japan while the body was made at the Cowley Pressed Steel factory. The car was then assembled at the Morris factory, also in Cowley. Having said all that, the car proved quite popular. Front wheel drive and fitted with a 1335cc twin-carb engine it was available in three levels of trim including the 'luxury' CD. An automatic was also offered which Honda had called the 'Hondamatic' so BL followed suit and called it the 'Triomatic'. The Acclaim was built from November 1981 until June 1984 and 133,000 were made, which is more than the number of Honda Ballades made in the same period.

When the Acclaim was dropped it was replaced with another Honda design, but this time it carried the Rover badge and was called the 213/216. Both the Standard and Triumph (car) brand names are now owned by BMW, who purchased the Rover Group in 1994. ✦

POWERING *the* FUTURE

The formation of British Leyland wasn't just an amalgamation of two large vehicle manufacturers – there was far more to its products than that. One such item it produced was even considered at the time to be the future power plant for virtually all transport – the gas turbine.

In 1928 a 21-year-old Cadet at RAF Cranwell named Frank Whittle wrote a remarkable thesis entitled 'Future Developments in Aircraft Design'. In it he envisaged a future where aircraft could top 500mph and reach the stratosphere. This showed real vision as at the time RAF fighters struggled to reach 150mph and had a ceiling of around 20,000ft. In his thesis Whittle realised that piston driven internal combustion engines could never achieve his goal – an alternative power source was needed. This was the start of his project which eventually led him to patent the world's first practical turbojet engine on January 16, 1930.

Looking back now at how the world has changed due to Whittle's invention it's unbelievable to find that it was originally met in Britain with almost total disinterest. Strangely, given its potential military uses, the patent wasn't even put on the 'restricted' list so it was there for all to see – both allies and enemies.

However, after a massive effort on Whittle's part he managed to obtain enough support to begin constructing his first engine in 1935, and it was successfully bench tested in 1937. This engine was subsequently developed and the first British aircraft with a jet engine finally flew in 1941. However, as a result of the earlier British indifference the first jet aircraft to fly ended up being a German Heinkel using an engine designed by Dr Hans Von Ohain.

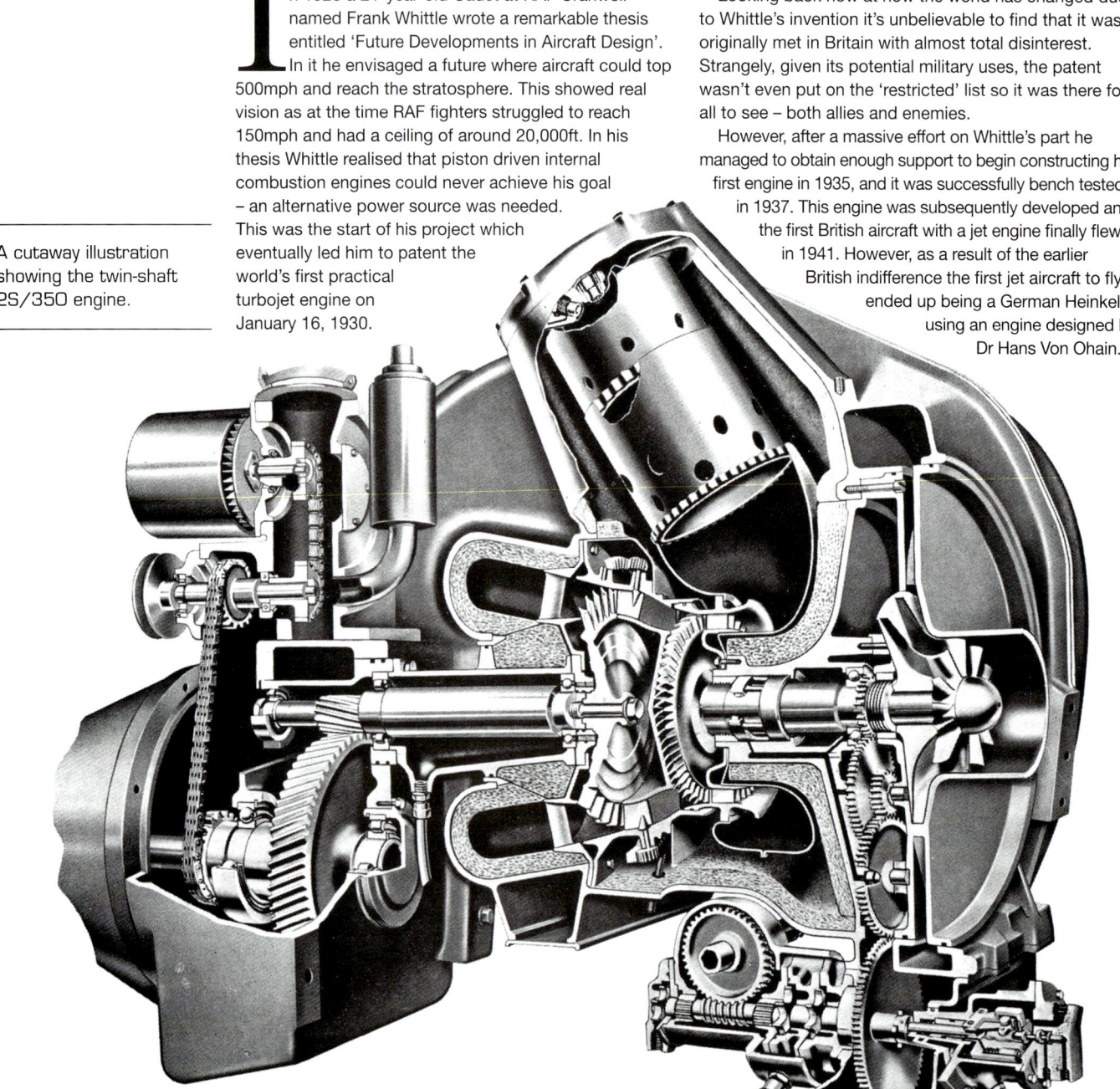

A cutaway illustration showing the twin-shaft 2S/350 engine.

The Rover JET 1, the world's first gas turbine engined car. *Photo National Motor Museum.*

ENTER ROVER

The connection with gas turbines to this book starts in 1940 when Rover was given contracts issued by the government to build a small batch of the W2 version of Whittle's engine.

The initial contract to Rover was for six engines – two at W2 specification and four at W2B spec – these ran at 14,500rpm and 16,500rpm (max) respectively. Other contracts soon followed, including doing development work, and in 1941 an order for 550 W2B engines for fitment to Gloster airframes was received. It's interesting to note that the government contracts at the time referred to the engines as 'superchargers'.

In 1945, with the war finally over, Rover realised they had the expertise to continue developing the gas turbine engine – and so they did. In fact, in March 1945 an internal Rover company memo looked at the possibility of producing a 90hp gas turbine for automotive use.

However, their first notable design appeared in 1949 in the shape of the twin-shaft 'T8', which could develop up to 200hp. Six of these engines ended up in marine use with four going to the Government Naval Research Laboratory and two being fitted to the 60ft launch 'Torquil', a boat that belonged to Rover boss Spencer Wilks. The other ended up in something far more spectacular – the world's first gas turbine car, JET 1.

AUTOMOTIVE USE

The Rover JET 1 (based on a Rover P4 car) was announced on March 8, 1950, when it underwent tests observed by the RAC at the Motor Industry Research Association test track in Warwickshire. The following day it had its press launch at Silverstone racing circuit, where it achieved a speed of 85mph.

There then followed a period of development work which culminated in June 1952 when the car was shipped to Belgium to set the first ever land speed record for a gas turbine powered car. The venue was a section of closed motorway between Ostend and Ghent, and the car undertook runs with both flying and standing starts. The final results were an average of 151.196mph for the flying mile, which it covered in 23.81 seconds and 95.668mph for the standing mile, covered in 37.63 seconds.

The car was then used for further demonstration work and in 1953 was donated to the Science Museum in London where it remains on show to this day.

TWIN-SHAFT ENGINES

In a basic gas turbine engine there is only one shaft on which is mounted the centrifugal compressor and the turbine rotor. In operation the compressor draws air into the combustion chamber where fuel is introduced and ignited. The hot gas produced then exits the combustion chamber and spins the turbine rotor before going to exhaust. However, this type of engine would be very unsuitable for road vehicle use, due to its power delivery. Basically the best use for a single shaft unit is where it will be run constantly at its maximum design speed, so would be perfect in applications such as generators or pumps. However, for road use it just wouldn't deliver the required power at lower engine revs. The answer was the twin-shaft engine, such as the T8. In this design the first shaft is there just to provide the hot gases to drive a second shaft. This turns and can be geared to drive a vehicle's wheels. ›

> IN 1945, WITH THE WAR FINALLY OVER, ROVER REALISED THEY HAD THE EXPERTISE TO CONTINUE DEVELOPING THE GAS TURBINE ENGINE – AND SO THEY DID.

> IN 1967 ROVER FOUND ITSELF AS PART OF LEYLAND AND WAS SOON EMBARKING ON A NEW AREA FOR THE GAS TURBINE – USE IN HEAVY TRUCKS.

With the success of the T8 engine Rover then embarked on more development work. These included twin-shaft units with 100hp and 140hp respectively, which were designated the 2S/100 and 2S/140. The first appeared in a 4x4 sports car in 1956, while the second was demonstrated in a saloon body in 1961. The turbine even entered motorsport when a 2S/150 engine was used to power the Rover-BRM which was entered in the 1963 Le Mans 24 hour endurance race. The car, which was developed in conjunction with British Racing Motors of Bourne in Lincolnshire, was driven by Graham Hill and Richie Ginther and reached speeds in excess of 140mph on the Mulsanne Straight. Even though it finished the race, as it was an experimental vehicle it was unplaced.

The Rover-BRM was further developed and took part in Le Mans again in 1964 and '65. It is interesting to note how far the design had moved on since JET 1. The early car's mpg figure was usually around 4mpg, while independent tests of the 1965 Rover-BRM after Le Mans recorded 30mpg at 50mph.

Single shaft engines were also developed by Rover and in 1954 the company launched the 1S/60. Several thousand were built over the coming years and mostly ended up driving pumps or generators, and some were used as auxiliary power units on Vulcan bombers.

LEYLAND GAS TURBINES

In 1967 Rover found itself as part of Leyland and was soon embarking on a new area for the gas turbine – use in heavy trucks.

A Leyland Super Comet tractor unit was fitted with a 2S/150R engine and four-speed semi-automatic gearbox in order to demonstrate its feasibility to the Leyland board. Despite a few problems the board decided to go ahead with the project and the Rover Turbine Research Group was renamed Leyland Gas Turbines.

The decision was made to develop a 350hp twin-shaft engine, and the board required that six engines, one of which should be fitted into a truck, should be ready within 18 months. The first 2S/350R engine was ready in mid 1968 and was fitted to a Leyland Lynx/Bison chassis. The reason a production chassis was used was because BL hoped that they would be able to sell gas turbines to companies to replace diesels in existing lorries.

The cab chosen was based on the 'Ergomatic' design already used on the V8 AEC Mandator, but fitted with a completely new interior and stainless steel outer panels. The first lorry, christened GT1, was unveiled at the 1968 Commercial Vehicle Show.

Altogether six trucks were built, three for BL to develop and one each for ESSO, Castrol and BP to use as tankers.

However, there were problems. Firstly these lorries proved very thirsty compared to diesel vehicles. In addition there were problems with the heat exchangers which proved quite unreliable. Despite this BL decided to go ahead and plans were made to start full scale production of a gas turbine powered truck in 1972/73.

In 1971 BL were approached by British Rail with a view to using the new gas turbine 2S/350R in their latest design – the Advanced Passenger Train. This train became famous the world over as it was so fast it had to 'lean' into corners like a motorcycle. BL agreed to supply engines for the prototype APT, eight to drive the train while the other two drove the auxiliaries such as the air conditioning and lighting. The prototype APT appeared in 1972 and clocked speeds of around 135mph.

By 1972/3 LGT had developed a Mk2 version of the S2/350 and under test it could produce around 400hp. However, BL had by now changed its mind about gas turbines. The engines were proving very costly to develop and were still thirsty compared to diesels. The fuel crisis of 1973 certainly didn't help with this last point. So, in 1974 the BL board made the decision to stop research into gas turbines and abandon the idea of full-scale production. The end had finally come for this futuristic vehicle power plant. ♦

The Leyland gas turbine truck, GT1 (later renamed GT11) has recently been restored to fully working order. *Photo Alan Barnes.*

INNOVATIONS

During its time in business, British Leyland introduced many innovations, one of which was a 'run-flat' tyre. This had actually been developed by tyre maker Dunlop and was marketed as the 'Denovo'. Basically, the design used a special wheel rim that kept the tyre on the rim in the event of a blowout, together with small glass cylinders fastened to the inner part of the rim. These would break if the tyre deflated and release a solution that would temporarily plug the puncture and a gas that would partially reinflate the tyre. This was available on the Rover P6, Wolseley 18/22, Austin Princess and Mini 1275 GT, and contemporary adverts said you could still drive 100 miles at 50mph before changing the tyre. Unfortunately, it was expensive to make and required specialist dealers to fit, so it was soon dropped.

THE DENOVO TYRE

Tyre deflation at high speed holds no terrors when Dunlop Denovo tyres and wheels are fitted as optional equipment (power-assisted steering comes as part of the package). The car remains controllable under almost any driving conditions and the tyres can be driven deflated for distances of up to 100 miles at speeds up to 50 mph. A network of more than 600 Denovo service centres has been set up and, in the United Kingdom, one centre will usually be within access of any normal travel route. A similar network has been set up in Europe.

TILLING *the* SOIL

Although the firm didn't have the following of the likes of Massey Ferguson, BL did produce tractors for several years, building on the work done by Nuffield. However, earlier agricultural machines had been made by other group members, notably Austin.

During the First World War, Austin had been involved with importing agricultural tractors from America. When the conflict ended the firm decided to manufacture its own tractor, the Model R, which went on sale in 1919. These tractors were exported around the globe and proved particularly popular in France. Unfortunately high French import duties started to hit sales and so Austin decided to set up a factory just north of Paris in order to assemble kits of parts sent from England. This French arm of Austin prospered and even developed its own models. Many were even exported to Britain.

By the mid 1920s it was decided to cease tractor production in Britain and henceforth the French company, Societe Anonyme Austin, became Austin's tractor builder. Tractors produced included diesels and, unsurprisingly, vineyard versions.

The firm did well until the Second World War when the Germans invaded France and the factory was seized. All tractor production then ceased, never to return.

However, in 1946 the Nuffield Organisation started testing its own design of agricultural tractor. Twelve more prototypes were then made which were tested in all manner of conditions including overseas, and by late 1946 the Nuffield Universal, as it had been named, was ready for production. Unfortunately the severe shortage of steel available straight after the war meant production had to be put on hold. In fact it would be the Smithfield Show of 1948 before it went on general sale.

The first tractors produced in 1948 were powered by a Morris Commercial four-cylinder, side-valve TVO (tractor vapourising oil) engine which produced 38hp at 2000rpm. There were two types, the four-wheeled M4 and the three-wheeled rowcrop M3.

The first tractors were sold to the UK market but by 1949 exports had started through Nuffield Exports Ltd.

Sales were further improved in 1950 when the options of a 45hp petrol and 48hp Perkins P4 diesel engine became available.

In 1952 the British Motor Corporation (BMC) was formed by the merger of the Austin Motor Company and the Nuffield Organisation. This didn't immediately change the tractors produced but in 1954 the Perkins engine was dropped in favour of a 56hp BMC diesel unit of 3.4-litres capacity. TVO powered tractors remained available until 1956, by which time the market for such fuel had virtually collapsed, as it was replaced by cheaper diesel.

In 1957 a three-cylinder 37hp, 2.55-litre BMC engine was introduced to meet the need for a smaller tractor.

A number of improvements were made in 1959, the main ones being the addition of a differential lock and independent wheel brakes. These just helped sales even more and by 1960 some 80% of production was being made for export.

The 1961 season saw the engine size increased and the model numbers changed to 3/42 & 4/60. These numbers represented the number of engine cylinders followed by the engine horsepower. Power steering was also offered as an option on the 4/60 for the first time.

In 1962 production of all Nuffield tractors was moved from Ward End in Birmingham to a new factory at Bathgate in Scotland that also produced lorries.

The construction of the Bathgate factory had started just one year previously on 250 acres of land just outside Edinburgh. This move was actually politically motivated by the government to replace the loss of jobs caused by closure of coal mines in central Scotland.

The move was heralded as a new beginning for industry in Scotland, particularly when you add the new Rootes Group Hillman Imp factory and Pressed Steel Fisher plant, which were both at Linwood, into the equation. It was hoped that local entrepreneurs would soon start producing components for these new plants but apart from a few suppliers, the Bathgate factory always had to rely on all its major components being brought up from England. This caused a massive increase in costs, even though Bathgate did machine all its own castings, gears and hydraulic valve blocks etc. This, along with the BMC lorries being produced at the plant, meant that at the time Bathgate had the largest machine shop in Europe. At one point Bathgate employed around 4500 people but it must be said that labour relations were, at times 'strained' to say the least.

1964 saw the introduction of the 10/42 and 10/60 models which featured a high/low range gearbox giving 10 forward and two reverse gears. The model designations were also changed to tell the number of forward gears and engine horsepower.

In contrary to other makers who were producing bigger tractors, 1965 saw Nuffield introduce its new 'Mini' tractor. It measured a mere 8ft 2¼in long and 3ft 8½in from the ground to the top of the bonnet. It only weighed 2098lb. A large amount of the development for this new tractor was done by Harry Ferguson Research of Coventry. It was offered initially with a BMC 950cc diesel engine which produced 15hp. In 1967 a 950cc petrol engine was also offered which produced 20hp. ›

Opposite: The 'Synchro' gearbox was available from 1978.

Above: The 'Mini' series of Leyland tractors was made for many years. The 154 was built from 1970 until 1984. *Photo Tractor Magazine.*

Below: A 1957 Nuffield Universal on display. *Photo Tractor Magazine.*

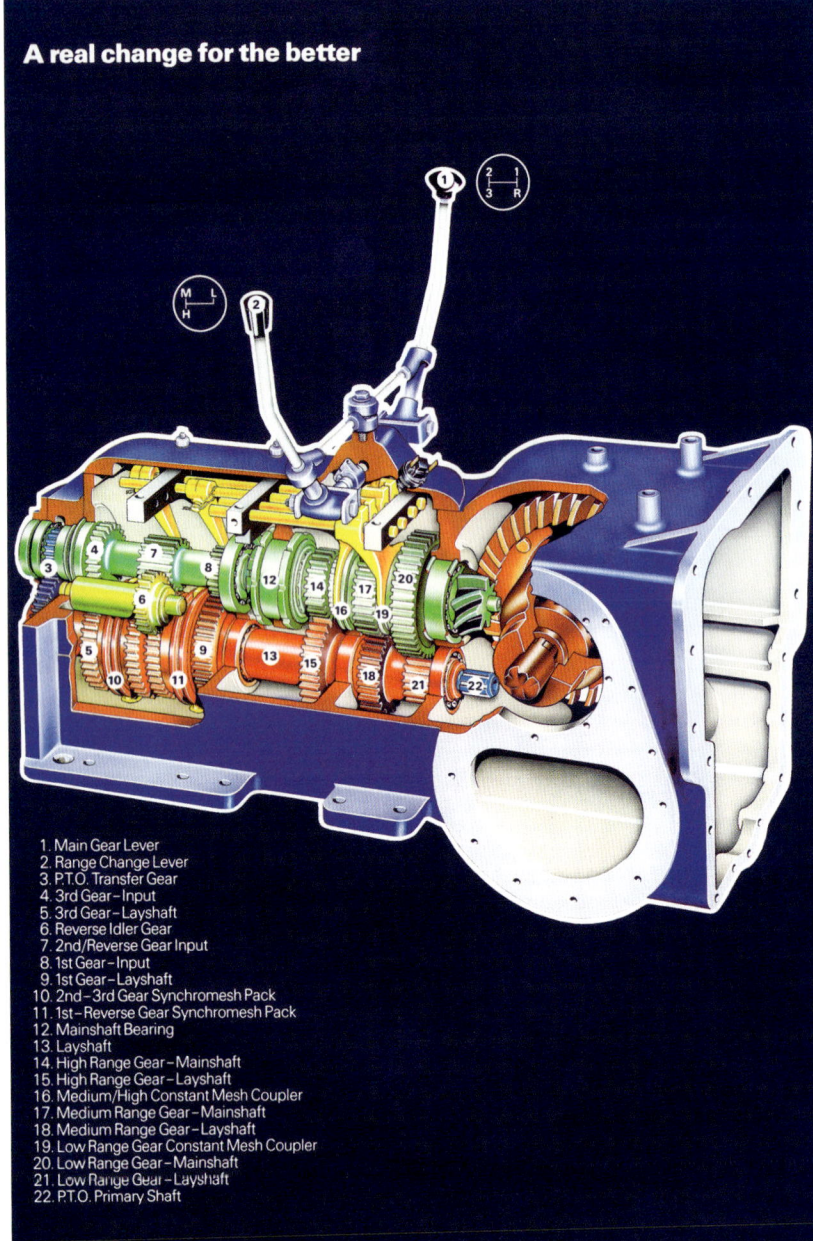

The 'Synchro' gearbox was a real improvement.

An early Leyland 502 tractor. The model made its first appearance in 1982.

In 1967 the 3/45 and 4/65 models were introduced. These tractors not only looked more modern, they also had many new features such as new hydraulics with a double acting top-link and dual chamber hydraulic pump. The fuel tank was also repositioned to the front of the tractor in front of the radiator and the steering was also redesigned. A new instrument panel, dry element type air-cleaner and front weight frame were also featured, as was a new bonnet, side panels and grille.

In 1968 the merger took place between British Motor Holdings, and the Leyland Motor Company, creating British Leyland. Therefore Nuffield tractors were redesigned as Leylands and were first seen at the Smithfield Show of 1969. The models introduced were 154, 344 and 384, the designations indicating engine capacity in litres and number of engine cylinders (so a 344 was a 3.4-litre with four-cylinders). The power outputs for these models were 25, 55 and 70 respectively. The three-cylinder engine fitted to the 3/45 was eventually dropped in favour of a 3.4-litre four-cylinder engine in the 344.

From 1968 to the late 1970s JCB used the Nuffield 'Skid Unit' as a base for its excavators – in fact it used so many that at times the entire production line was just units for JCB!

In 1971 a completely new tractor was introduced, the 253. This was designed as competition to the very successful Massey Ferguson 135.

1972 was an important year for BL tractors, as a new Bathgate designed and built engine was fitted to the 344 and 384. The model designation numbers were also changed again, from engine capacity and cylinders to the number of driving wheels and horsepower. Therefore the 253 became the 245 etc.

Other new tractors were also introduced, these being the 285, 485, 2100 and 4100. These models had two-speed PTOs, wet disc brakes and hydraulically operated clutch and brakes. All the driven axles, both front and rear, were sourced from County.

In 1975 the 255 and 270 were uprated to 62 and 72hp respectively, with their model numbers changing to 262 and 272. A silver cab roof and decals identified the new models.

Another BL company involved in agricultural machinery was Barfords of Belton in Lincolnshire which manufactured agricultural implements. For a while during the 1970s a range of its implements was sold under the Leyland name such as ploughs and a seed drill.

From 1976 Leyland introduced the new 'Q' cab. This was due to a new law that had been introduced to give tractor drivers a quieter workplace, with a maximum limit of 87dB. In addition 1976 also saw items that were previously available as just an option become standard, including power steering.

In March 1978 the Leyland 'Synchro' gearbox was introduced. This had nine forward and three reverse synchromesh gears. Each range had three gears and it was possible to change ranges while in motion. In addition a synchromesh was also featured between forward and reverse, giving a 'shuttle change' from forwards to reverse which was useful, for example, when loading trailers. These tractors could easily be identified by a red stripe decal with the word 'Synchro' in red.

Later that year two new four-wheel drive middleweight tractors were also launched, the 462 and 472.

The 1979 Smithfield Show saw the introduction of the 82hp turbocharged 4/98 TT engine. The tractors fitted with this engine were designated 282 and 482.

By the start of the 1980s it was realised that the Leyland range of tractors really wasn't that good when compared to other manufacturers' offerings. It was therefore decided to give the range a bit of a makeover by introducing new house colours, something that would really stand out. After a few trials 'Golden Harvest' was chosen for the tinwork and black for the chassis and engine.

The 1980 Smithfield Show was the debut for the 'new' tractor range. These were designated the 500, 600, 700 and 800.

However, there were some other changes apart from a new colour and badge. These included a fully live engine-driven twin-chamber hydraulic pump, oil-immersed multi-plate disc brakes, two-speed PTO, as either standard or optional, heavy duty linkage and improved levelling box either with or without assistor ram. Two cabs were also now available, the improved Leyland 'QM' with sound deadening down to 85dB or the Danish 'Sekura' deluxe designated as the 'Explorer Cab'. That year also saw a Leyland 'import' in the shape of the 235 tractor, which was built in Turkey by BMC. This was given a facelift and sold in the UK as the 302.

1981 was a terrible year for Leyland tractor production. The labour relations between management and the workers at Bathgate were at an all-time low and production was frequently halted due to strike action. There is little doubt that this hastened the end of Leyland's tractor production, as in 1982 the business, designs and all rights were sold to Charles Nickerson, who also owned Marshall Tractors at Gainsborough. Six hundred completed tractors were also included in the deal, some of which were rebadged as Marshalls before sale.

All production of Leyland Tractors at Bathgate ceased on January 15, 1982. Production was then switched to Gainsborough where the tractors were made as Marshalls. Lorry production continued at Bathgate until 1985 when it closed for good. There had been plans for Land Rovers to be made there but it came to nothing. The site has been redeveloped as housing. ✦

The Leyland 502 appeared in 1982. It was painted the new house colours of 'Golden Harvest' tin-work and black for the chassis and engine.

ROVER'S ICON

Of all the products manufactured by BL there really was one true icon – but it wasn't a car. The item in question was the legendary Rover V8 engine. However, the origins of this world famous engine lie not in Britain but over the 'pond' in the spiritual home of the V8 – America.

The States have had a love affair with V8 engined cars for decades, but in the late 1950s things were starting to change. After years of having things virtually all their own way America's car producers realised they were losing market share to large numbers of smaller, more efficient vehicles being imported from Europe. However, typical of the American psyche, this threat was also viewed as a new challenge – here was a new market for US producers to enter. So the idea for the 'compact' was born – smaller American cars that were more economical to run.

At General Motors the Buick division soon set to work on a 'senior compact' design that was to be launched in 1961. However, unlike the European cars that were then starting to flood into the US, this would not be powered by a four or six cylinder engine – only a V8 would do for a Buick!

The engine the company came up with was an all-aluminium unit of 215 cubic inch capacity, with a bore of 3.5in and a 2.8in stroke. Buick's sister company, Oldsmobile also came up with its own version based on this design, which differed in several areas such as pistons and valve gear.

Designated the 'Aluminium Fireball V8' by Buick this engine had one major advantage over its competitors – weight – just 318lb compared to 575lb for a cast iron, small block Chevrolet of 265 cubic inch capacity.

However, despite this advantage, there were many manufacturing problems to attend to, notably due to the use of cast-iron dry liners in the aluminium block. The major concern was how to prevent the liners becoming displaced during production. This proved so difficult to overcome that in the early days as many as 90% of new Fireball blocks produced were rejected and scrapped. Other problems included preventing threads from being stripped as bolts were tightened, and matching of the main bearing caps.

After much development work the engine was finally ready for mass production in the autumn of 1960 and it was announced it was to be available in three new GM cars from 1961. These were the Buick Special, where it was the standard engine, the Pontiac Tempest (as an option), and the Oldsmobile F85, although, as already mentioned, the Oldsmobile unit differed in several ways to the Buick lump.

Initially there was great praise for these new cars and their exotic aluminium engines. However, this did not last. The main technical problem was cooling – but it wasn't due to the design. These new aluminium engines required special antifreeze which could only be bought from General Motors. Failure to use the correct coolant resulted in a reaction with the aluminium block which created an aluminium-silicone oxide which quickly clogged the radiator. This led to overheating which could warp the cylinder heads. ›

Left: The engine was originally designed by General Motors and was first fitted in the 1961 Buick Special. *Photo National Motor Museum.*

The Rover V8 engine was in production for over 35 years and grew from 3.5-ltrs to 5-ltrs capacity. *Photo National Motor Museum.*

However, there was another reported problem that few could have foreseen – the negative reaction of the very powerful American steel industry. This combined with improvements in thin-wall steel casting, and an upturn in the US economy, suddenly made the aluminium engine seem far less attractive.

GM finally ceased production of the engine in 1963 after just two years of manufacture. Some 750,000 units had been built – a pitiful amount by GM standards. However, the idea did live on in the US for a while longer, as the engine was redesigned as a V6 and eventually became a power unit used by Jeep.

ROVER TO THE RESCUE

In the mid 1960s Rover was having problems exporting its vehicles to the States. This wasn't really surprising as it only had two vehicles to sell – the Land Rover and the Rover P5 3-litre saloon. The man in charge of the US operation was one J Bruce McWilliams, who had previously been with Mercedes-Benz. He recognised the main problem selling Rovers over there – the old fashioned image of the P5 and lack of power in the Land Rover.

He started by trying to encourage Rover to put a bigger engine into the Land Rover, such as a straight-six or better still a small American V8. His boss over in Britain, William Martin-Hurst, agreed with the idea and so the search began.

Above: Rover bought the rights to the Buick engine in 1965. The first car it fitted the V8 to was the Rover P5B in 1967. *Photo National Motor Museum.*

Below: The new engine was used in many different BL cars over the years including the MGB GT V8 introduced in 1973. *Photo National Motor Museum.*

McWilliams' first port of call was Chrysler, who said it may have a suitable engine, and so he soon found himself travelling to New York to have a look. While there he decided to call on his friend Karl Kiekhaefer, who worked for Mercury Marine, the world famous builders of boat engines. While at Mercury, McWilliams noticed a Buick Fireball V8 sat in the workshop, and thought it could possibly be suitable for Rover. On asking about the engine he found out that it was no longer in production but that the tooling still existed.

He reported his find to Martin-Hurst in the UK who became very enthusiastic and made contact with General Motors, and eventually managed to buy the rights to the Fireball, together with technical assistance and some tooling. Rover even got a batch of assembled engines to experiment on, and, most importantly, GM sent Buick Chief Engine Designer, Joe Turley, over to the UK to help get production underway. It really does seem a very generous deal in favour of Rover – perhaps GM couldn't believe that they'd found a buyer for such a 'lame duck'!

UK PRODUCTION

With the negotiations finished Rover finally got the production rights in January 1965. However, there were still quite a few problems to overcome. For example many of the drawings supplied by GM turned out to be wrong. These errors were not deliberate but turned out to be changes made on the shop floor to rectify problems encountered during production. It seems many just never got reported back to the drawing office! The other major problem was the manufacturing process itself.

GM had used semi-permanent moulds to form the block etc, and used die-casting as much as possible. In Britain this technology was virtually unknown, and so Rover decided to sand-cast the whole block. The dry liners were then pressed into the block when it had been pre-heated to 160 degrees C in order to expand it. However, the cylinder heads were die-cast with sand cores being used for the water cooling passages.

With production of the engine sorted the next problem was fuelling. Buick had used a Rochester carburettor, but it was decided that they weren't suitable for UK use as there was no service back-up and there was very little experience of that type of carb over here. The replacement was a pair of SU carbs mounted on a 'pitched roof' style inlet manifold, similar to those used on V8 Rolls-Royces of the day.

The Earls Court Motor Show held in September 1967 saw the debut of the 'Rover V8' engine, which was fitted to the Rover P5B, an updated version of the old P5 3-litre. It's interesting to note that the new 3.5-litre V8 engine weighed some 200lb less than the 3-litre's straight-six, while its output of 158hp was 40hp up on the older unit.

The launch of the new engine was only a few months since Rover had been taken over by Leyland in March '67, and there were high hopes of the engine being used in many different designs. However, this was a turbulent time for the company and most of the proposed ideas were eventually scrapped.

One of these plans had been the 'Rover P8', which was to be fitted with a 4.4-litre version of the new V8 and would have been a top of the range luxury car.

Unfortunately it never saw the light of day. However, the 4.4-litre engine did end up 'down under' in the Australian built Leyland P76.

Over the years the Rover V8 engine (in various forms) found its way into many different BL and Rover Group designs including the Rover P5B Coupe, MGB GT V8, Rover P6, Range Rover, Land Rover Military 101 Forward Control, Rover SD1 3500, Land Rover Stage 1 V8, Triumph TR8, Land Rover 90 and 110, Freight Rover Sherpa, Land Rover Defender and Land Rover Discovery. In addition it was bought by several specialist vehicle makers such as Morgan, TVR, Bowler and Marcos, and to this day forms the heart of thousands of kit cars, racers and specials all over the world.

During its production run the Rover V8 grew in stages from 3.5-ltrs to 4.6-ltrs (although TVR took it to 5-ltrs!), went from carburettors to electronic fuel injection and there were even experimental diesel variants. Production of the Rover V8 finally ended in 2004. ♦

Above: Under the bonnet of an MGB GT V8. Only right-hand-drive versions of this car were made and production ran for just three years. *Photo National Motor Museum.*

Below: Outside manufacturers also purchased the Rover V8, including Morgan for its Plus 8 model. This is a 1990 version and uses the 3.9-ltr engine and electronic fuel injection. *Photo National Motor Museum.*

OVERSEAS

As well as being a massive exporter of vehicles, BL also had overseas factories and even licensed some other companies to assemble their products. Here's just a few.

It's perhaps obvious that BL vehicles would be assembled in Australia, after all it was traditionally one of the UK's major export markets. One of the first firms to open a plant there was Austin who in 1949 purchased the Ruskin Body Works to build touring bodies and pick-ups (Utes!) on to Austin A40 chassis imported from Britain. Morris also opened a facility and when the companies amalgamated they moved to the Nuffield plant in Zetland, New South Wales. The first cars produced were the Austin Lancer and Morris Major, which were badge engineered versions of the Riley 1.5 and Wolseley 1500.

Other vehicles followed including the front-wheel-drive models such as the 1100 and Mini. The Mini was incredibly popular, and there was even an Australian only version which had wind-up windows years ahead of the UK built ones. The 1800 was also made there and typical of Australian needs there was also a pick-up version, which was certainly something that was never offered in Britain. The Mini-Moke was also made in Australia from 1966, but with slight differences to the UK Moke such as 13in wheels.

In 1970 the Australian BL operation brought out the X6, which was developed from the Austin 1800, and had a longer wheelbase, revised bonnet and boot styling and a transverse 2227cc straight-six 'E' Series engine. This was marketed as Tasman (basic) or Kimberley (deluxe).

The Marina joined the range in 1972, initially fitted with either a 1485 or 1750cc engine. However, there was soon a version available with a 2623cc straight-six.

In 1973 the names 'Austin' and 'Morris' were dropped and all vehicles were renamed as Leyland's.

One car worthy of note was the P76, which was solely an Australian design and had no UK equivalent. This car's basis came from a UK Rover idea for the 'P8' which was never made. It was to have been fitted with a 4.4-ltr version of Rover's V8 engine, and this was what went on to power the P76.

The P76 went on sale in 1973 and was also available with the option of an 'E' series straight-six. The car was designed by Giovanni Michelotti and was very light for its size. It also had rack and pinion steering. One was even entered in the 1974 World Cup Rally where it won the Targa Florio section – an event win which inspired a special edition.

The Australian Leyland P76 was designed by Michelotti. It was powered by a 4.4-litre version of the Rover V8 engine. *Photo National Motor Museum.*

The Innocenti Mini 120 used a three-door hatchback body made by Bertone. *Photo National Motor Museum.*

However, there were problems, notably in the supply of the V8 engine. Nobody really wanted the six-cylinder engine and in addition the world fuel crisis at the time really hit the demand for large cars. A station wagon version and a coupe were being readied for production but due to the world economy it was really no surprise when it was decided that production would cease and the factory shut down. Around 19,000 P76 cars had been produced.

Leyland Australia's subsidiary, the Pressed Metal Corporation, then started producing Mini's and Mokes from kits supplied from the UK. Mini production ceased in 1978 and the last Moke was made in 1982.

THE ITALIAN JOB

In 1946 Italian industrialist Ferdinando Innocenti started manufacturing Lambretta scooters. The firm also made heavy presses for Fiat, Ford and Volkswagen among other makers. In 1961 it decided to add cars to its list of products and took out a licence to produce the Austin A40. The same year the company signed an agreement to allow it to make the Austin Healey MkII Sprite. However, being Italian, they were fitted with a very pretty two-door sports body designed by Ghia. This was sold as the Innocenti Spyder and was made until 1970.

In 1963 the company added the Austin 1100 to its list and in 1965 took on production of the best known of Innocenti's cars, the Mini.

In common with most other industrialised countries at the time, the Mini was a cult car, so it was a wise move by Innocenti, and some 150,000 Minis were produced by the end of 1966.

In 1972 Innocenti's car plant was purchased by British Leyland for a cost of around £3million. At the time BL was not involved in the Italian market so had great hopes for Innocenti, which had sales in Italy second only to Fiat, and far ahead of other rivals.

In 1974 the Innocenti company started producing the Allegro, which was re-badged as the Regent. However, the following year came something far more interesting – a completely new Mini-based car fitted with a three-door hatchback body designed by Italian designer Bertone. There were two versions of this new car, the 90, which had the 998cc 'A' Series engine and the 120 which used the 1275cc unit.

However, in 1975 BL had serious financial problems which resulted in it being nationalised. As a result Innocenti was sold in December of that year to Alessandro de Tomaso.

The new company was called Innocenti de Tomaso and it soon stopped production of both the Regent and ordinary Mini. The firm then concentrated just on producing and developing the Bertone bodied Mini. This included fitting three-cylinder Daihatsu petrol engines of 993cc from 1982, and increasing the wheelbase in 1986. In 1990 a diesel unit was also added to the options list, as was a 548cc twin-cylinder petrol.

In 1990 the company was purchased by Fiat which, three years later, decided to close the factory. The Innocenti name survived for a while being used as just a badge fitted to some vehicles imported into Italy, notably the Yugo 45, but in 1996 it too disappeared. ›

The Innocenti Spyder used a Ghia body on an Austin Healey Sprite chassis. It was made until 1970. *Photo National Motor Museum.*

IRELAND

In the 1960s several BMC/Leyland Motors car types were assembled in Ireland from CKD (completely knocked down) kits. Austins were assembled by Lincoln & Nolan while Morris cars were made by Brittains of Naas Road in Dublin. Both of these firms also had agencies for other BMC cars imported complete and ready to go from Britain, such as Rover. Eventually however, Brittains took over Lincoln & Nolan. It also ended up purchasing Booth Poole who had been assembling Rileys and MGs in Ireland. Other separate companies also imported other group cars such as Jaguar and Triumph so when BL was formed the Irish operation looked a bit of a mess.

In order to simplify things a deal was struck where all Austin, Morris and MG cars would be the responsibility of Brittains but all other vehicles would be handled by a new company, British Leyland (Ireland) Ltd.

However, things did not go well. Brittains took on the franchise for the Japanese Datsun marque (With hindsight who can blame them?) and in 1974 BL severed its contract with the firm. Despite continuing to sell Datsuns, Brittains ceased trading in 1977. BL then started exporting CDK Minis to Ireland which were assembled by the Reg Armstrong company. This lasted until 1978. After this all BL cars were imported from Britain although some interior trim was made in Ireland until 1979.

It must be noted that in the early 1960s Triumph Heralds were also assembled in Belfast by a firm called the Clarence Engineering Company.

ISRAEL

The Israeli company Autocars was formed in 1955 in order to assemble Reliant three-wheelers. The firm soon started making four-wheeled cars as well and in 1965 entered into an agreement with Triumph. After this all the Autocars range would use Triumph engines and certain other components.

Two years later Autocars began assembling CKD kits of the front-wheel-drive Triumph 1300, an arrangement that continued until 1973. Triumph engines and components were also used in a variety of other glass fibre bodied Autocars including the Sussita that could be purchased as a saloon, estate, van or pick-up.

In 1974 the firm changed hands and production ceased in 1980.

The Austin Apache was built in South Africa. It was based on an Austin 1100/1300.

The Austin Apache was also built in Spain as the Authi Victoria.

IRAN

Leyland cars and commercial vehicles were both assembled in Iran from CKD kits imported from Britain. In addition Spanish-made Santana Land Rovers were also exported in CKD form to Iran where they were assembled and sold under the brand name Morattab.

SOUTH AFRICA

Leyland Cars set up a South African division in 1971 that was to survive until 1978. During this period it produced several different types of BL cars including Jaguars, Minis and Rovers. The company also made Austins, including some local designs such as the Apache. This was based on the 1300 body shell and was styled by Michelotti. Marinas fitted with six-cylinder engines were also made before the plant was shut down.

It should be noted that the South African plant actually produced its own engine blocks and other castings as, due to import restrictions imposed by the government in the 1960s, at least 85% of a vehicle's weight had to be locally produced in order for it to be classed as South African.

TURKEY

In 1964 BMC Group commercial vehicles began being assembled in Turkey by BMC Sanayi ve Ticaret AS. Later on vans, buses, tractors and engines joined the range. By 1968 the firm was producing a version of the normal control Austin WE lorry.

Like most other overseas operations the company soon became independent of BL but have kept the BMC name to this day. In fact since 2003 Turkish BMC lorries and buses have been available in the UK.

INDIA

There were two main India concerns with links to British Leyland. The first was Ashok Motors who was set up in 1948 just after Indian independence in order to assemble Austin cars. In 1955 the firm was renamed Ashok Leyland as it had moved on to the production of Leyland lorries and buses. The basic business idea was to take over production of Leyland models as they ceased production in the UK. So, for example, when the Titan bus was axed in Britain in 1968, Ashok Leyland started making it. It must be said that most of the commercials made by Ashok Leyland used cabs and bodywork of Indian design. The company survives to this day and sells around 60,000 commercial vehicles each year. Since 1987 the firm has been owned by the London-based Hinduja Group, so technically you could say it is a British company. Strangely all Ashok Leyland vehicles still carry the British Leyland 'L and wheel' logo.

The other Indian company was started in 1948 by the Standard Motor Company, which began assembling cars at a plant near Madras. These included the Vanguard and Pennant and later on the Triumph Herald, which was re-badged as a Standard. As the years passed the cars got more local content and relied less on imports from Britain. Finally the company parted from British Leyland in 1973.

Up until 1971 the main product had been the Herald but from then until 1977 it produced a redesigned version called the Gazelle. After this the company just produced the Standard 20, a van which was based on the Leyland 20, which in turn was originally the Standard Atlas.

However, the firm was eventually to return to car building with a real BL classic– the Rover SD1. ›

The Apache engine block etc were made in South Africa due to government import quotas.

ONE WAS EVEN ENTERED IN THE 1974 WORLD CUP RALLY WHERE IT WON THE TARGA FLORIO SECTION – AN EVENT WIN WHICH INSPIRED A SPECIAL EDITION.

> **AND SO STANDARD APPROACHED BRITISH LEYLAND WITH A VIEW TO ASSEMBLING ONE OF THEIR CAR DESIGNS. THE VEHICLE CHOSEN WAS THE ROVER SD1**

Ashok Leyland usually fitted its own cabs and bodywork to Leyland chassis assembled in India. *Photo Rupert Burrows.*

In the early 1980s the Indian Government decided to allow a little more foreign involvement in the car industry and so Standard approached British Leyland with a view to assembling one of its car designs. The vehicle chosen was the Rover SD1 and a deal was struck by 1984 when Rover body shells and panels started to be shipped to Madras. The plan was to assemble these cars and fit them with Standard's own 2.5-litre diesel or 2-litre petrol engine.

The car was named the Standard 2000 and was launched in April 1985 at a price of around 212,000 Rupees, which was approximately £12,000, and this made it a very expensive vehicle.

By this time Rover was gearing up to replace the SD1 with the new 800 and so UK production of panels was ceased and restarted in India – in fact some of these were exported to the UK as replacement items.

However, the car was just too expensive for the local market, and was not a particularly pleasant vehicle to drive either. And so in 1988 production ceased.

However, there is a twist to this story. When Standard shut down in 1988 the plant contained vast quantities of SD1 body panels, shells etc. After many years in dry storage these have recently been purchased by the Lincoln based classic car parts supplier Rimmer Bros, who has shipped them back to the UK. So, with this large supply of body parts, we may perhaps look forward to seeing a few more SD1's back on the roads of Britain soon.

YUGOSLAVIA

In 1967 the company of Industrija Motornih Vozil or IMV, signed an agreement with BMC to assemble Austin cars that would be shipped in CKD form from Britain. Production started in 1969 with the Austin 1300 and the following year the Mini and Maxi 1500cc were added to the range. In 1971, the Austin 1750 Maxi was also produced, as was the Austin 1300 Special in 1972. However that year saw IMV sign an agreement with Renault to produce its cars and so production of the BL models ceased.

SPAIN

There were several companies in Spain connected with BL, one of the most prominent being Metalurgica de Santa Ana (MSA), who in 1958 began assembling CKD Land Rovers.

This firm continued just assembling Land Rovers (approximately 600 per year) until 1967 when it

announced its first independent design. This was the Santana 1300 and was its take on the British Forward Control. The following year MSA brought out its 109in Station Wagon, which had subtle differences to the UK model.

These vehicles were basically an answer to Spanish Government import restrictions, which meant more Spanish produced components had to be used.

As time went on the Santana vehicles became even more different to the Solihull product and this even went as far as the design and manufacture of engines, including six-cylinder variants of the familiar 2286cc Land Rover four-cylinder units. These engines had a capacity of 3429cc.

In the early 1980s Land Rover was busy developing its coil-sprung 90/110 models. However Santana decided to stick with leaf springs and instead brought out the Series IIIA. This differed from the Series III in many ways such as the fitment of front disc brakes, new parabolic leaf springs, power steering and five-speed gearboxes.

However, by this time Santana had also obtained financial support from the Japanese motorcycle and car maker Suzuki, and in 1984 began assembling the Suzuki SJ range of 4x4s.

The Santana company continued to develop its Land Rover based designs over the next few years, but as the designs were becoming so different the models offered by the two firms were now competing against each other in various markets. So in 1990 the Rover Group, who BL had become, sold its 25% shareholding in MSA.

Santana continued manufacturing vehicles with obvious Land Rover styling until 2011 when it ceased trading.

Another Spanish connection was with Automoviles de Turismo Hispano Ingleses of Navarra. This company started assembling Morris and MG 1100s in 1966 under the Authi name. It went on to assemble Minis and manufacture the Authi Victoria, which was the same as the South African Austin Apache. Production ceased in 1976 when Seat took over the factory. When Volkswagen eventually took over Seat, the plant went over to the production of the VW Polo.

SOME OF THE REST

As well as the above, BMC/Leyland/BL Group vehicles were also assembled at various times from CKD kits in Belguim, Chile, Columbia, Costa Rica, Equador, Malta, Morocco, Rhodesia, Trinidad, Uganda, Uraguay, Zaire, Zambia and other places. ✦

The Mini Moke was made in Britain and Australia, and finally in Portugal. Photo National Motor Museum.

SCAMMELL

The lorry producing firm of Scammell really needs no introduction. It started in the early days of mechanised road haulage, prospered independently and then as part of Leyland Motors, and only disappeared after it left the British Leyland empire.

A preserved 1929 Scammell 'Articulated Six' with frameless bitumen tanker. *Photo Alan Barnes.*

The roots of Scammell go back to before 1900 when a wheelwright named George Scammell set up in business at Fashion Street, Spitalfields, in London's East End. This firm became G Scammell and Nephew, and expanded into the manufacture of horse-drawn carts. Further expansion in the early 1900s saw the company start to sell Foden steam wagons.

One of Scammell's customers at this time was a haulage contractor named Edward Rudd, and he had started using an American Knox-Martin tractor unit which he had recently imported. This used a trailer coupling mounted on semi-eliptic leaf springs fixed to the tractor unit's rear axle. This meant the weight was carried on the axle and not on the chassis. Rudd was very impressed with his new vehicle and suggested that Scammell should make something similar.

However, it would be 1920 before the first Scammell lorry, which was inspired by the Knox-Martin vehicle, took to the road. This was developed by George Scammell's great nephew, Alfred George Scammell, who had been invalided out of the army and joined the firm.

The new lorry was the 'Articulated Six-wheeler' and could carry a 7½-ton payload. It could also do a legal 12mph due to its low axle weight, instead of the 5mph that lorries of this size were normally restricted to. It was advertised by Scammell as '7½-tons at 3-ton speed and cost'. It should be noted that the Scammell was a 'matched' vehicle, where the 'tractor unit' and 'trailer' remained coupled all the time. You could not readily uncouple the trailer and couple up to another.

Orders for these lorries came flooding in and it soon became obvious that the works were not big enough to cope. So in 1921 a new firm was formed, Scammell Lorries Ltd, and a new site was purchased on Tolpits Lane in Watford, where a new factory was constructed.

During the 1920s Scammell's tractor unit remained virtually unchanged, but the company put a lot of effort into the design and construction of a wide range of trailers. These included tankers and the Scammell soon became a favourite with oil and fuel companies such as Shell-Mex. This connection saw Scammell go on to produce and

patent the world's first chassisless tanker trailer in 1926. A new lorry, and a totally new concept, was launched in 1927 in the shape of the on/off road 'Pioneer'. This was a 6x4 rigid and had a 'walking-beam' bogie which allowed any of the four driving wheels to be raised by up to two feet without the bogie losing traction. Its front undriven axle was centrally pivoted. A driven front axle, making the lorry a 6x6, was available from 1929.

In 1928 a four- and a six-wheel rigid was added to the range but the following year came something far more spectacular – the 'Hundred Tonners', which at the time were the biggest lorries in the world. Two of these massive machines were constructed for Marston Road Services Ltd for the transportation of railway locomotives, and each was fitted with a Scammell seven-litre petrol engine giving 86bhp. This was a thirsty unit to say the least and after a few years both lorries were rebuilt and fitted with Gardner 6LW diesel engines, which as well as improving fuel consumption also increased the power to 105bhp.

Loaded with a 100-ton payload the gross train weight of these Scammells was 130 tons. The weight on the front axle was 10 tons while the chain-driven rear drive axle, which was fitted with four wheels shod with solid tyres, carried 40 tons. The remaining load was carried on an eight-wheeled steerable bogie. The brakes on this bogie were controlled by a steersman, who was in contact with the driver via a telephone.

As spectacular as the 'Hundred Tonners' were, one of Scammell's best known products was soon to appear, but it would be at the other end of the weight range. In 1932 Scammell purchased the design for a three-wheeled tractor unit from D Napier & Son Ltd. Scammell developed this design into the famous Mechanical Horse. This used a new automatic trailer coupling designed by Oliver North, and the whole artic was able to turn in less than its own length. Launched in 1933 there were two versions, the three tonner with a 1.13-litre four-cylinder petrol engine, and the six tonner which used a 2.04-litre petrol engine. These lorries became very popular, particularly with the railway companies. Over the years the Mechanical Horse was developed into the Scarab and then the Townsman, with production ending in 1968. ›

Top: Scammell started making the three-wheeled 'Mechanical Horse' in 1933. This is an example of the last version, the Townsman. *Photo Stephen Pullen Collection.*

Above: The Scammell Highwayman appeared in 1957 and used either Leyland or Gardner engines. *Photo Gyles Carpenter.*

Despite the success of the Mechanical Horse, Scammell found itself in financial difficulties due to the 1930s depression. In the end it was one of its customers, Shell-Mex, who came to the rescue and invested some much needed capital. This led to the 'Artic-Six' and the 'Artic-Eight' models being developed into the 'Lightweight' range, most of which were fitted with Gardner 6LW diesel engines. An eight-wheeled rigid also joined the range in 1937.

WAR PRODUCTION

During the Second World War Scammell was kept very busy, mostly with the manufacture of Pioneers, which were used as tank transporters, gun tractors and heavy recovery lorries. The firm also took on other war work including the production of fire pumps.

With the war over in 1945 Scammell was keen to build on the reputation it had earned during the war for heavy specialised lorries, and the first new vehicle was the 'Showtrac'. This was a combined drawbar haulage vehicle and generating set designed for fairgrounds and aimed squarely at replacing the Showman's steam traction engine.

The other market Scammell particularly concentrated on was off-road transport, particularly for the oil industry and the military. The vehicles produced included the 4x4 Mountaineer, and the Meadows engined 6x6 Explorer. Heavy haulage was another Scammell specialisation and the 1950s saw the arrival of the Rolls-Royce engined Super Constructor.

In 1955 Scammell became part of Leyland Motors which led to more new Scammell vehicles, many of which were available with Leyland engines, gearboxes and axles. The Lightweight range soon gave way to the normal control Highwayman tractor unit, and the forward control Routeman eight-wheeler. New off-roaders were also launched including the 4x4 Sherpa and 6x4 Himalayan dump trucks.

The 1960s brought something a bit different for Scammell in the shape of a new cab designed by Italian Giovanni Michelotti, who was more famous for his car designs including the Triumph Herald and Spitfire as well as all manner of Italian exotica for Lancia and Maserati.

These cabs were striking to say the least and were constructed from glass fibre reinforced plastic. They were fitted to the Routeman, Handyman and the twin-steer 6x2 Trunker tractor unit.

Throughout the rest of the 1960s other new models were produced including the heavy-haulage 6x4 Contractor which could be used at a GTW of 240 tons. The other major product launched came in 1969 – the Crusader. Initially this was only available as a Rolls-Royce powered 6x4, and many ended up in service with the British Army. However, a 4x2 tractor unit was soon developed and became very popular, particularly with British Road Services. It must be said though that it did have a few flaws, particularly the fixed cab which made engine access difficult. The Crusader ended up being produced at the Guy Motors plant in Wolverhampton, which was another member of the BL group.

In 1972 BL decided to shut another of its specialist heavy vehicle makers, Thornycroft. After this the production of the Nubian 6x6 airfield crash tender and LD55 dump truck were transferred to Scammell.

Also during this period the Michelotti-cabbed range of Scammells was revised producing the Handyman 4, Trunker 3 and double-drive Routeman 3.

The late 1970s saw the introduction of the heavy haulage Contractor Mk2, which used a Cummins KT450 engine that developed 425hp. Work also started on a new tank transporter for the army. This was the 100-ton GTW Commander. It was fitted with a Rolls-Royce CV12TCE 26-litre twin-turbo engine that developed 625hp. After acceptance the new vehicle was in service by 1983. Other new military vehicles soon followed, as the

The last Watford-built Scammell was 'Evening Star', a 400bhp S26 made for Econofreight. *Photo Gyles Carpenter.*

Nubian range of airfield crash tenders was also redesigned. These new models had rear-mounted engines producing up to 540hp.

During the late 1970s BL decided to produce two completely new lorry designs – the normal control Landtrain for export and the forward control Roadtrain, which would initially be just for UK use. In view of the company's experience of export specials, Scammell was given the job of developing the Landtrain. It also used the Landtrain cab and bonnet on its replacement for the Contractor, the S24. This could be ordered as a 6x4 or 6x6, with either manual, automatic or torque converter/manual transmissions. The weight range went from 40 tonnes GVW to more than 200 tonnes GTW, and the engine options were the Cummins NT350 or 400.

Leyland also tasked Scammell with the development of the eight-wheeled 'Roadtrain' which went on sale as the 'Constructor 8'.

Scammell then went on to produce the forward control S26 which used the 'Roadtrain' cab, and was to replace the Crusader and Michelotti cabbed 'A' range.

A 6x6 version with a Rolls-Royce 350 engine, ZF automatic gearbox and Kirkstall axles was also designed. An 8x6 was also made which was tested by the British Army in 1986 for its hooklift-equipped DROPS (Demountable Rack Offload and Pickup System) vehicle requirement.

The test was successful and Scammell was awarded the contract in February 1987 to build 1522 DROPS vehicles. However, Scammell had recently been taken over by DAF, together with the rest of Leyland Trucks, and the new owners decided that production would be transferred to the Leyland plant and the Scammell works at Watford would be closed. The Watford plant ceased production in July 1988, with the last lorry made being a 6x4 S26 heavy haulage tractor for Econofreight. This was to be named Evening Star, after the last ever British Railways steam locomotive.

Since then the Scammell name has only been used once by DAF on a batch of aircraft refuelling tankers made for the RAF in the early 1990s.

The rights to the S24, Nubian, Crusader and Commander were bought by Unipower Ltd who opened a new plant in West Watford. Again military vehicles were the speciality and in 1994 the firm was purchased by military equipment maker Alvis, who itself had once been part of BL. Unfortunately Unipower's bid to produce a new tank transporter failed in the late 1990s and instead the British Army contract was given to the American maker Oshkosh, resulting in the end of Unipower vehicle production. ✦

Top left: The Crusader was launched in 1969. Initially it was only available as a 6x4, but a 4x2 followed later.

Top right: The Michelotti-designed cab was fitted to the 4x2 Handyman, 8x4 Routeman and 6x2 Trunker. *Photo Stephen Pullen Collection.*

Left: The Scammell name was last used on a batch of refuelling tankers for the RAF. *Photo Bob Tuck.*

A few ODDS & ENDS

While researching this publication I came across many companies and products which I was surprised to find were connected with British Leyland. Here's just a few.

Over the years British Leyland did experiment with electric cars. However, many do not realise that for a while it actually owned part of a specialist maker of such vehicles.

This firm was Crompton Leyland Electricar Ltd, a company that could trace its history back to 1890, when one Alfred Morrison was given £22 (worth around £1300 in today's money) by his father and set up a small engineering works in Leicester. Here he worked mainly on bicycles but in later years he patented an independently sprung-wheel motorcycle sidecar.

This sold well and soon the firm expanded into other areas including gas-powered stationary engines and generator sets. The company also made Tiger motorcycles.

The JOY 4 pedal car was made from 1949 until BL axed production in 1971. *Photo National Motor Museum.*

During the First World War the company worked on agricultural machinery and when the conflict ended continued making generators, bicycles and motorcycles.

Eventually the production of two-wheelers was stopped and the firm moved into making battery chargers and installing cinema equipment.

The first electric vehicle appeared in 1933. This was a 10cwt truck that was used as the works runabout. However, later that year full scale production started, with the first sale being to a local baker.

Soon the generators and other products were phased out and other electric commercial vehicles introduced. These had capacities of up to 30cwt and could be bought with a variety of bodies including milk floats.

It must be noted that Morrison was keen to make as many components as possible including the chassis, controller and drive motor.

In 1936 several companies involved in the manufacture and sales of electric vehicles formed a new company called Associated Electric Vehicle Manufacturers Ltd. This included Morrison, Electricars of Birmingham and the Young Accumulator Company of New Maldon.

Electricars had been founded in 1919 and began importing American-made Edison electric vehicles before starting to make its own designs.

Morrison and Electricars soon started working together instead of making competing models. However, in 1941 AEVM Ltd was purchased by Crompton Parkinson Ltd, and this led to the amalgamation of the two firms as Morrison-Electricar Ltd.

One interesting introduction by the new company was the 'route survey', which was to see if, firstly, an electric vehicle was suitable for a particular delivery job and, secondly, to work out the optimum battery and motor required if it was. To do this an engineer in a car equipped with a mileometer and gradient meter would go to a respective customer's depot and follow the current delivery vehicle – even if it was a horse and cart – on its round. On return to the factory the engineer could then work out what type of vehicle was required. Sometimes however, this did lead the firm to decline orders as it considered an electric vehicle was not suitable.

The company continued to grow and in 1948 Austin purchased a 50% share in AEVM and a new firm Austin Crompton Electric Vehicles Ltd was formed. After this the vehicles were sold as Austin Electricars.

More new products soon appeared including small pedestrian-controlled vehicles aimed at moving goods around factories, hospitals etc. The firm also converted some Austin three ton chassis to electric power for the chain store John Lewis.

The mid-1960s saw the firm introduce a very popular vehicle when the three-wheeled milk float returned. It also started making an off-road car called the Midge.

All these new products and increasing sales led the firm to build a new factory at Tredegar in South Wales. Construction started in February 1967 and the first complete vehicle left the site in April 1968.

By now the range of electric commercials made was vast. These included milk floats, general goods vehicles, mobile shops, refuse collection trucks, buses and even armoured security vans.

With the formation of British Leyland in 1968 the 50% share bought by Austin in the electrical vehicle business passed across and so the firm was renamed Crompton Leyland Electricars Ltd. In 1970 the company brought out the A1 model. This could be bought as a van or pick-up and could carry a load of 500lb. Its top speed on the flat was 33mph and it had a range of 25 miles. A lot of the mechanical components came from the Mini, as they did on a proposed two-seat car brought out shortly afterwards.

This was designed by Michelotti and the prototype was first seen at the 1972 Geneva Motor Show. However, later that year BL decided to sell its shares in CLE to Hawker Siddeley, which already owned several other electric vehicle makers including Brush of Loughborough. The company then became Crompton Electricars Ltd and went on to concentrate solely on goods vehicles.

The company continued in production until 1983 when production ceased and the factory closed down.

KEEPING THE KIDS HAPPY

In 1945 Austin chief Leonard Lord decided to set up a factory in South Wales to manufacture children's pedal cars. This was to give employment to former miners who had been struck down with what they called 'the dust', or the respiratory disease pneumoconiosis to give it its correct medical name, which was caused by breathing in coal dust over a period of years.

The brief for these pedal cars was that they should be suitable for children from ages four to nine, there must be enough room to carry a second child, the bonnet and boot were to open, it had to have working lights and a pretend engine and finally, that the body was to be made from the off-cuts of steel from Austin's car factories. ›

The Crompton Leyland Electricar prototype was unveiled in 1972. Most of its mechanical components came from the Mini.

Forklift maker Coventry Climax was part of BL until 1982. This 'blinged up' example was built for an advert in 1977.

A prototype, christened JOY 1, was soon made. This followed Austin design practice at the time with a chrome grille and alligator bonnet. It also had a dashboard with a dummy speedometer and a combined ammeter, oil pressure and fuel gauge. The car was driven by a bicycle type crank mechanism.

JOY 2 was basically the development prototype. It was a lot lighter than the first car and the drive was changed from a bicycle crank to two pedals that the child pushed backwards and forwards.

The next pedal car was JOY 3 and this was the first to go into production. However, instead of the saloon car designs produced up to now this was a small replica of a single-seat Austin Seven 'special' racing car, which had become famous on racing circuits prior to the Second World War. This pedal car went on sale as the Pathfinder.

Shortly after the racer was introduced JOY 4 was ready for production. This used the styling cues from the new Austin A40 Devon saloon.

To produce the Pathfinder and JOY 4 a new factory was built at Bargoed in South Wales which was completed by January 1949. This had some fairly advanced equipment such as a 'Rotodip' paint system, which as its name suggests, dipped the bodies in the paint and rotated them so everything was coated. Also, given the illness the workers were suffering from, the factory also had a fully staffed medical centre.

The first Pathfinders went on sale in the middle of 1949 at a cost of £25-4s, with the saloons going on sale just before Christmas priced at £20. These prices would translate to around £575 and £455 in today's money respectively.

These little cars sold well and the workforce grew from just over 100 to a peak of 514 in 1965.

The last pedal car was produced in September 1971 when BL decided to close the Bargoed factory. Total production from 1955 until 1971 topped 32,000 cars. Unfortunately no figures were kept prior to 1955 but it is believed that around 1500 saloons and 3000 Pathfinders left the works during that period.

> **UNFORTUNATELY PROBLEMS SOON STARTED TO EMERGE WITH THESE TRAINS VERY SOON AFTER THEY ENTERED SERVICE, PARTICULARLY WITH THE SLIDING DOOR MECHANISMS**

ON RAILS

From 1987 until 1988 British Leyland/Rover Group manufactured the Class 155 Super Sprinter at the Workington plant in Cumbria, using components from Leyland National buses. These trains were diesel multiple units – which is defined as a train made up from multiple carriages that is driven by a diesel engine on board one or more of the carriages. Altogether 42 of these two car trains were made. Each was fitted with two Cummins NT855-R5 diesel engines, one in each car, that produced 285hp each.

Unfortunately problems started to emerge with these trains very soon after they entered service, particularly with the sliding door mechanisms. This led to 35 of them being withdrawn from service and rebuilt as Class 153, which is a single car vehicle, so the 35 Class 155s made 70 Class 153s. The other seven Class 155 trains were owned by the West Yorkshire Passenger Transport Executive and it decided not to convert them but instead to modify the doors. These seven are still in service at the time of writing.

LIFT AND CARRY

Coventry Climax started out as a producer of automotive engines, but then went on to specialise in fire pump engines and forklift trucks.

The company started as Lee Stroyer in 1903 as a partnership between Englishman Henry Pelham Lee and

Jens Stroyer, who was from Denmark. Pelham Lee had been born in 1877 and after leaving school studied electrical engineering. He then joined the British Army and served in the Boer War before returning to England – finishing his engineering training with Daimler. While there he realised his real interest lay in mechanical engineering, particularly the internal combustion engine, and so in 1903 he left to set up his own firm with Stroyer as his business partner.

In 1905 Stroyer left the company so Lee relocated the firm to Paynes Lane in Coventry and renamed it as Coventry-Simplex.

Coventry-Simplex supplied engines to various car makers including GWK. This firm made cars from 1911 until 1915 and one of the company's service agents became particularly interested in them. This was Bamford & Martin of Buckinghamshire that had been started by Robert Bamford and Lionel Martin. In his spare time Martin raced cars at the local Aston Hill and one of the cars he made for racing was an Italian Isotta-Fraschini chassis fitted with a Coventry-Simplex engine. This was named the Aston Martin and became the first ever version of a car that went on to become a favourite of fictional super-spy James Bond.

Coventry-Simplex engines also found their way into the sledge-hauling tractors used by Ernest Shackleton in his 1914 Imperial Trans-Arctic Expedition, and the engines were also used in their hundreds to power searchlights throughout the First World War.

Such was the success of the firm that in 1917 it relocated to larger premised on East Street in Coventry and was renamed as 'Coventry Climax Ltd'.

Throughout the 1920s and into the 30s Coventry Climax continued to supply engines to many light car makers including Standard and Triumph, and so expanded into two new premises in Coventry. However, the depression soon hit the firm. One of the casualties was Swift, which had been buying Coventry Climax engines for quite a while. The closure of Swift meant that Coventry-Climax had a stock of engines it couldn't sell so Leonard Pelham Lee, who had by now taken over control of the firm from his father Henry, had them converted to drive generators. Soon after he decided to make engine-driven water pumps and so devised the Godiva series of pumps and engines. This would become very important due to the outbreak of war in 1939 as fire pumps were in great demand.

In 1946 Coventry Climax made the first British produced forklift truck, the ET199. This could lift 4,000lb to a height of nine feet. This truck was so popular that the company soon went on to dominate the British forklift market. ❯

42 of the Class 155 Super Sprinter diesel multiple unit train were made at the Workington plant in Cumbria in 1987/88 using Leyland National bus components. *Photo courtesy Railway Magazine.*

But the company didn't give up on its other products.

In 1950 an engineer named Walter Hassan joined the firm. He had learned his trade at Bentley before going on the work at the Lincolnshire-based racing car maker ERA and then SS. During the war he had worked at Bristol on aircraft engine development and returned to his prewar firm, now renamed Jaguar, in 1945. Here he helped develop the legendary XK engine. ❯

At Coventry Climax Hassan worked with another very talented engineer named Harry Mundy, who had also previously worked at ERA and also the postwar racing car maker BRM. Together they designed the FW fire pump engine. This was a very light four cylinder, single overhead cam unit of 1020cc. This engine was developed into the FWA, and subsequent engines, that were used very successfully by many racing car builders including Cooper and Lotus. Car engines continued to be made into the 1960s and one was developed into a road car power unit for the Hillman Imp.

In addition to competition engines, forklifts and fire pumps Coventry Climax also made engines for marine and military use.

In 1963 Coventry Climax was purchased by Jaguar so in 1968 became part of the British Leyland Motor Corporation. Here it was part of the Special Products Division, but the firm was soon changed. In the early 1970s the fire pump business was sold off and became Godiva Fire Pumps of Warwick. In 1977 however, the firm expanded by purchasing the Warrington-based forklift maker Rubery Owen Conveyancer Ltd, which was renamed Climax Conveyancer.

In 1982 BL sold the entire Coventry Climax business and three years later the forklift side of the business was purchased by Kalmar Industries.

KEEPING COOL

In 1934 the car body building division of Morris, The Pressed Steel Co Ltd, started manufacturing refrigerators that were sold under the Prestcold brand name.

This firm ended up producing fridges at several different factories in the UK such as Theale near Reading and in 1961 opened a new factory at Crymlyn Burrows in Wales. Shortly after this the company began the manufacture of the Rolls Rapide washing machine for the Rolls Razor Company.

The Rolls Rapide was sold at around half the price of other similar machines on the market. In addition Rolls Razor sold them direct to the customer – not from shops but via coupon advertising in the national and local press. Things went well for a while but then a price war began with other retailers, as the market was starting to slow down. On top of this a postal strike in 1964 caused a long period of time with no orders. Later that year Rolls Razor went in liquidation.

With the loss of the Rolls Razor business the Crymlyn Burrows factory was sold to Ford. Thereafter the company continued to make just refrigerators. However, after the Ryder Report in 1975 Prestcold was placed into the Leyland Special Products division and ended domestic refrigerator manufacture and concentrated on commercial refrigeration.

In May 1979 Prestcold acquired fellow refrigeration equipment maker Searle, but just two years later BL sold Prestcold to Suter plc.

A BIT MORE LUXURY

Avon Bodies was set up in Warwick in 1919. Two years later the firm was reorganised as The New Avon Body Company Ltd. Until 1927 the firm only made bodies for Lea-Francis and Hampton cars, but after then became one of the many companies around Britain that built them on the ubiquitous Austin Seven chassis. It also built bodies designed by Jensen on Standard chassis.

During the 1930s Avon also built bodies on Wolseley and Lanchester chassis, and also made some taxis, but in 1937 the company hit financial trouble when it couldn't pay Standard for the chassis it had recently taken. This led the business to go bankrupt, but it was bought by Maudslay Motors and re-branded as Avon Bodies Ltd.

The new company's first job was to modify its existing stock of Standard bodies to fit on Triumph Dolomite chassis.

During the Second World War Avon was contracted to repair aircraft and when the conflict ended it constructed some drophead coupe bodies on Hillman Minx chassis. However, the car world was changing and moving away from coachbuilt bodies, and the firm soon just ended up as a body repair company – although it did construct a few hearses over the next few years.

In 1973 the firm was bought by Ladbroke and renamed Ladbroke Avon Ltd. Initially the firm continued in vehicle body repairs but in 1979 Avon Special Products was formed and the company started to build convertible versions of the XJ6 Jaguar. An XJ6 estate car soon followed but in the early 1980s something very different

Avon Coachwork received a Gold Medal at the 1980 Birmingham International Motor Show for its Jaguar XJ6 estate conversion.

The Avon Collection

A unique assembly of coachworked cars for connoisseurs and enthusiasts

> AGAIN THIS CAR FEATURED TWO-TONE PAINT AND LEATHER SEATS BUT IT ALSO HAD AN AIRESEARCH T3 TURBOCHARGER

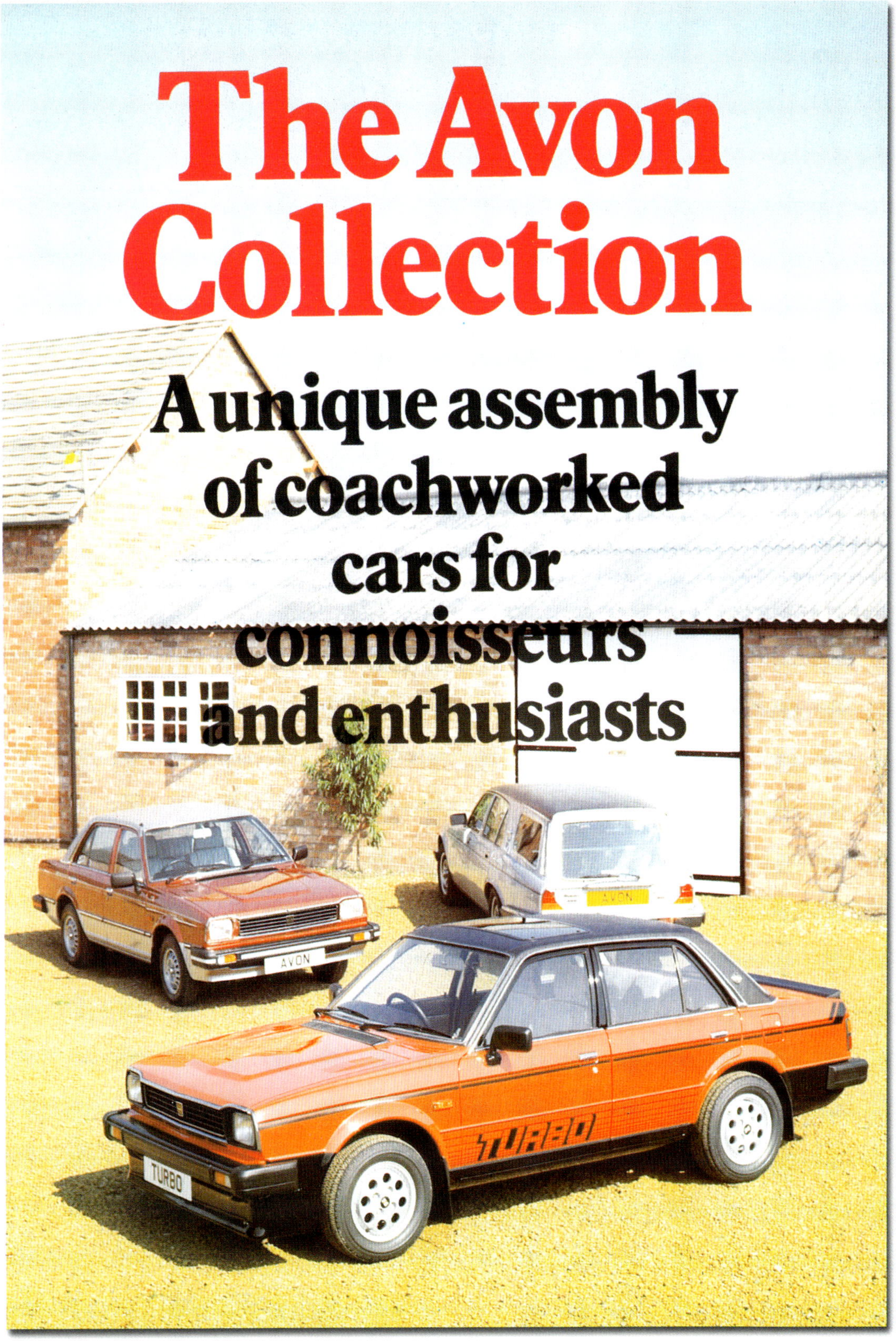

Avon also made luxury and turbocharged versions of the Triumph Acclaim. These were BL approved conversions.

appeared. This was a luxury version of the Triumph Acclaim that featured two-tone paintwork, a vinyl roof and an interior trimmed with Connolly leather and burr walnut. The conversion was approved and available through British Leyland dealers, and basically you would buy a new Acclaim, pay an extra £1365 and it would be shipped to Avon for the work.

Soon after the luxury version was made available came the Turbo. Again, this car featured two-tone paint and leather seats but it also had an AiResearch T3 turbocharger. This fitment was engineered by Turbo Technics of Market Rasen in Lincolnshire and boosted the engine's output to 105bhp at 5500rpm and gave 123lb-ft of torque at 3500rpm. This would power the car to a top speed of 115mph and give a 0-60 time of a shade under nine seconds. In order to improve road holding the ride height was lowered, but contemporary road tests still described the handling as 'floppy'.

The car was available until 1984 when the Acclaim was dropped and replaced by the Rover 213/216. The following year the company was sold and eventually went into liquidation. ✦

SAFETY FAST!

The MG marque became synonymous with low cost, high performance cars. These were sports cars for the ordinary person – but what is their history?

The firm was started by Cecil Kimber, who was born in 1888, the son of an engineer in the printing industry. In his teenage years he became a keen motorcyclist but unfortunately he had a serious accident which meant he had to switch to four wheels. After working at his father's company for a while he left and became the assistant to the chief engineer of Sheffield-Simplex, who made cars and also the unusual Ner-a-Car motorcycle.

During the next few years he worked for a few different engineering companies including AC Cars, but in 1921 he moved on and became sales manager at the Oxford branch of Morris Garages. He became general manager the following year.

Kimber soon began to design bodies to be fitted to Morris Cowley cars called the 'Chummy'. This design was what would now be called a 2+2 and had a full length folding hood. These bodies were made by Carbodies of Coventry and were finished off at the Morris Garages site at Longwall Street in Oxford.

These cars sold very well and by 1923 a 19ft x 100ft workshop had been acquired in Alfred Lane in Oxford just to assemble Chummys.

Later in the same year Kimber entered a mildly tuned Chummy-bodied Cowley in the Land's End Trial and won a Gold Medal. This was the spur to start production of something a bit more sporty.

The result was a Cowley fitted with a special two-seater body built by Charles Raworth of Oxford. Six of these cars were sold before Kimber designed a body for the Oxford 14/28 chassis. This was advertised as the 'MG Super Sports Morris' and was the first car ever to be sold under the MG name, although it still said Morris on the radiator grille.

An MG M-Type Midget pictured on the 1929 Edinburgh Trial. *Photo National Motor Museum.*

Top left: An MG Magnette K3 pictured at Donington in 1933. *Photo National Motor Museum.*

Top right: The MG TA was launched in 1936. *Photo National Motor Museum.*

Above left: The MG TD appeared in 1949. This one is shown taking part in the 1952 RAC Rally. *Photo National Motor Museum.*

Above right: MG has a long history of saloon car making, such as this YA of 1951. *Photo National Motor Museum.*

In 1924 Kimber built some 'special' cars to order, one of which was made for racing driver Billy Cooper, which used a 14/28 Oxford chassis. This polished aluminium-bodied car created a bit of a stir in racing circles at the time and led to many requests for replica vehicles.

Several similar cars had been made by October 1924 when Morris increased the length of the Oxford. However, this just led to more Kimber designed cars that, if anything, looked better than the previous models.

In 1925 Kimber issued his first brochure that made no mention of Morris – the car was just called the MG Super Sports. There were three versions available, a two seater, a four-seater and the Salonette which was a 2+2.

As well as new bodies, Kimber also altered the mechanics by including a higher final drive ratio and flattened springs to lower the ride height.

By now the Alfred Lane workshop was just not big enough to cope and so Morris allowed Kimber to move production into part of his radiator factory. This improved matters immensely and soon there were 50 staff working on MG production, which now went beyond just fitting new bodies and included stripping and rebuilding the new Morris engines before use. All this work meant that the Morris and MG cars were becoming increasing different so in 1927 the cars started to be fitted with the famous octagonal MG badge on the radiator grille. Morris Garages also became a limited company and later in the year moved to a purpose built factory on Edmund Road in Cowley.

The following year MG had its first stand at the Motor Show held at Olympia, where the company exhibited three cars. Two of these were completely new. The first was the M-Type Midget and the second was the 18/80 MG Six which used a six-cylinder overhead cam engine of 2468cc.

At the time of the show neither of these new cars was in production – in fact the Midget on display didn't even have an engine. However, there was enough interest generated for both to go on sale.

The 18/80 was incredibly well made and is regarded by many as the first 'real' MG as it wasn't just an upgraded Morris.

Over the next few years the car was improved but production ceased in 1932/33, although they were still available from stock into 1934, such was the depressed state of the car market following the Wall Street Crash of 1929.

The Midget however was a far bigger success. The car was based on the Morris Minor that had gone on sale the previous year as competition to the best-selling Austin Seven. However, the Morris was a bit more technically advanced than the Austin as it had an overhead camshaft as opposed to the Seven's side-valve setup. Morris had obtained this engine design from Wolseley, a company he purchased in 1927.

Production of the Midget began in March 1929, which apart from the two-seat MG body was virtually identical to the Minor except for some suspension modifications. ›

Below: The ZA Magnette of 1954 used the body from the Wolseley 4/44 and a BMC 1498cc 'B' series engine. *Photo National Motor Museum.*

Bottom left: There were also MG versions of the 1960s Farina saloons, such as this 1100. *Photo National Motor Museum.*

Bottom right: The MBG could be bought as a roadster or, as pictured here, a GT coupe. It was made until 1980.

Orders flooded in for the new Midget and over the next few years MG initiated a series of improvements. The car also found its way into motorsport and a modified version fitted with a supercharger was driven by Captain George Eyston to a new Class H land speed record of over 100mph. To celebrate this MG produced a short run of C-Type cars which were better known as the 'Montlhery Midgets', named after the French racing circuit where the record attempts were held.

Production of M-Types ceased in 1932 when 3235 cars had been made. Compare this to the 741 18/80 cars produced over a slightly longer period of time and you can see how popular the Midget had become.

All this extra work meant that in 1929 MG had to move again, this time to Abingdon just outside Oxford.

After the M-Type Midget came the J-Types. These were the J1 four-seater and J2 two-seater which used an 847cc engine and four-speed gearbox. The J3 and J4 were the motorsport versions and were fitted with supercharged 746cc units.

A very important car for MG during this period was the K series Magnette. As well as road going versions the firm also offered the K3 racing version. This had a highly tuned 1271cc engine with a balanced crankshaft and a Powerplus supercharger giving 120bhp. This car was incredibly successful in motorsport and one was even driven by the great Italian driver Nuvolari.

With all these sports and racing cars it's no wonder the MG slogan became 'Safety Fast!' However things were set to change. Up until 1935 MG had been the personal property of William Morris, or Lord Nuffield as he had now become, but in that year he sold the business to Morris Motors. Straight away the new management closed the MG competition department and axed the overhead cam engines from the range. From then on MGs would be fitted with overhead valve units from other Morris vehicles.

This resulted in the end of the ohc Midgets, by now called the P series, in 1936 to be replaced with the T series, starting obviously with the TA. This used a 1292cc engine very similar to that used in the Wolseley Ten.

Despite what some saw as MG now producing less sporty cars, the firm remained successful. However, Kimber himself was about to make an error of judgment that would cost him dear. With the outbreak of war in 1939 he realised that the company would have to go over to making war materials, and contracts were obtained to make sections of fuselage for the Armstrong Whitworth Albemarle transport aircraft. However, he did this without consulting the board and so he was asked to resign in 1941.

After this Kimber went to work for Charlesworth, a coachbuilder who had just taken on aircraft production work, followed by a spell at Specialloid Pistons. Unfortunately in February 1945 he was travelling on a train leaving Kings Cross Station when the carriage he was in was derailed. Two people lost their lives, one of whom was Kimber.

MG POSTWAR

With the war over, during which time MG had not only made aircraft parts but also that military essential, frying pans, the firm launched the TC Midget. As with most car makers this was basically the same as the company's prewar car, but did have a wider cockpit and different suspension. Production lasted until 1949 by which time some 10,000 had been produced. As this was Britain's 'export or die' period, over 6500 had gone abroad, many to America.

The TD that replaced the TC used the same engine but had rack and pinion steering, coil-spring independent front suspension and a restyled body.

MG also introduced new saloon cars after the war including the Y-Type which appeared in 1947. This was developed and was produced until 1954 when it was replaced with the ZA Magnette. In keeping with many other cars in the group this was a bit of badge engineering. The body came from the Wolseley 4/44 and the engine was the 1498cc 'B' series that went on to be fitted in the Austin Cambridge.

Other MG saloons followed over the next few years, all basically examples of badge engineering. These included the Magnette III that used the Austin Cambridge Farina body, and MG versions of the Austin 1100/1300. It must be said that as well as an MG grille these cars did have other modifications including the fitment of twin carbs. The last of this line, the 1300, ceased production in 1971.

One of the real MG classics appeared in 1955 in the shape of the MGA. This used the 1489cc 'B' series engine in a sleek two-set body. This car was an instant success and 13,000 were sold during the first year of production alone.

Other MGA variants soon followed including the 1588cc Twin Cam which gave 108bhp as opposed to 72bhp for the 1955 car. A coupe body also became available. Production ceased in 1962 when over 101,000 cars had been made. ›

Above left: The founder of the MG marque, Cecil Kimber. *Photo National Motor Museum.*

Above right: The final version of the Midget was fitted with the 1493cc engine from the Triumph Spitfire. It also had to comply with new American safety and crash regulations, and so had large black 'rubber' bumpers and a higher ride height.

1961 saw the welcome return of the Midget. This was the same car as the Mark Two Austin Healey Sprite, with just a few detail changes. They were even made side by side at the Abingdon factory. The following year both cars were uprated with the 1098cc engine and front disc brakes.

The Mk3 Midget was made from 1964 until 1969 and was fitted with the 1275cc engine from the Mini Cooper S, although slightly detuned to 65bhp. The Mk4 version was basically just a facelift, but the final version, made from 1974 until 1979, was fitted with the 1493cc engine from the Triumph Spitfire. The vehicles also had to comply with new American safety and crash regulations, and so the car now had large black 'rubber' bumpers and a higher ride height.

MGB

With the demise of the MGA in 1962 the company came up with something even more successful to replace it, the MGB. This two-seater sports car appeared in September of that year and used a B series engine that had been increased to 1798cc. Top speed was 104mph. Such was the demand for the MGB that in 1963 it helped push MG's total output up by almost 75%.

The MGB GT coupe was added to the range in 1965, and two years later both the roadster and coupe models were uprated with the fitment of an all-synchromesh gearbox.

In 1967 the firm brought out the MGC although this wasn't to take the place of an MG car, but instead was to replace another car in the BMC group, the Austin Healey 3000. This used the big Healey's 2912cc straight-six engine fitted into an MGB body. This propelled the car to 118mph but the weight of the engine did require the suspension to be re-engineered. Unfortunately the MGC did not sell well, as it just didn't handle as well as the MGB. Therefore in late 1969 after just 8999 had been produced the MGC was dropped.

The MG body did receive a larger engine a few years later when in 1973 the MGB GT V8 was launched. This car was capable of 125mph and was fitted with the Rover 3528cc V8 engine. However, the car was dropped some two years later, mainly due to the fact that Rover could not produce enough engines. Only 2591 cars were made, all of them being right-hand drive coupes.

In 1974 the MGB also received similar modifications to that already inflicted on the Midget to comply with US regulations. Again these included an increased ride height and 'rubber' bumpers. It would have been far better to have either replaced or restyled the entire vehicle but at this time British Leyland was having financial troubles and there was just no money in the MG pot.

The MGB soldiered on until 1980 when production ceased and the Abingdon factory closed. Well over 500,000 MGBs had been produced since 1962.

It then appeared that 1980 would mark the end of the MG name and so several attempts were made to purchase the designs and brand, including one involving Aston Martin. Unfortunately BL wanted to keep the name, which was really what people wanted, so all the attempts failed.

However, the name did survive and in May 1982 BL launched a high performance version of the Metro hatchback that carried the famous name. This used a 1275cc 'A+' engine tuned to 72bhp. Later that year the MG Metro Turbo appeared. This had a Garrett turbocharger that increased the top speed to 112mph, some 12mph up on the standard MG Metro.

Many were critical of the MG badge being used on these little hatchbacks but in 1984 came something that was far more in keeping with MG's original sporting credentials. This was the MG Metro 6R4, which had been developed by Williams, much better known for its Formula One cars. The designation '6R4' meant 6-cylinders, Rally car, 4-wheel drive, and the engine was a mid-mounted V6 of 2991cc. This car could be bought in one of two trims. The first was the 'Clubman' which produced 250bhp at 7000rpm, and could yours at the time for a 'mere' £40,000. The other was the 'International' which produced between 380 or 410bhp at 8500 or 9000rpm depending on how you wanted it tuned. This really was an 'off the shelf' Group B rally car, and its first outing in anger was the 1984 York Rally, when it set the fastest times in the first eight stages before an overheating alternator forced it to retire.

The following year a 6R4 driven by Tony Pond finished third in the Lombard RAC Rally. Other rallies were then entered but teething problems with the car never meant victory. However, in 1985 a 6R4 won the Gwynedd Rally, finishing almost two minutes ahead of an Audi Quattro. Unfortunately this was probably the highpoint for the 6R4 as in 1986 Group B was banned due to the high number of fatalities involving both spectators and participants. Austin-Rover abandoned motorsport that year but the

The MG Metro 6R4 was an 'off the shelf' Group B rally car.

technology for the 6R4 was sold to Tom Walkinshaw Racing. This company used the 6R4 engine, with added turbochargers, in a car it developed for Jaguar in the early 1990s – the XJ220, the world's fastest production car at the time.

BACK TO THE NORMAL WORLD

The two MG Metro versions remained in production until 1991 and were soon joined by MG versions of Austin-Rover's bigger cars, the Maestro and Montego. These were available over the next few years in both turbocharged and naturally aspirated forms – but don't underestimate them. The Maestro Turbo for example could do 0-60mph in 6.7 seconds and had a top speed of 128mph.

MG road-going sports cars returned in 1992 in the form of the MG RV8. This was basically an MGB fitted with the latest 3.9-litre version of the Rover V8 engine and a limited slip diff, and definitely aimed at the 'retro' market. Around 2000 were made, with most being exported to Japan, before production stopped in 1995.

In 1994/95 the Rover Group was taken over by BMW, and that year also marked a new car for MG. This was the MGF which used a mid-mounted 1.8-litre twin-cam K series engine, which was also available with variable valve control. Over the next few years this car was available in various guises, including some fitted with a 'Steptronic' paddle-shift gearbox.

Other cars also carried the MG badge during this period including sporty versions of the Rover 45 and 75 which were called the MG ZS and MG ZT respectively.

However, in 2000 MG Rover, as it was now known, was sold by BMW to the Phoenix Consortium. From the start the whole group ran at a loss but gradually managed to reduce the deficit.

However things did not go well over the years and in 2005 MG Rover was placed into administration. The firm had tried to form an alliance with the Chinese car maker SAIC (Shanghai Automotive Industry Corporation) but the offer of help from the British Labour government failed to materialise. Later that year MG Rover collapsed.

But that is not the end of the MG story. The rights were bought by the Chinese car maker, Nanjing Automobile Corporation, and in 2008 assembly of a revised MGF started again at Longbridge, lasting until 2011. MG Motor, now a division of Chinese state-owned SAIC Motor, is based in Shanghai. The first new MG-branded model for 16 years, the MG6, was launched in June 2011. MG Motor finally ended Longbridge production in 2016 with all manufacturing moved to China.

The firm saw substantial growth in the UK and Europe during the 2020s, with success in other markets too, and the current range of electric and hybrids includes the MG3 compact and the MG Cyberster sports car. ✦

Above left: The MG Maestro Turbo could do 0-60mph in 6.7 seconds and had a top speed of 128mph. Photo National Motor Museum.

Above right: The MG name returned in 1982, after a two year absence, and was used on the MG Metro.

The MG ZT of 2002 was the sports version of the Rover 75. *Photo National Motor Museum.*

FROM THE ARCHIVE

When Leyland merged with British Motor Holdings they issued a brochure to inform people of the state of Leyland at the time. Here are just a few pages from it showing the factory locations and some of the products made back in 1968.

CORPORATION FACTORIES IN THE U.K.

1. **Leyland Motors Limited** Leyland, Lancashire
2. **Standard-Triumph International Limited** Canley, Coventry, Warwickshire
3. **AEC Limited** Southall, Middlesex
4. **Rover Company Limited** Solihull, Warwickshire
5. **Albion Motors Limited** Scotstoun, Glasgow W.4
6. **Scammell Lorries Limited** Watford, Hertfordshire
7. **Alvis Limited** Coventry, Warwickshire
8. **Standard-Triumph (Liverpool) Limited** Woodend Avenue, Speke, Liverpool 24
9. **Transport Equipment (Thornycroft) Limited** Basingstoke, Hants
10. **Beans Industries Limited** Tipton, Staffordshire
11. **West Yorkshire Foundries Limited** Sayner Lane, Leeds 10
12. **Park Royal Vehicles Limited** Abbey Road, Park Royal, London N.W.10
13. **Butec Limited** Leyland, Lancashire
14. **Aveling-Barford Limited** Grantham, Lincolnshire
15. **Maudslay Motor Company Limited** Castle Maudslay, Alcester, Warwickshire
16. **Alford & Alder (Engineers) Limited** Maylands Avenue, Hemel Hempstead, Herts
17. **Forward Radiator Company Limited** Bordesley Green Road, Birmingham 9
18. **Self-Changing Gears Limited** Lythalls Lane, Coventry, Warwickshire
19. **Charles H. Roe Limited** Cross Gates Carriage Works, Leeds 15
20. **Power Jacks Limited and Newton & Bennett Limited** Agnes Road, Acton, London W.3
21. **Auto Body Dies Limited** Luton Road, Dunstable, Bedfordshire
22. **British Gear Grinding and Manufacturing Company Limited** Standard Road, Park Royal, London N.W.10
23. **Leyland Gas Turbines Limited** Leyland, Lancashire
24. **Aveling-Barford Limited** Newburn, Newcastle-upon-Tyne
25. **Goodwin Barsby & Company Limited** Leicester
26. **Barfords of Belton Limited** Belton, Grantham, Lincolnshire
27. **Invicta Bridge and Engineering Company Limited** Hoveringham, Nottinghamshire
28. **Grantham Electrical Engineering Company Limited** Grantham, Lincolnshire
29. **Rover Gas Turbines Limited** Solihull, Warwickshire

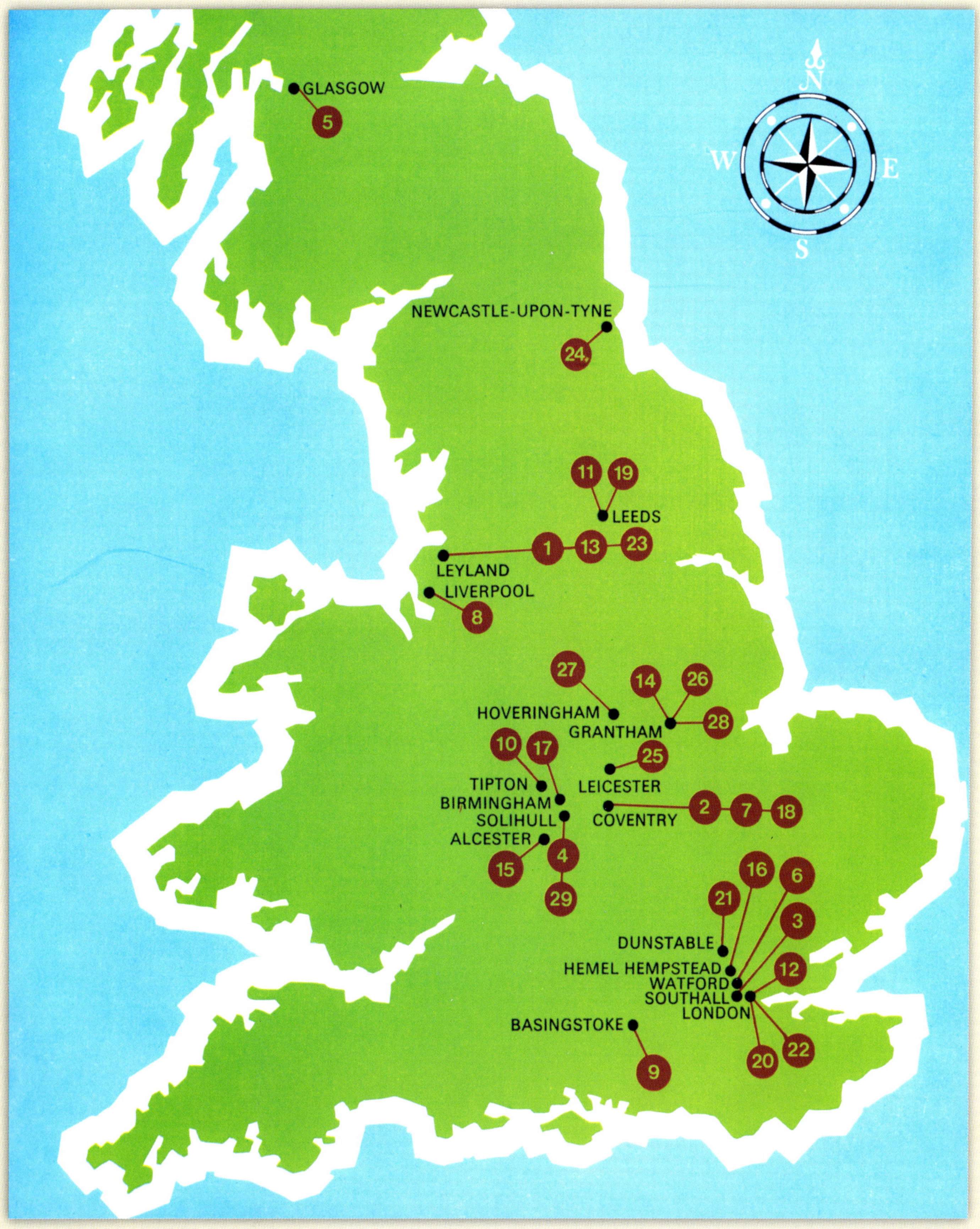
N
W
E
S
GLASGOW
5
NEWCASTLE-UPON-TYNE
24
11
19
LEEDS
LEYLAND
1
13
23
LIVERPOOL
8
27
14
26
HOVERINGHAM
GRANTHAM
28
10
17
25
TIPTON
LEICESTER
BIRMINGHAM
SOLIHULL
COVENTRY
2
7
18
ALCESTER
4
15
29
16
6
21
3
DUNSTABLE
HEMEL HEMPSTEAD
WATFORD
SOUTHALL
LONDON
12
BASINGSTOKE
9
20
22

Corporation's range of goods vehicles

Scammell Townsman
available in 1 model
G.T.W. 5 383 kg (11 872 lb)

Scammell Scarab
available in 2 models
G.T.W. 9 851 kg (21 728 lb)

Land-Rover Light Commercials up to 1 524 kg (3 360 lb)
load carriers in Regular and Long Wheelbase, normal and forward
control forms, with diesel or petrol engine

Leyland Light Commercial 1 016 kg (2 240 lb)
available as a Van, Pick-Up or Chassis-and-Cab, with diesel or petrol engine

Leyland '90'
available in 2 models
G.V.W. 4 572 kg (10 080 lb)

Albion Victor
available in 4 models
G.V.W. up to 10 363 kg (22 848 lb)

Albion Chieftain Super Six
available in 9 models
G.V.W. up to 12 697 kg (28 000 lb)
G.T.W. up to 19 305 kg (42 560 lb)

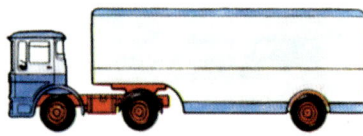
Leyland Comet
available in 3 models
G.V.W. 13 209 kg (29 120 lb)
G.T.W. 20 320 kg (44 800 lb)

Albion Chieftain 51
available in 7 models
G.V.W. up to 13 717 kg (30 240 lb)
G.T.W. up to 20 320 kg (44 800 lb)

Albion Chieftain 53
Available in 1 model
G.T.W. up to 19 305 kg (42 560 lb)

Leyland Bonneted Super Comet
available in 1 model
G.V.W. 14 225 kg (31 360 lb)

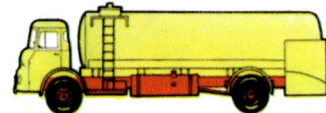
Albion Clydesdale
available in 10 models
G.V.W. up to 16 256 kg (35 840 lb)
G.T.W. up to 22 352 kg (49 280 lb)

Albion Super Clydesdale
available in 5 models
G.V.W. 16 256 kg (35 840 lb)
G.T.W. up to 22 352 kg (49 280 lb)

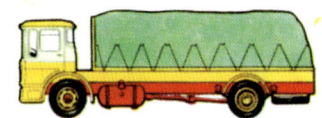
Leyland Super Comet
available in 22 models
G.V.W. up to 16 256 kg (35 840 lb)
G.T.W. up to 22 352 kg (49 280 lb)

AEC Mercury
available in 5 models
G.V.W. 16 256 kg (35 840 lb)
G.T.W. 25 401 kg (56 000 lb)

AEC Monarch (Export)
available in 4 models
G.V.W. up to 16 256 kg (35 840 lb)
G.T.W. 25 401 kg (56 000 lb)

Leyland Badger
available in 2 models
G.T.W. 24 384 kg (53 760 lb)
26 416 kg (58 240 lb)

Leyland Beaver
available in 10 models
G.V.W. 16 256 kg (35 840 lb)
G.T.W. up to 32 512 kg (71 680 lb)

Leyland Beaver (14BT 28R) (BETRIPR)
G.T.W. 32 512 kg (71 680 lb). 14BT28R 1 model with
semi-automatic transmission. BETRIPR 1 model
with semi-automatic transmission with integral
splitter and full torque P.T.O.

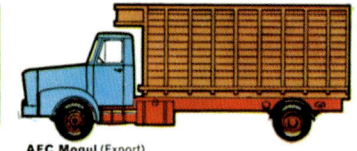
AEC Mogul (Export)
available in 2 models
G.V.W. up to 16 357 kg (36 176 lb)
G.T.W. up to 37 267 kg (79 970 lb)

AEC Mandator
available in 4 models
G.V.W. up to 16 256 kg (35 840 lb)
G.T.W. up to 36 576 kg (80 640 lb)

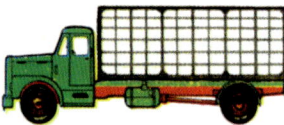
Leyland Super Beaver (Export)
available in 6 models
G.V.W. 18 289 kg (40 320 lb)
G.T.W. 36 576 kg (80 640 lb)

Scammell Handyman III
available in 2 models
G.T.W. up to 32 512 kg (71 680 lb)

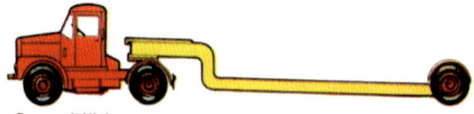
Scammell Highwayman
available in 11 models
G.V.W. up to 42 674 kg (94 080 lb)
G.T.W. up to 52 834 kg (116 480 lb)

Thornycroft 4 x 4 Nubian
available in 2 models
G.V.W. 10 410 kg (22 960 lb)

Albion Chieftain 71 4 x 4
Available in 3 models
G.V.W. up to 12 193 kg (26 880 lb)

Scammell 4 x 4 Mountaineer
available in 3 models
G.V.W. 20 320 kg (44 800 lb)
G.T.W. 60 963 kg (134 400 lb)

Albion Reiver
available in 3 models
G.V.W. up to 17 273 kg (38 080 lb)

Albion Super Reiver
available in 5 models
G.V.W. up to 20 320 kg (44 800 lb)

Albion Super Reiver 20
available in 5 models
G.V.W. up to 22 352 kg (49 280 lb)

Leyland Super Comet '20'
available in 1 model
G.V.W. 20 320 kg (44 800 lb)

AEC Marshal
available in 11 models
G.V.W. 22 352 kg (49 280 lb)

Leyland Retriever
available in 4 models
G.V.W. 22 352 kg (49 280 lb)

Leyland Hippo
available in 13 models
G.V.W. 22 352 kg (49 280 lb)
G.T.W. 32 512 kg (71 680 lb)

AEC Mammoth Minor
available in 2 models
G.T.W. 32 512 kg (71 680 lb)

AEC Mammoth Major 6
available in 14 models
G.V.W. up to 25 400 kg (56 000 lb)
G.T.W. 56 896 kg (125 440 lb)

Leyland Super Hippo (Export)
available in 6 models
G.V.W. 30 482 kg (67 200 lb)
G.T.W. 48 768 kg (107 520 lb)

Scammell 6 x 2 Trunker II
available in 1 model
G.V.W. 32 512 kg (71 680 lb)

AEC Majestic (Export)
available in 4 models
G.V.W. 25 293 kg (55 776 lb)
G.T.W. 56 700 kg (124 992 lb)

Thornycroft 6 x 6 Nubian and Nubian Major
available in 3 models
G.V.W. up to 25 400 kg (56 000 lb)

AEC 6 x 6 Militant
available in 2 models
G.V.W. 24 889 kg (54 880 lb)
G.T.W. 40 640 kg (89 600 lb)

Scammell 6 x 4 Contractor
available in 5 models
G.T.W. up to 304 814 kg (672 000 lb)

Scammell 6 x 6 Constructor
available in 4 models
G.T.W. up to 182 880 kg (403 200 lb)

Scammell Routeman Mark II
available in 3 models
G.V.W. 24 384 kg (53 760 lb)

AEC Mammoth Major 8
available in 8 models
G.V.W. 28 448 kg (62 720 lb)
G.T.W. up to 56 896 kg (125 440 lb)

Leyland Octopus
available in 9 models
G.V.W. 26 416 kg (58 240 lb)
G.T.W. 32 512 kg (71 680 lb)

61

Construction equipment

Corrugated Plate Apron Feeder
Available in 5 sizes up to 1·37 m (54 in) wide
Belt Feeders up to 0·91 m (36 in) wide
also available

'Ajax' Impact Breaker
available in 4 sizes,
outputs up to 60 962 kg/h (134 400 lb/h)

Crushing Rolls
available in 4 sizes up to
1·01 m × 0·6 m (40 in × 24 in)

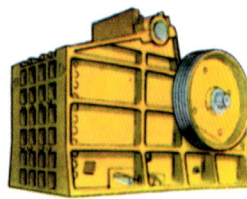

Blake Primary Crusher
Available in 5 sizes up to
1·2 m × 0·96 m (48 in × 38 in)

'Accra-Batch' Proportioner Unit
available in 2 sizes,
outputs up to 243 840 kg/h
(537 600 lb/h)

'Acme' Stonecrusher
available in 8 sizes up to
1·2 m × 0·91 m (48 in × 36 in)

Mobile 'Vitex' Vibrating Screen
Single, double or triple deck models up to
4·87 m × 1·52 m (192 in × 60 in)

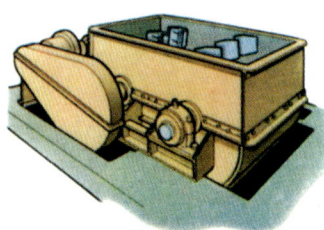

Rota-Mixer
available with batch capacities up to
4 535 kg (10 000 lb)

Scrubber
available in sizes up to
1·98 m (78 in) dia.

'Goliath' Mobile Primary Crushing Unit
available in 4 sizes incorporating 'Acme' crushers
up to 1·06 m × 0·76 m (42 in × 30 in)
Secondary crushing and screening plants also available.

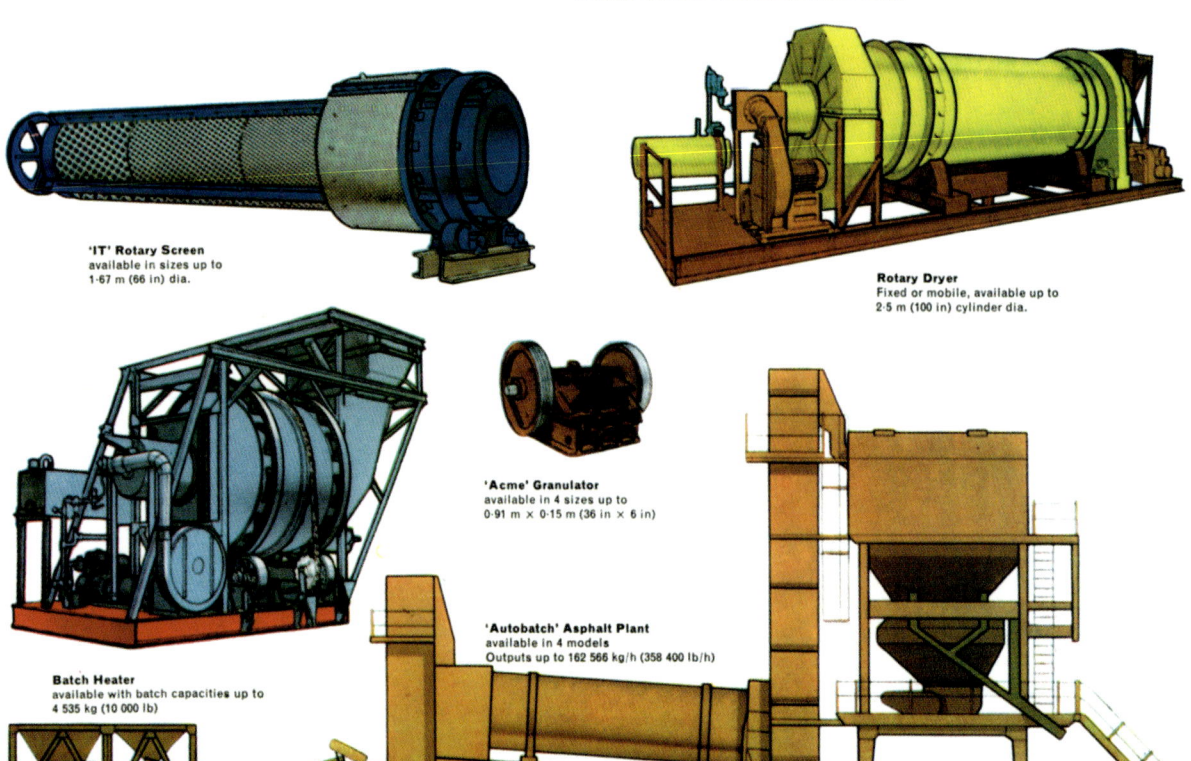

'IT' Rotary Screen
available in sizes up to
1·67 m (66 in) dia.

Rotary Dryer
Fixed or mobile, available up to
2·5 m (100 in) cylinder dia.

'Acme' Granulator
available in 4 sizes up to
0·91 m × 0·15 m (36 in × 6 in)

Batch Heater
available with batch capacities up to
4 535 kg (10 000 lb)

'Autobatch' Asphalt Plant
available in 4 models
Outputs up to 162 566 kg/h (358 400 lb/h)

74

Construction equipment

'Rocket 6' Truck Mixer
available in 1 model of 4·6 m³ (6 yd³) capacity

Concrete Mixer
available in 4 sizes up to 10/7

'Hydra-Ditcher'
available in 1 tractor-mounted model with wide range of attachments for multi-purpose use

Mobile Tubular Conveyor
available in sizes to suit wide range of applications

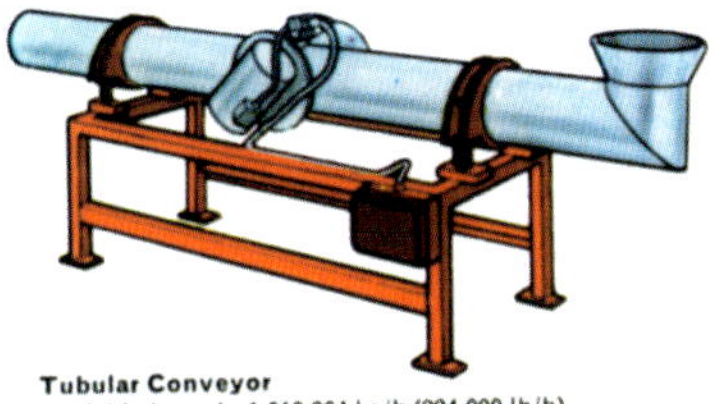

Tubular Conveyor
available in up to 1 016 064 kg/h (224 000 lb/h) conveying rate

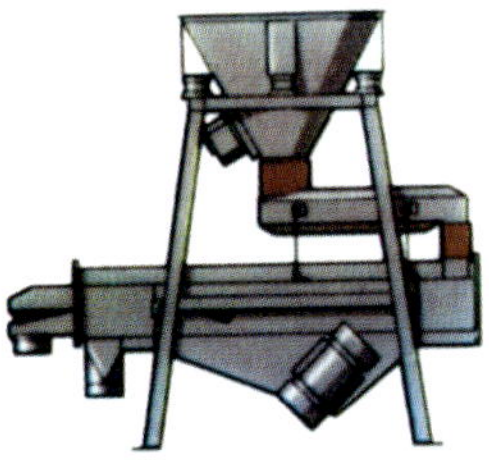

Totally-enclosed Hopper/Feeder/Screen Unit
available in 3 models with either single or double deck screen.

Control Panel
Standard or special electrical/electronic control panels supplied to customer requirements

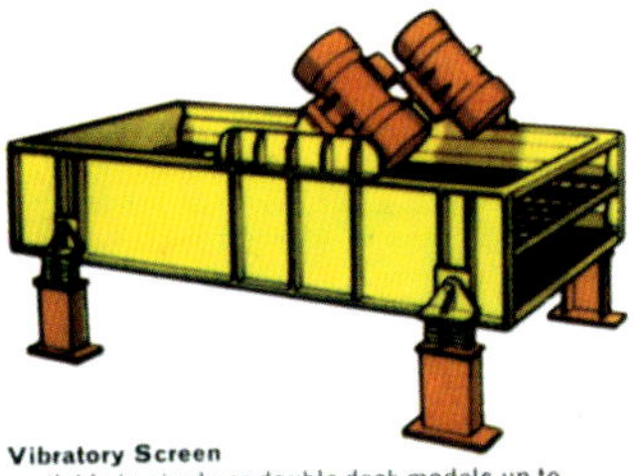

Vibratory Screen
available in single or double deck models up to 2·4 m × 1·2 m (96 in × 48 in)

Vibratory Table
available in light, medium and heavy duty models

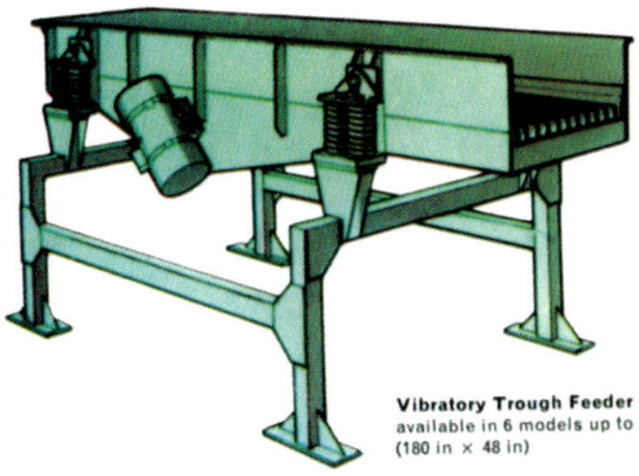

Vibratory Trough Feeder
available in 6 models up to 4·6 m × 1·2 m (180 in × 48 in)

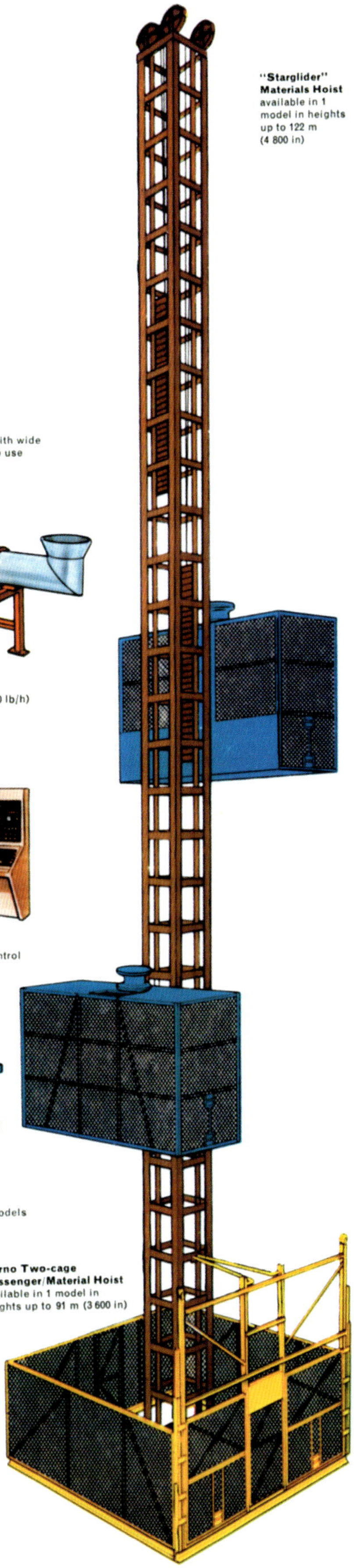

"Starglider" Materials Hoist
available in 1 model in heights up to 122 m (4 800 in)

Torno Two-cage Passenger/Material Hoist
available in 1 model in heights up to 91 m (3 600 in)

LEYLAND NATIONAL

The Leyland National bus was designed in conjunction with a large bus user – a recipe for success you would think. However, BL's initial design left a lot to be desired.

In 1966 the Labour party was victorious in the general election and appointed Barbara Castle as Minister for Transport. At the time the British government owned the Transport Holding Company that had been set up in 1962 and consisted of all manner of transport related companies including the haulage company British Road Services and even the travel agent, Thomas Cook. It also owned many regional bus companies that were becoming increasingly unprofitable due to the rise in ownership of the private car.

Castle's first idea to combat this was to form regional transport authorities that would take control of bus services in their areas and build the business up. However, in 1967, British Electric Traction approached the government and offered to sell them its portfolio of bus companies.

BET had started in 1895 setting up the electrification of tramways and in later years also bought several motorbus companies. When the electricity generating side of its business was nationalised just after the Second World War it ended up with loads of bus companies and loads of cash! It then set about investing in all manner of businesses from plant hire to printing. But in 1967 it decided to dispose of the bus side.

The government agreed to the purchase, which consisted of 25 companies and over 11,000 buses, at a cost of around £35 million.

The BET bus holding was then merged with the bus companies in the Transport Holding Company to form the National Bus Company on January 1, 1969.

It was then decided that the National Bus Company should work with another nationalised firm, British Leyland, on the design of a single deck bus.

The prototype appeared in 1970 and was shown at that year's Commercial Motor Show. This was an integral chassisless vehicle with a rear mounted engine, styled by the Italian designer Giovanni Michelotti, who had also penned the Triumph Herald and Stag, together with the 'finned' GRP (glass fibre) cab used on various Scammell lorries. Technical features included air suspension and a roof-mounted ventilation/heating pod. The other thing the makers were keen to stress was the ease of body repairs due to its simple design.

The first Leyland Nationals, which were built at the Workington Plant in Cumbria, entered service in 1972 but problems soon developed. The weak point was the Leyland 510 engine. This was a horizontal fixed-head turbocharged straight-six unit of 8.3-litre capacity. The problem was the 'fixed head', as this meant if you needed to work on the valves for example you had to strip the entire engine including removing the crankshaft and pistons.

Unsurprisingly this engine became very unpopular with operators, as it was also very thirsty and gave out heavy smoke if not looked after well – and it was such a difficult engine to work on that many weren't. To help reduce the smoke, the power of the engine was capped, which really seems quite a lame fix.

In 1978 Leyland brought out an economy version of the National Bus, the 10351B/1R. This dispensed with the roof mounted heating and ventilation pod and also had a revised interior. The heating was now a basic under-seat system, but it was adequate. However, the main 'carrot' for the bus companies was that it was cheaper. This helped to increase sales by quite a bit.

Despite all the problems, the National Bus was made until 1979 when the 'National 2' appeared. This bus had the Leyland 680 engine although this was soon developed into the L11. Three years later Gardner diesels were offered as an option.

Going back now to the early days, it is interesting to note that only three colours were available at the start – National Bus green, National Bus red and ordinary white. Unfortunately they had neglected to include London Transport red and so it would be 1973 before the National was seen in the capital, when other colours became available. By the way, London Transport had actually purchased 500 of these buses by 1980.

Despite the engine problems, the actual bus design was very good, and they were exported as far afield as Australia, Jamaica and Holland. The largest export order actually came from Venezuela, ordering 450 in 1975. Leyland National bus components were also used to construct the 'Pacer' and Class 155 'Super Sprinter' trains, which you'll find elsewhere in this publication.

Over the years this bus was developed into many different vehicles including mobile banks and a mobile disaster headquarters. One was even constructed as a 'double ended' bus with controls at either end for use in tunnels.

Production of the Leyland National 2 ended in 1985, although some buses remained in service until as late as 2007. It must be noted that many of these buses were rebuilt during their service lives with the fitment of modern engines, particularly from Volvo and DAF. However, it should be noted that two of the longest serving buses kept their original Leyland 510s – perhaps I was a bit harsh on this engine after all. ✦

Above: *Photo Mortons Media Archive*

Opposite: *Photo Alan Barnes*

RILEY MOTORS LTD

The roots of the Riley company could be traced back to the 1890s but that didn't stop it from becoming one of the first marques to completely disappear under BL ownership.

In 1896 William Riley set up the Riley Cycle Co Ltd in Coventry. Shortly afterwards his son Percy left school and entered the business, but his interest wasn't really in bicycles and he started to experiment with cars. He produced his first in 1898, but he had to keep it a secret from his father as he didn't approve.

The car Percy designed was a two-seater fitted with a single cylinder engine. This engine was quite advanced for the time as it had mechanically operated inlet valves. Despite this the car did not go into production and it would be 1900 before the first Riley motor vehicles were sold, and these were tricycles and quadricycles.

In 1903 the firm started producing tricars, which had two wheels at the front and one at the back. Steering was by handlebars. These initially used De Dion Bouton engines, but later that year Percy, together with his brothers William and Victor, set up the Riley Engine Company to make engines for the cycle company's vehicles.

The first four-wheeled production car appeared in 1907. This was powered by a mid-mounted 9hp V-twin engine of 1034cc capacity, driving through a three-speed gearbox, with chain final drive. As an aside, one of these, Riley's, was the first car ever owned by WO Bentley.

Larger cars soon followed of up to 2075cc. These had constant-mesh gearboxes and shaft drive, but it was another Riley product that really helped the firm's success – its design of detachable wire wheels. These were very popular and were sold to other manufacturers including Rolls-Royce, Napier, Hispano-Suiza and Mercedes.

In 1911 the Riley Cycle Co was so busy that the business had to be reorganised. The first step was to stop making bicycles. A few months later in 1912 a new company was formed to take on the production of cars, called the Riley Motor Manufacturing Co Ltd. This left the cycle company with the wheel business, but as it was no longer making bicycles its name was changed to Riley (Coventry) Ltd.

In 1914 the company launched the 17/30 which was powered by a four-cylinder, 2949cc engine. However, few were made due to the outbreak of war, after which Riley went over to military production.

FAME AT LAST

The 1920s brought two new Riley models which were to achieve great success. These were the Riley 10.8 and the Nine.

The 10.8 could be bought as an open two-seater or tourer, but in 1923 a sports model was introduced. This had a polished alloy body and red wings. These 'Redwingers' were an instant success and took Riley cars into motorsport. One stripped down version even lapped Brooklands at 103mph. A supercharged version was planned but was never launched due to patent difficulties.

The Riley Nine was launched at the 1926 Motor Show and had a 1087cc overhead valve four cylinder engine which developed 32bhp in standard tune.

These models too also entered motorsport, and the legendary Parry Thomas (see chapter one) started developing a very low-slung sports car from a Nine. After his death in 1927 this work was carried on by Thomson & Taylor. Altogether around 100 'Brooklands Nine' cars were produced from 1928 until 1932.

The Nine was produced until 1938 and developments over the years included coil ignition in 1933, and the option of a pre-selector gearbox from 1934.

Another well-known Riley user was Freddie Dixon who raced them successfully for several years achieving wins at Brooklands and at the TT.

Riley's from this period also formed the basis of the famous ERA racing car and one launched the post-Second World War career of Britain's first Formula One World Champion, Mike Hawthorn.

Despite all this Riley found itself in financial trouble in 1938 and the company was bought by Lord Nuffield for £143,000 and promptly sold on to Nuffield's company, Morris Motors. Riley was immediately reorganised. One of the criticisms leveled at the firm in the past was that it made too many different cars. It agreed and in the past had even used it in advertising. Nuffield changed all that – it would now concentrate on two new models, one of 12hp and one of 16, both figures being the RAC rating for tax. However, war soon stopped production.

POSTWAR CHANGES

With the war over Riley brought out the RMA saloon. This was a very elegant design and had torsion-bar independent front suspension and the prewar 1496cc high-camshaft engine. In 1946 the RMB arrived on the scene. This was basically a lengthened RMA fitted with the Riley 'Big Four' engine of 2443cc. Both of these

models were made until 1952. In addition there were two drophead versions of the RMB, the three-seat RMC roadster and the four-seat RMD.

In 1952 the RME and RMF cars appeared. These were very similar to the RMA and B but had different rear axles and full hydraulic brakes instead of hydro-mechanical systems.

The Pathfinder was introduced in 1953 which replaced the RMF. The RME continued in production for another two years. The Pathfinder was the first Riley to share a body with its Nuffield stablemate, Wolseley, although it did keep the Riley 'Big Four' engine. This was the first sign of the end of Riley's individuality. When the Pathfinder was dropped in 1957 it was replaced by the 2.6 and this not only used the Wolseley 6/90 body but the same engine as well.

Similarly, when the RME finally disappeared it was replaced by the 1.5, which was basically a Riley version of the Wolseley 1500. This in turn was an enlarged and restyled Morris Minor fitted with a 'B' Series 1489cc engine.

The final Riley's were just badge engineered versions of Wolseley's Farina models, which were in turn just re-styled Austin/Morris designs. These three were the Kestrel, based on the Austin 1100/1300, the 4/68 and 4/72 based on the Morris Oxford/Austin Cambridge and the Elf, based on the Mini. These three cars carried this once proud name until 9 July 1969 when BL ceased production. The Riley name is now owned by BMW. ♦

Opposite: Glory days – a 1929 Riley Nine Brooklands doing the sort of thing it did best. *Photo National Motor Museum.*

Above: The RMA was introduced in 1945. *Photo National Motor Museum.*

Below: The last Riley's were just badge-engineered versions of other BL group cars, such as this Mini based Elf. *Photo National Motor Museum.*

FROM THE ARCHIVE

Here's what you would have paid for your new Leyland back in 1978.

Model	List Price £	Special Car Tax £	VAT £	Max. Rec. Retail Price £
MINI				
850 Saloon	1787·00	148·92	154·87	2090·79
1000 Saloon	1879·00	156·58	162·85	2198·43
Optional Extra:				
1000 Model only				
Automatic transmission	299·73	24·98	25·98	350·69
Clubman Saloon (1098 c.c.)	2083·00	173·58	180·53	2437·11
Clubman Estate (1098 c.c.)	2232·00	186·00	193·43	2611·44
1275 GT	2323·00	193·58	201·33	2717·91
Optional Extras:				
Clubman Models				
Automatic transmission with 998 c.c. engine (except GT)	299·73	24·98	25·98	350·69
Denovo wheels and tyres (Clubman Saloon and Estate)	36·77	3·06	3·19	43·02
Metallic paint finish (except Estate)	26·04	2·17	2·26	30·47
ALLEGRO				
1100 De-luxe 2-door	2148·00	179·00	186·16	2513·16
1100 De-luxe 4-door	2233·00	186·08	193·53	2612·61
1300 Super 2-door	2398·00	199·83	207·83	2805·66
1300 Super 4-door	2483·00	206·92	215·19	2905·11
1500 Super 4-door	2556·00	213·00	221·52	2990·52
1500 Special 4-door	2797·00	233·08	242·41	3272·49
1750 HL 4-door	2967·00	247·25	257·14	3471·39
1300 Super Estate	2644·00	220·33	229·15	3093·48
1500 Super Estate	2745·00	228·75	237·90	3211·65
Optional Extras:				
Automatic transmission (1300 and 1500 models only)	299·73	24·98	25·98	350·69
Laminated windscreen (1750 HL only)	40·82	3·40	3·54	47·76
Metallic paint finish (except 1100 models)	26·04	2·17	2·26	30·47
VANDEN PLAS 1500 SALOON	3377·00	281·42	292·67	3951·09
Optional Extras:				
Automatic transmission	299·73	24·98	25·98	350·69
Head restraints	34·97	2·91	3·03	40·91
Metallic paint finish	26·04	2·17	2·26	30·47
MARINA (1979 model)				
1300 2-door	2314·00	192·83	200·55	2707·38
1300 4-door	2412·00	201·00	209·04	2822·04
1300 L 2-door	2502·00	208·50	216·84	2927·34
1300 L 4-door	2570·00	214·17	222·73	3006·90
1300 HL 4-door	2845·00	237·08	246·57	3328·65
1700 4-door	2589·00	215·75	224·38	3029·13
1700 L 4-door	2760·00	230·00	239·20	3229·20
1700 HL 4-door	3039·00	253·25	263·38	3555·63
1300 Estate	2751·00	229·25	238·42	3218·67
1700 Estate	2888·00	240·67	250·29	3378·96
1700 L Estate	3090·00	257·50	267·80	3615·30
Optional Extras:				
Automatic transmission (L & HL models except 1300 L 2-door)	269·41	22·45	23·25	315·21
Laminated windscreen	34·15	2·85	2·96	39·96
Metallic paint finish (L & HL models)	26·04	2·17	2·26	30·47
Tinted glass (standard on HL models)	38·40	3·20	3·33	44·93
Vinyl roof (1300 L & 1700 L 4-door models)	42·65	3·55	3·70	49·90
MAXI				
1500 Saloon	2818·00	234·83	244·23	3297·06
1750 Saloon	2948·00	245·67	255·49	3449·16
1750 HL Saloon	3204·00	267·00	277·68	3748·68
Optional Extras:				
Automatic transmission (1750 only)	318·34	26·53	27·59	372·46
Metallic paint finish	26·04	2·17	2·26	30·47
PRINCESS 2				
1700 L	3184·00	265·33	275·95	3725·28
1700 HL	3402·00	283·50	294·84	3980·34
2000 HL	3470·00	289·17	300·73	4059·90
2200 HL	3752·00	312·67	325·17	4389·84
2200 HLS	4179·00	348·25	362·18	4889·43
Optional Extras:				
Automatic transmission	338·38	28·20	29·33	395·91
Cropped nylon seat facings plus rear centre armrest (1700 L only)	48·38	4·03	4·19	56·60
Denovo wheels and tyres	84·98	7·08	7·36	99·42
Head restraints (standard on 2200 HLS)	29·57	2·46	2·56	34·59
Metallic paint finish	26·04	2·17	2·26	30·47
Power assisted steering (standard on 2200 HL and 2200 HLS)	194·70	16·23	16·87	227·80
Tinted glass (standard on 2200 HLS)	48·82	4·07	4·23	57·12
Vinyl roof (HL models only)	44·73	3·73	3·88	52·34
MG SPORTS CARS				
MG Midget	2395·00	199·58	207·57	2802·15
MGB Sports	3225·00	268·75	279·50	3773·25
MGB GT	3625·00	302·08	314·17	4241·25
Optional Extra:				
Painted wire wheels (MGB models only)	89·99	7·50	7·80	105·29
TRIUMPH				
DOLOMITE				
1300 Saloon	2684·00	223·67	232·61	3140·28
1500 Saloon	2870·00	239·17	248·73	3357·90
1500 HL Saloon	3192·00	266·00	276·64	3734·64
1850 HL Saloon	3560·00	296·67	308·53	4165·20
Optional Extras:				
Automatic transmission (except 1300)	283·98	23·67	24·61	332·26
Overdrive (except 1300)	188·49	15·71	16·34	220·54
Tinted glass (standard on 1850 HL)	49·20	4·10	4·26	57·56
Sprint Saloon	4340·00	361·67	376·13	5077·80
Optional Extras:				
Automatic transmission in lieu of overdrive	95·49	7·96	8·28	111·73
Limited slip differential	147·00	12·25	12·74	171·99
SPITFIRE 1500				
Soft Top Model	2774·00	231·17	240·41	3245·58
Hard Top Model	2854·00	237·83	247·35	3339·18
Optional Extra:				
Overdrive	188·49	15·71	16·34	220·54
TR7	3648·00	304·00	316·16	4268·16
Optional Extras:				
Automatic transmission	270·66	22·56	23·46	316·68
Five speed gearbox (including 185/70 HR—13 tyres and uprated rear axle)	175·72	14·64	15·23	205·59
Metallic paint	35·12	2·93	3·04	41·09
Sun roof	90·62	7·55	7·85	106·02
ROVER				
2300 Saloon	5051·00	420·92	437·75	5909·67
2600 Saloon	5521·00	460·08	478·49	6459·57
3500 Saloon	6462·00	538·50	560·04	7560·54
Optional Extras:				
Alloy wheels and 195/70 tyres (2600/3500)	213·57	17·80	18·51	249·88
Automatic transmission (2600/3500)	182·25	15·19	15·80	213·24
Automatic transmission (2300)	295·44	24·62	25·60	345·66
Denovo wheels and tyres	84·98	7·08	7·36	99·42
Electrically operated front and rear windows (2600)	127·18	10·60	11·02	148·80
Five-speed gearbox (2300)	142·70	11·89	12·37	166·96
Front fog lights (2300/2600)	32·22	2·69	2·79	37·70
Halogen headlights (2300)	30·66	2·56	2·66	35·88
Inertia reel rear seat belts (2300/2600)	42·71	3·56	3·70	49·97
Leather seat facings	182·75	15·23	15·84	213·82
Metallic paint (2300/2600)	44·08	3·67	3·82	51·57
Power assisted steering (2300)	180·60	15·05	15·65	211·30
Radio-cassette player plus rear speakers (2300/2600)	138·24	11·52	11·98	161·74
Remote control passenger door mirror (2300)	24·85	2·07	2·15	29·07
Sliding steel sun roof (3500)	172·72	14·39	14·97	202·08
Tinted glass (2300/2600)	66·89	5·57	5·80	78·26

— 108 —

Model	List Price £	Special Car Tax £	VAT £	Max. Rec. Retail Price £
RANGE ROVER	7821·00	651·75	677·82	9150·57
Optional Extras:				
Head restraints (pair)	37·95	3·16	3·29	44·40
Inertia reel front seat belts	24·65	2·05	2·14	28·84
Nylon fabric trim	32·64	2·72	2·83	38·19
Power assisted steering	255·53	21·29	22·15	298·97
Tinted glass	78·93	6·58	6·84	92·35
Option Pack comprising:				
Tinted glass, Head restraints, Nylon fabric trim, Inertia reel front seat belts	145·77	12·15	12·63	170·55
JAGUAR				
XJ 3·4 Saloon Automatic or five-speed Manual	8258·00	688·17	715·69	9661·86
XJ 4·2 Saloon Automatic or five-speed Manual	8726·00	727·17	756·25	10209·42
XJ 5·3 Saloon Automatic	10629·00	885·75	921·18	12435·93
XJS Automatic or Manual	12948·00	1079·00	1122·16	15149·16
Optional Extras:				
(Prices apply to items fitted to new cars during production)				
Air conditioning (XJ 4·2 and 5·3—Standard on XJS)	740·75	61·73	64·20	866·68
Front fog lights (except XJS)	55·86	4·66	4·84	65·36
Grab handles per pair (XJ 3·4 only)	5·46	0·46	0·47	6·39
Halogen headlights (standard on XJS)	75·24	6·27	6·52	88·03
Head restraints (XJ 3·4 only)	60·58	5·05	5·25	70·88
Inertia reel rear seat belts (except XJS)	45·42	3·79	3·94	53·15
Lap and diagonal rear seat belts (all models)	27·58	2·30	2·39	32·27
Limited slip differential (standard on XJ 5·3 and XJS)	97·72	8·14	8·47	114·33
Remote control passenger door mirror	28·12	2·34	2·44	32·90
Tinted glass (XJ 3·4 and 4·2)	100·11	8·34	8·68	117·13
Wheel trim rings (XJ 3·4 only)	27·06	2·26	2·35	31·67
Wheels—chrome plated pressed steel (except XJS)	134·58	11·22	11·66	157·46
Wheels—light alloy (standard on XJS)	314·24	26·19	27·23	367·66
Whitewall tyres (available only with light alloy or chrome plated pressed steel wheels)	49·31	4·11	4·27	57·69
Audio Equipment.—All models are fitted with a Philips AC460 mono radio/stereo cassette player plus manual aerial and four speakers as standard equipment—except XJS where two speakers are fitted.				
Electric aerial	35·88	2·99	3·11	41·98
Philips AC860 stereo radio and cassette player plus electric aerial	167·08	13·92	14·48	195·48
Paint and Trim				
Black upholstery (no extra charge on XJS)	23·70	1·98	2·05	27·73
Cloth upholstery (XJ 4·2/5·3 and XJS)	(alternative at no extra charge)			
Leather upholstery (XJ 3·4 only)	267·41	22·28	23·18	312·87
Signal Red or Yellow Gold paint with any available trim colour (no extra charge on XJS)	136·98	11·42	11·87	160·27
DAIMLER				
Sovereign 4·2 Saloon Automatic or five-speed Manual	9174·00	764·50	795·08	10733·58
Double-Six 5·3 Saloon Automatic	11104·00	925·33	962·35	12991·68
Vanden Plas 4·2 Saloon Automatic	12223·00	1018·58	1059·33	14300·91
Double-Six Vanden Plas 5·3 Saloon Automatic	14352·00	1196·00	1243·84	16791·84
Optional Extras:				
(Prices apply to items fitted to new cars during production)				
Air conditioning (standard on VDP)	740·75	61·73	64·20	866·68
Front fog lights (standard on VDP)	55·86	4·66	4·84	65·36
Halogen headlights (standard on VDP)	75·24	6·27	6·52	88·03
Inertia reel rear seat belts	45·42	3·79	3·94	53·15
Lap and diagonal rear seat belts (except VDP)	27·58	2·30	2·39	32·27
Limited slip differential (standard on 5·3 models)	97·72	8·14	8·47	114·33
Remote control passenger door mirror	28·12	2·34	2·44	32·90
Tinted glass (Sovereign 4·2 only)	100·11	8·34	8·68	117·13
Wheels—chrome plated pressed steel	134·58	11·22	11·66	157·46
Wheels—light alloy	314·24	26·19	27·23	367·66
Whitewall tyres (available only with light alloy or chrome plated pressed steel wheels)	49·31	4·11	4·27	57·69
Audio Equipment.—All models are fitted with a Philips AC460 mono radio/stereo cassette player plus four speakers and manual aerial as standard equipment—except Vanden Plas models which are fitted with an electric aerial.				
Electric aerial (standard on VDP)	35·88	2·99	3·11	41·98
Philips AC860 stereo radio and cassette player (VDP models)	131·20	10·93	11·37	153·50
Philips AC860 stereo radio and cassette player plus electric aerial (other models)	167·08	13·92	14·48	195·48

Model	List Price £	Special Car Tax £	VAT £	Max. Rec. Retail Price £
Paint and Trim—(excluding Vanden Plas models)				
Black upholstery	23·70	1·98	2·05	27·73
Cloth upholstery	(alternative at no extra charge)			
Signal Red or Yellow Gold paint with any available trim colour	136·98	11·42	11·87	160·27
Limousine	14091·00	1174·25	1221·22	16486·47
Chassis only	9467·00	—	757·36	10224·36
Power assisted steering, automatic transmission, front seat inertia reel safety belts and wing mirrors are fitted as standard equipment.				
Optional Extras				
(Prices apply to items fitted to new cars during production)				
Air conditioning	1222·77	101·90	105·97	1430·64
Badge bar	15·91	1·33	1·38	18·62
Blind to division	93·07	7·76	8·07	108·90
Clock to rear—electric	34·07	2·84	2·95	39·86
Clock to rear—mechanical	47·18	3·93	4·09	55·20
Cocktail cabinet	1102·06	91·84	95·51	1289·41
Electrically operated division	415·84	34·65	36·04	486·53
Electric windows—front	248·89	20·74	21·57	291·20
Electric windows—rear	228·84	19·07	19·83	267·74
Fire extinguisher	34·07	2·84	2·95	39·86
Flagmast to bonnet or roof	39·18	3·27	3·40	45·85
Flagmast to wing	59·59	4·97	5·16	69·72
Footrests—rear compartment	77·23	6·44	6·69	90·36
Front fog lights	55·86	4·66	4·84	65·36
Halogen headlights	75·24	6·27	6·52	88·03
Hazard warning lights	44·94	3·75	3·90	52·59
Inter comm telephone	299·97	25·00	26·00	350·97
Laminated glass all round	213·60	17·80	18·51	249·91
Nylon rug—rear compartment	94·79	7·90	8·22	110·91
PVC washable headlining	66·59	5·55	5·77	77·91
Radiator blind	47·63	3·97	4·13	55·73
Reading lamps—per pair	50·58	4·22	4·38	59·18
Remote control door mirror	49·99	4·17	4·33	58·49
Rubber mats front—per pair	25·06	2·09	2·17	29·32
Rubber mats rear—per pair	21·67	1·81	1·88	25·36
Rear seat belts—per pair inertia	45·42	3·79	3·94	53·15
Rear seat belts—per pair static	27·58	2·30	2·39	32·27
Side flashers to front wing	15·91	1·33	1·38	18·62
Side flashers to centre pillar	21·67	1·81	1·88	25·36
Tinted glass all round	234·86	19·57	20·35	274·78
Tinted glass windscreen only	129·60	10·80	11·23	151·63
Tinted glass backlight only	22·74	1·90	1·97	26·61
Tinted glass front doors	32·53	2·71	2·82	38·06
Tinted glass rear doors	49·99	4·17	4·33	58·49
Warning triangles per pair	21·07	1·76	1·83	24·66
Writing tables per pair	247·66	20·64	21·46	289·76
Paint and Trim				
Listed optional paint colours	202·23	16·85	17·53	236·61
Non listed paint colours	Individual quotation			
Duo-tone paint colours	291·54	24·30	25·27	341·11
Non-standard trim—front compartment	154·19	12·85	13·36	180·40
Non-standard trim—rear compartment	202·23	16·85	17·53	236·61
Audio Equipment				
Radio front compartment (with manual aerial and speakers)	100·47	8·37	8·71	117·55
Radio rear compartment (with manual aerial and speakers)	128·92	10·74	11·17	150·83
Philips AC460 mono radio/stereo cassette player, 4 speakers and electric aerial	306·66	25·56	26·58	358·80
Philips AC860 stereo radio and cassette player, 4 speakers and electric aerial	437·86	36·49	37·95	512·30
Electric aerial in lieu of manual	35·88	2·99	3·11	41·98
Electric aerial only	51·67	4·31	4·48	60·46

Austin Morris
Jaguar
Rover
Triumph

Price List
Effective from 18th October 1978

The Associated Equipment Company

AEC was once one of, if not the, biggest competitor of Leyland Motors. So how did it come to be owned by its deadly rival?

1920 AEC K-Type double decker. *Photo Mortons Media.*

It's strange to think that the company of AEC, maker for so long of the British icon that is the red London bus, owes its existence to three French entrepreneurs from the Victorian age. However, this is just the case, as in 1855 Leopold Foucaud, Joseph Orsi and Felix Carteret came to Britain and set up the Compagnie Generale des Omnibuses de Londres or the London General Omnibus Company for us 'rosbifs'. In fact the company wasn't officially given its British name until 1859. Even then the annual company report continued to be printed in both English and French until 1911 when it went over to just English.

In the early 1900s LGOC started to experiment with motor buses, including some steam powered vehicles, and by 1907 had some 200 motorised buses on the road. These included Wolseleys, Straker-Squires and French De Dions.

The following year LGOC took over two rival bus operators, increasing its fleet to almost 900 vehicles. However, a new series of regulations was introduced in 1909 regarding the maximum weight of buses. At a stroke many of the company's fleet were now off the road and new vehicles were needed. Therefore the decision was made by LGOC to try producing its own buses. Two prototypes had been produced by August 1909 and were passed for use and on the road in December.

More of these buses, named the X-Types, were produced into 1910 when the improved 34-seat double-deck B-Type appeared.

However, LGOC didn't have the London passenger transport business to itself, and due to threats from various other firms in 1911 LGOC accepted a takeover offer from the Underground Electric Railways Company of London.

The takeover was completed by April 1912 and one of the first decisions taken was to separate the Walthamstow-based vehicle building side of the business and set it up as an LGOC subsidiary. And therefore on June 13, 1912, the Associated Equipment Company Ltd was formed. The logo for the new firm was taken from UERCL 'Underground' symbol of a red circle with horizontal bar, with the word 'Underground' replaced with 'AEC'.

Production of the B-Type chassis continued into 1913, and by now some were being sold to firms outside the capital, with some even going to New Zealand. It is interesting to note that all sales were handled by Daimler.

The outbreak of war in 1914 greatly increased the need for motor vehicles and so AEC set to with an urgent expansion of their manufacturing facilities. This need for motor vehicles didn't just come direct from the War Office as almost 1200 LGOC buses were commandeered for military service leading to a shortage of buses in the capital.

In 1916 AEC was taken under temporary War Office control and in January 1917 began the production of the Tylor-engined Y-Type lorry specifically for the military. By the end of hostilities, around 5200 of these lorries had been produced.

With the war over, AEC looked to the future. Although the government had cancelled its orders for several

1939 AEC Mammoth Major. *Photo Gyles Carpenter.*

thousand vehicles, the LGOC was desperate for vehicles – in fact it was having to use some old army lorries as buses in some areas.

However, by the early 1920s things had changed and a deep economic recession brought a sharp drop in orders for vehicles. To try and improve things AEC looked to export markets and also experimented with an articulated lorry design similar to the Scammell Artic Six.

In 1925 the board commissioned a study of working practices at AEC and the conclusion was that the company should move to more modern premises. Eventually a suitable plot was purchased in Southall, Middlesex, and construction of a new factory incorporating a moving-track production line was started.

1944 AEC Matador 4x4 in Royal Artillery colours. *Photo Gyles Carpenter.*

1928 was a big year for AEC. Firstly its agreement with Daimler, which not only concerned sales but also the production of certain vehicles, was severed. AEC also altered its logo which saw the circle and bar placed on an inverted blue triangle – a badge it would use until AEC was closed many years later. However, the biggest news was that the firm finally moved to its new premises in Southall.

1928 also saw AEC start development work on an agricultural tractor designed by company works manager George Rushton. These tractors initially went on sale under the 'General' name but this was eventually changed to Rushton. Production ended in 1932 due to poor sales.

A new engine was also developed in 1928. This was a six-cylinder overhead camshaft unit and was first fitted into the Reliance bus chassis.

For 1929 AEC announced seven new commercial vehicle chassis, three bus and four lorry. The lorry chassis included the 4-ton Monarch, 6-ton Majestic and 8-ton Mammoth.

By now things had really improved at AEC, and in 1931 some 2000 chassis had been produced. In addition the firm were now also supplying components to the Four Wheel Drive Lorry Company Ltd and Hardy Rail Motors Ltd.

FWD had started producing off-road lorries in the US in 1910 and became a major supplier to the allies in the First World War. With the war over there was a market to rebuild and sell these lorries to the civilian market, which is how the British Four Wheel Drive Lorry Co came into being.

However, by the end of the 1920s the firm decided to start manufacturing its own vehicles, hence the need for AEC. To avoid confusion with the American FWD company these vehicles were sold as Hardys, this being the name of the railway vehicles produced by the company's associate firm. ›

However, the company soon ran into financial difficulties and was eventually taken over by AEC. This led AEC into the production of four-wheel-drives, notably the Matador that appeared in 1938 and went on to see extensive service with the British and Allied forces during the Second World War.

Also in 1938 a very important vehicle saw the light of day. This was a prototype bus designated A185. This became world famous as the RT – London's standard red double-decker, some of which were used until well into the 1970s.

After the war AEC looked to expand and in 1948 purchased two fellow commercial vehicle makers, Crossley Motors Ltd and Maudslay Motors Ltd. A new firm, Associated Commercial Vehicles Ltd, was set up to handle the sales from the group.

CROSSLEY

Crossley's history goes back to the late 1860s when brothers William and Frank Crossley started producing gas-powered stationary engines. In 1904 they were approached by a firm of London car dealers who wanted Crossley's to build cars for it to sell alongside the American Oldsmobiles it then imported. The car was designed by Daimler's former works manager, JS Crichley, and featured a 4760cc engine of 22hp and four-speed gearbox.

Over the next few years several different cars and engines were introduced and so in 1910 the vehicle side of the business was split from the stationary engines and set up as Crossley Motors Ltd. At the same time it also purchased the car sales company that had started them in the motor business, Jarrott & Letts.

Crossley became particularly well known during the First World War for the 20/25hp cars and lorries it produced for the military, particularly the Royal Flying Corps.

After the war, car production continued and in the early 1920s the firm also signed an agreement to produce the Bugatti Type 22 at Gorton from components shipped from France. Another company was also formed called Willys-Overland-Crossley Ltd which assembled various cars from the American-made Willys-Overland range at a separated Manchester factory. This factory also made the Manchester light lorry and from 1931 until 1933 it also made AJS cars. This factory was closed in 1933.

1965 AEC Mercury. *Photo Gyles Carpenter.*

1960 AEC Mammoth Major Mk5. *Photo Gyles Carpenter.*

The main Gorton works however, continued producing vehicles including sports cars. In fact one of Crossley's engines actually ended up being specified by Lagonda for its 16/80 model made from 1933 until 1935.

As well as cars, Crossley also made all manner of commercials. As well as the RFC tenders already mentioned it also made a 1.5-ton 'subsidy' lorry in 1923 and in 1925 its military 6x4 lorry was available fitted with the Kegresse rear bogie to make it into a half-track. In 1928 the firm made its first bus in the shape of the 32-seat single-deck 'Eagle'.

During the Second World War Crossley produced the forward control Q-Type 4x4 for the RAF, but after the conflict ended it decided to move to new premises in Stockport in Cheshire and concentrate on just bus production. As we've seen, Crossley became part of ACV in 1948. Initially it continued to produce its own vehicles but in 1951 the name was used on badge-engineered AEC vehicles. The last vehicle to carry the Crossley badge was produced in 1956.

MAUDSLAY

The Maudslay Motor Company Ltd was founded in 1902 and had a great deal to live up to from the very start, as the founder was the great grandson of one Henry Maudslay, inventor of the screw-cutting lathe and micrometer. He was also the engineer who helped the likes of Marc Brunel (father of Isambard Kingdom Brunel) put his mechanical ideas into practice.

The story starts in 1900 when Walter H Maudslay set up a company to manufacture marine engines. He was soon joined in the business by his sons Cyril and Reginald, although Reginald soon left to set up Standard. Cyril on the other hand saw that the marine engines weren't selling and so it was decided that Maudslay's should go into car production and so the Maudslay Motor Co was set up. Its first car was soon produced, using a 20hp three-cylinder engine and chain drive. It was entered in the Welbeck Speed Trials that year, where it did well enough to be put into production.

Left: 1966 AEC Mammoth Major eight-wheeler. The cab is an 'Ergomatic'. *Photo Gyles Carpenter.*

Below: 1960 AEC Routemaster. *Photo Mortons Media.*

The following year the company launched a 40hp car fitted with what is believed to be the world's first overhead camshaft six-cylinder engine. That year also saw Maudslay produce its first commercial vehicle, which was a van based on the 20hp chassis. A small bus was produced the following year.

However, after a few years of producing both cars and commercials, the firm switched to just cars, which were by far the bigger sellers. These included the 'Sweet Seventeen' of 1910 which had a 3308cc 17hp four-cylinder single overhead cam engine. A petrol-electric version was also experimented with.

This situation continued until 1912 when two new commercial chassis were introduced, a 1.5- and a 3-tonner. A 3-ton 40hp 'subsidy' lorry soon followed which was made throughout the First World War.

After the war, Maudslay decided to concentrate on commercials, although the company did exhibit a new car called the 15/80 at the 1923 London Motor Show but it never went on sale.

Over the years Maudslay's vehicles gradually moved up the weight range and the smaller models were abandoned, and by the end of the 1920s the firm had a 10-ton six-wheeler in production. ›

1973 AEC Mandator. *Photo Gyles Carpenter.*

Above left: A Maudslay Mogul circa 1949/50. *Photo National Motor Museum.*

Above right: Maudslay made 'subsidy' lorries during the First World War. *Photo National Motor Museum.*

In the early 1930s the firm brought out the 'Six-Four' which weighed less than four tons but could carry six. It could be specified with a four-cylinder ohc petrol or Gardner 4LW diesel engine. At this time Maudslay also started the tradition of naming its vehicle models with words beginning with 'M'. Initially this was just on the buses and included Majestic and Meteor. The lorries followed suit in 1937 with the 'Six-Four' becoming the Mogul.

At the beginning of the Second World War Maudslay set up a second factory at Alcester in Warwickshire. However, the original works in Coventry was soon damaged by enemy bombs and so production was switched to the new site. During this period Maudslay produced the Militant lorry for the army, which was a military version of the Mogul.

In 1948 when Maudslay became part of ACV, the range consisted of four different 4x2 rigids, a tractor unit and an eight-wheeler among others. However, the new owners were keen not to have competing models on their books and so several of Maudslay's designs were dropped. Soon the various Maudslay factories found themselves just producing components and the last real Maudslay was made in 1951. After this the name was used on badge-engineered AECs until 1960 when the name was dropped. The Castle Maudslay factory however did continue to produce commercial vehicle axles and in 1972 British Leyland sold the factory to the American axle maker Rockwell. The factory was eventually shut down in 1987.

THE ROAD TO LEYLAND

In 1949 AEC acquired Park Royal Vehicles and its associate company Charles H Roe Ltd. These were long standing coachbuilders and had been building bus bodies on AEC chassis for years. Under their new ownership Park Royal began to work very closely with AEC and together designed a chassisless bus. The team also started producing some lorry cabs.

1949 also saw AEC produce the first production underfloor bus in Britain – the Regal IV. This was soon joined by other new models such as the Mercury 8-ton lorry.

The firm soon started to try new markets including supplying chassis to Merryweather for use as fire appliances and the introduction of the 'Dumptruk' range of quarry dumpers. The initial version was a half-cab version of the Mammoth Major but by 1959 this had been joined by the normal control 690 'Dumptruk'. This vehicle was manufactured for many years and after AEC came under British Leyland control its production was switched to Aveling Barford of Grantham in Lincolnshire.

The early 1960s were the big turning point for AEC. Firstly after several years of exporting vehicles to Spain, where they were sold under the ACLO name, an agreement was signed in 1961 to allow them to be manufactured there by Barrerios Diesel SA. In addition certain models would also be assembled in Argentina.

1961 also saw ACV acquire Transport Equipment (Thornycroft) Ltd. The origins of this firm go back to 1864 when John Isaac Thornycroft set up in business as a shipbuilder with a factory on the Thames at Chiswick. This business flourished and is recorded as making all kinds of vessels from tugs to destroyers.

However, in 1896, Thornycroft decided to branch out and made a steam powered van with front wheel drive and rear wheel steering. Two years later the vehicle manufacturing side of the business split from the shipbuilding company and set up in a new factory in Basingstoke. Production of steam wagons soon got under way, and later that year Thornycroft produced what was possibly the world's first articulated lorry. In 1900 it produced its first bus but by now the firm was becoming more interested in the internal combustion engine than steamers.

Its first petrol-engined cars appeared in 1903, a twin-cylinder model of 20hp and a four-cylinder with 40hp. These cars were developed and by 1906 were also being sold under licence in Italy. By 1909 a range of three cars was offered, with the biggest having an overhead valve six-cylinder engine producing 45hp.

A 1938 Crossley IGL8 lorry pictured with a 1932 Crossley 4-seat tourer. *Photo Dave Bowers.*

A 1949 Thornycroft Nippy coach.
Photo Mortons Media.

1915 Crossley 20/25 bus. *Photo Dave Bowers.*

The cars were exceptionally well made but in 1913 the company decided to concentrate just on commercial vehicles. Altogether it is believed that some 450 cars were made during their 10-year production run.

By then Thornycroft was producing a three-ton 'subsidy' lorry which proved popular with the British military during the First World War.

After the war the firm brought out several new models including Britain's first production four-wheel drive lorry, the 'Hathi', which was introduced in 1924.

1927 saw the first six-cylinder petrol Thornycroft engines fitted into a coach sold as the 'Lightning', while in 1933 the firm offered Thornycroft diesel engines for the first time on models like the six-wheeled 'Amazon' and 'Stag' lorries. Shortly after this a proprietary engine from Dorman was available as an option on the 'Bullfinch' three-tonner.

During the Second World War Thornycroft manufactured some 20,000 military vehicles including the 4x4 'Nubian' and 6x4 'Tartar'.

1953 Thornycroft Nubian MkV. *Photo Alan Barnes.*

With the war over the company continued in commercial vehicle production but in 1948 the firm changed its name to Transport Equipment (Thornycroft) Ltd to make it clear that it was separate from the shipbuilding firm.

As well as producing normal road haulage vehicles Thornycroft began to develop heavy haulage lorries for oilfield use, particularly the 'Mighty Antar'. This was a 6x4 85-ton tractor unit fitted with the 18-litre V8 Rover Meteorite petrol engine developing 250bhp. This went on to become the standard tank transporter for the British Army, although later versions used Rolls-Royce diesel engines.

The takeover by AEC in 1961 marked a change of direction for Thornycroft, which now gradually dropped production of normal road-going lorries and concentrated on specialist vehicles such as the 6x6 Nubian Major airfield crash tender that was launched in 1964.

However, the Leyland takeover of ACV in 1962 meant that many Thornycroft vehicles were competing with another company in the Leyland empire, Scammell.

Gradually specialist vehicle production was moved away from Thornycroft and taken on by Scammell. The factory was finally shut in 1969 and the Thornycroft name used for the last time the following year on an export model 6x4 tractor unit.

AEC'S FINAL YEARS

In 1962 ACV became part of Leyland Motors (see chapter one). Two years later the group announced the 'Ergomatic' lorry cab. This ended up on both Leyland and AEC vehicles and was hailed as a breakthrough in cab design with ergonomic design looking after the driver. However, there were problems such as lack of airflow causing engine overheating on some models and odd design features like windscreen wipers that tried to push water UP the windscreen!

A new model of note at this time was the Mandator V8 tractor unit which given a bit more development time and money could have been a winner. Unfortunately both were sadly lacking.

Following the formation of BL, production continued at Southall until 1979, although the AEC name had been dropped two years earlier. After that the factory produced the Leyland Marathon, but when it was announced that this model was due to be replaced with the T45 'Roadtrain' the Southall plant was closed. ✦

Sure as the SUNRISE

One of the first companies to be taken over by Leyland Motors was the Scottish Albion concern. Although BL dropped the name in 1972, Albion would continue for another 52 years.

There is a bit of confusion about the official start date for the Albion Motor Car Company but most scholars pin it down to 1899. That was when Norman Osborne Fulton and Thomas Blackwood Murray built a small car with two transverse rear seats that was defined at the time as a 'dogcart'. Both men had previously worked at The Mo-Car Syndicate Ltd of Camlachie, Glasgow. This company by the way went on to become the car maker Arrol-Johnston, later renamed as Arrol-Aster.

The Albion dogcart used a horizontally opposed twin-cylinder engine and was fitted with a unique engine governor and chassis lubricator, both of which had been patented by Murray.

By mid-1903, it is recorded that Albion, which at the time had just seven employees, had produced some 160 cars. That year also saw the company move to larger premises in Scotstoun, Glasgow.

The following year the dogcart design, that could be bought with either an eight or 10hp engine, was dropped and replaced with a more modern-looking car fitted with a 16hp vertical twin-cylinder engine of 3115cc. Initially only solid tyres were available but pneumatics were offered as an option later. This car was also used as the basis for Albion's first commercial vehicle, a two-tonner that was available until 1914.

The firm's next vehicle was a large touring car that featured double chain drive and a 24hp four-cylinder engine of 4175cc capacity.

Its last car design appeared in 1912. This was a 15hp model that used a 2490cc four-cylinder engine and shaft drive. However, by this time Albion had decided that its future lay in commercial vehicles, as demonstrated by the fact that of the 553 vehicles that left the factory in 1912, only 150 were cars. Albion axed car production altogether in November 1913.

While car production was winding down, Albion was having increased success with its commercial designs. These included the 32hp A10 which had been introduced in 1910. This was soon followed by a new two-tonner that was also available as a charabanc.

Over the next few years the A10 lorry became very popular and during the First World War some 6000 were used by the British armed forces. Production actually continued until 1926.

Left: An Albion HD57 of 1954. *Photo Gyles Carpenter.*

Opposite: A late 1960s Albion Super Clydesdale with Ergomatic cab. *Photo Gyles Carpenter.*

In 1923 the company brought out a new 'subsidy' vehicle that was successfully used by many fitted with a 20-seat bus body. This was developed into the 30-seat Model 26 low-chassis bus, and was later renamed as the Viking.

In 1930 the company name was changed to Albion Motors Ltd. The following year saw several new models including two 32-seat buses that were available as the six-cylinder Valiant and the four-cylinder Valkyrie. It's strange that the firm was now giving names starting with the letter 'V' to its bus models while the lorries just received a model number, such as the 5.5-ton '127' that appeared in 1935. This lorry had an unladen weight of less that 2.5 tons and so could legally do 30mph.

HALLEY

Later in 1935 Albion purchased Halley Motors Ltd. This firm had been started in 1901 as The Glasgow Motor Lorry Company Ltd to make steam wagons. The first prototypes were given the brand name 'Glasgow' but the production models were sold as Halleys. It wasn't long before Halley dropped the steamers and went over to the internal combustion engine and in 1906 the firm moved to Yoker in Glasgow on the north bank of the Clyde and was renamed as Halley Industrial Motors Ltd.

In 1907 Halley took part in the RAC Trials and won two top medals, a gold in the 1.5-ton class and a silver for their two-tonner.

Over the next few years municipal vehicles such as fire appliances and refuse collection vehicles became very important to the firm. It also made around 400 3-ton 'subsidy' lorries for the British Army during the First World War.

With the war over, the firm concentrated on one model which could be bought as either a 3.5-ton lorry or 25/35 seat bus.

However a new range appeared in 1922, and by 1925 it included the 31-seat 'Kenilworth' coach and 'Ivanhoe' charabanc.

In 1927 the company was renamed as Halley Motors Ltd and the following year the firm launched the 'Conquerer' bus.

Over the next few years various new models were introduced, but in the early 1930s, when other makers started offering diesel-powered vehicles, Halley stuck with petrol. This lost the company many sales, and in 1934 Halley did fight back by offering a Perkins diesel in a four-ton lorry, but it was too late. The business went into liquidation in 1935 and was purchased by Albion.

DIESEL ENGINES

In the mid-1930s, Albion specified Gardner diesel engines in both lorries and buses such as the Venturer, which was its first double-decker. The firm also started mounting the engines and gearboxes together, rather than them being connected via a separate drive shaft. After the initial success of the Gardner-engined vehicles, the firm decided to develop a diesel engine of its own and these vehicles proudly displayed the 'Albion oil engine' badge on their radiator grilles. ›

1939 Albion FT3. *Photo Gyles Carpenter.*

Right: 1970 Albion Chieftain with LAD cab. *Photo Gyles Carpenter.*

Below right: 1936 Albion KL127. *Photo Gyles Carpenter.*

Bottom: Late 1920s Albion LB41. *Photo Gyles Carpenter.*

During the Second World War Albion took on various war contracts including the production of Enfield revolvers, and by the end of the conflict it had actually produced around 24,000 of these 0.38in calibre pistols. It also produced lorries including three-ton 4x4s, 10-ton 6x4s and the FT15N six-wheel drive low-silhouette artillery tractor.

After the war Albion introduced some new lorries, this time with names from Scotland's rich heritage which had often been previously used by Halley. These included the Chieftain, Clansman and Clydesdale.

When Albion became part of Leyland Motors in 1951, it sadly lost much of its individuality, as many of the components were from the Leyland parts bin.

Despite this, the Scottish names continued including the Claymore of 1955. This used an underfloor engine and was very popular.

In 1960 the LAD 'Vista View' cab was launched and was fitted to many Albion models. LAD, by the way, stood for 'Leyland Albion Dodge', those being the three makes that used the cab. This cab was very well received by Albion customers and continued to be used on the Reiver model for quite a while when other Leyland group lorries had gone over to the 'Ergomatic' cab in 1964.

By now Albion was but a shadow of its former self and the vehicles that were often sold fitted with the Albion badge were usually just Leylands, such as the 'Lowlander' double-decker bus of 1961 that was really just a modified Leyland Titan.

However, there was one thing that Leyland couldn't take away from Albion – its fantastic reputation for drive axle construction. And that is what would secure the firm's future.

In 1969 the firm purchased a nearby factory previously owned by The Coventry Ordnance Works. The Albion name was dropped from BL lorries in 1972 but the firm continued to make Leyland lorries until 1980 when production was switched to the BL Bathgate plant.

However, the Albion works survived and continued to make axles for group vehicles, including into the DAF years. In 1993 the firm was the subject of a management buyout and the firm was renamed Albion Automotive. In 1998 the company was purchased by the American Axle and Manufacturing Company. It remained in business until 2024 when the closure of Albion Automotive was announced. ✦

READS FOR RIDERS

Discover the world of two-wheeled adventures with our cracking collection of motorcycle books. From legendary riders to the history of motorcycles, we have a read for everyone!

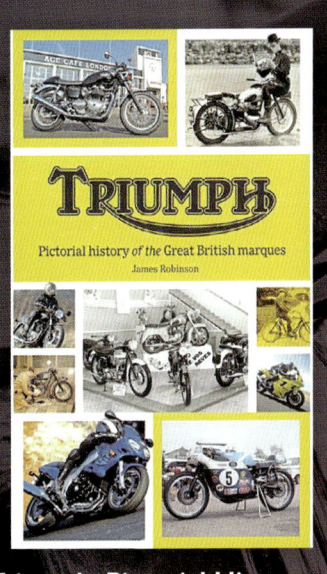

Triumph: Pictorial History of the Great British Marque
James Robinson
£25

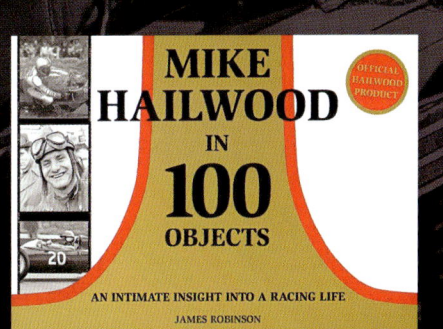

Mike Hailwood in 100 Objects
James Robinson
£30

Café Racer International Vol. 2
Mike Cowton
£8.99

Classic Superbikes 2
Frank Melling
£8.99

The Evolution of the Custom Scooter
Stuart Owen
£14.99

Le Vack's Legacy
Brian Thorby
£50

ORDER TODAY

www.mortonsbooks.co.uk

FREE UK DELIVERY

To find out more about our latest releases, join our book club at www.mortonsbooks.co.uk/book-club

ROVER

The first Rover car appeared in 1904 and from then on the firm was a fairly successful – if quite conservative – vehicle maker. The company became a minor part of Leyland Motors in 1967, but the name would eventually take the place of the British Leyland brand.

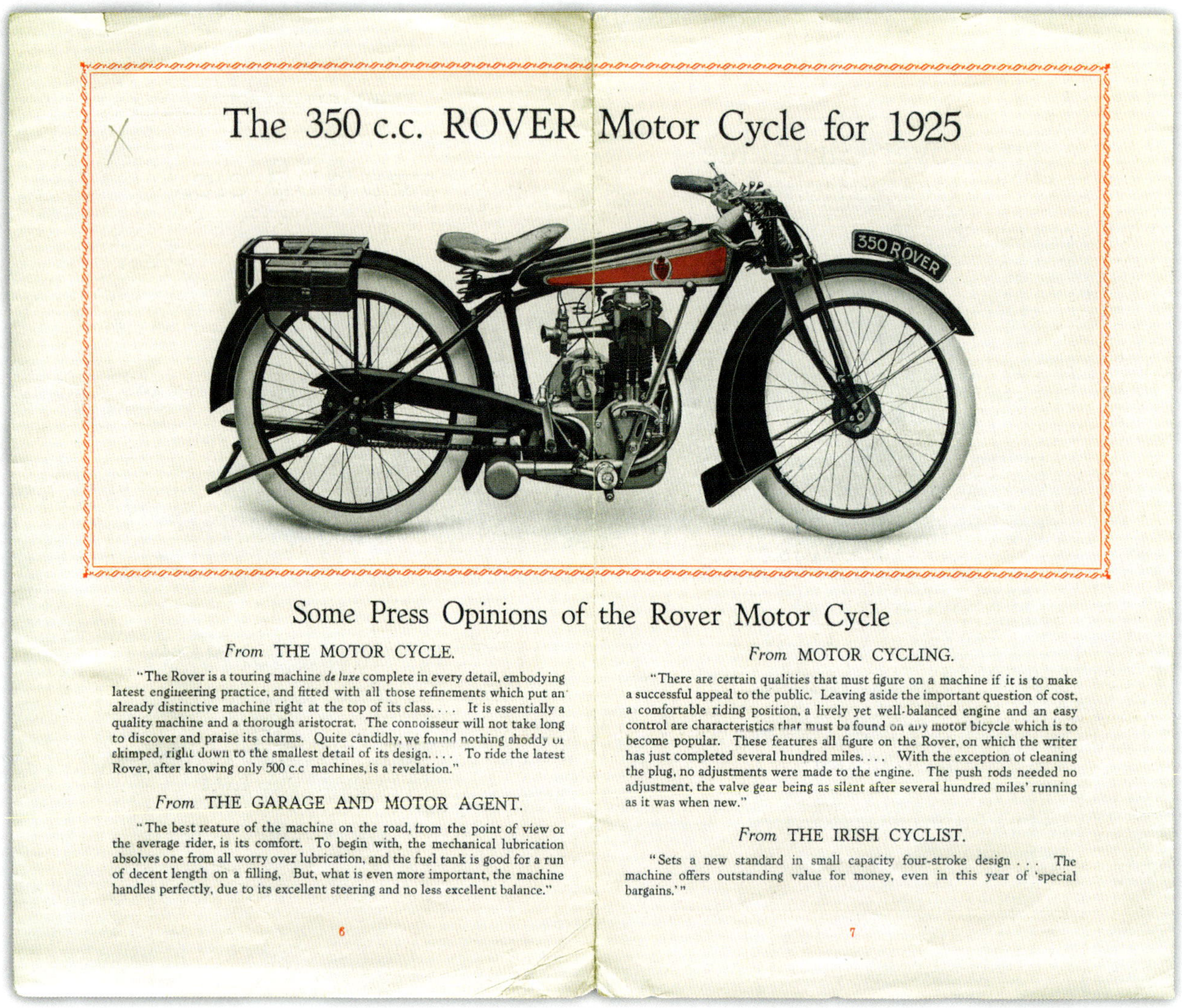

The 350 c.c. ROVER Motor Cycle for 1925

350 ROVER

Some Press Opinions of the Rover Motor Cycle

From THE MOTOR CYCLE.

"The Rover is a touring machine *de luxe* complete in every detail, embodying latest engineering practice, and fitted with all those refinements which put an already distinctive machine right at the top of its class. . . . It is essentially a quality machine and a thorough aristocrat. The connoisseur will not take long to discover and praise its charms. Quite candidly, we found nothing shoddy or skimped, right down to the smallest detail of its design. . . . To ride the latest Rover, after knowing only 500 c.c machines, is a revelation."

From THE GARAGE AND MOTOR AGENT.

"The best feature of the machine on the road, from the point of view of the average rider, is its comfort. To begin with, the mechanical lubrication absolves one from all worry over lubrication, and the fuel tank is good for a run of decent length on a filling. But, what is even more important, the machine handles perfectly, due to its excellent steering and no less excellent balance."

6

From MOTOR CYCLING.

"There are certain qualities that must figure on a machine if it is to make a successful appeal to the public. Leaving aside the important question of cost, a comfortable riding position, a lively yet well-balanced engine and an easy control are characteristics that must be found on any motor bicycle which is to become popular. These features all figure on the Rover, on which the writer has just completed several hundred miles. . . . With the exception of cleaning the plug, no adjustments were made to the engine. The push rods needed no adjustment, the valve gear being as silent after several hundred miles' running as it was when new."

From THE IRISH CYCLIST.

"Sets a new standard in small capacity four-stroke design . . . The machine offers outstanding value for money, even in this year of 'special bargains.'"

7

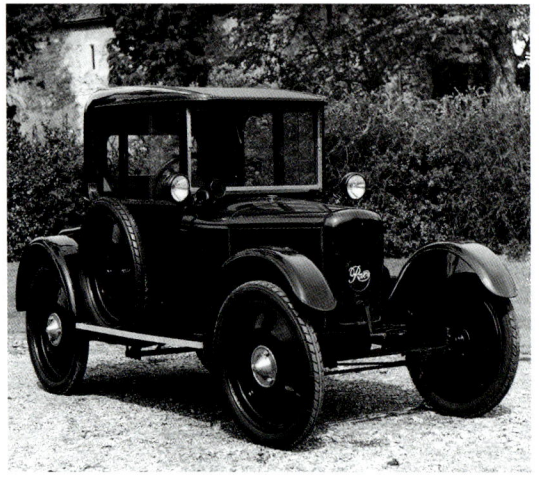

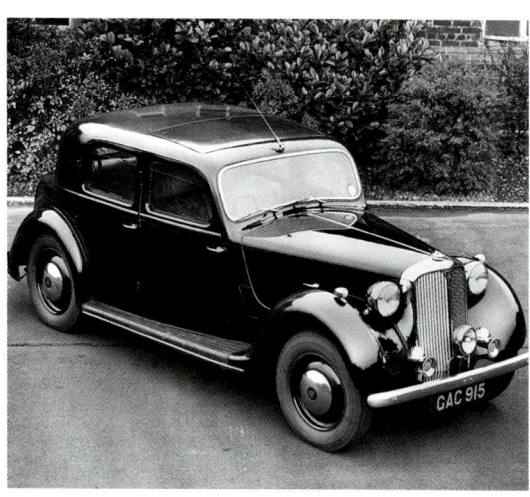

Above: Rover produced motorcycles until 1925. *Picture Mortons Media Archive.*

Left: The Rover Eight of the early 1920s used a 998cc flat-twin engine designed by Jack Sangster. *Photo National Motor Museum.*

Right: The P3 was a 'stop gap' car made in 1948/49. *Photo National Motor Museum.*

The first versions of the P4 had a three-headlight setup and gained the nickname Cyclops. *Photo National Motor Museum.*

The history of Rover begins in 1877 when John Kemp Starley and William Sutton set up in business in Coventry to manufacture tricycles.

In 1884 the firm started selling its machines under the name 'Rover', and the following year came up with a very important transport innovation. At the time the only two-wheeled bicycles were the 'ordinary' machines – which these days would be called a 'penny-farthing'. However, these bikes could be very dangerous and so Starley launched the Rover Safety Bicycle, which was far more stable and looked very similar to today's bikes.

This really kick-started the cycling craze of the late Victorian period and the business flourished.

In 1889 the firm of Starley & Sutton was renamed as J K Starley & Co Ltd, and then in 1896 it became the Rover Cycle Co Ltd.

Towards the turn of the century Rover imported some Peugeot motorcycles from France and was considering going into production. However, things were delayed as in 1901 John Starley suddenly died at the age of just 46.

Despite this the firm continued to prosper and in 1902 its first motorcycle, the 3.5hp Rover Imperial, was launched.

This had many advanced features for its day including 'springer' front forks and a spray carburettor.

Around 1250 of these machines were made until 1905 when the firm decided just to concentrate on bicycles and cars.

Rover's first car had appeared in 1904 and was christened the Rover Eight. This had been designed by Edmund Lewis who had previously worked at Daimler. The Eight was an unusual design even then. Instead of a conventional chassis it had a tubular 'backbone' that had the three-speed gearbox mounted at the front and the drive axle bolted directly to the rear. This meant there was no suspension at the rear but it did have a transverse leaf spring at the front. The engine was a vertical single-cylinder design of 1327cc. The selling price was £200.

The Rover Eight was soon joined by other designs including a 6hp car with a metal reinforced wooden chassis, and the four-cylinder 16/20. This car was made until 1910 and was even entered by Rover in the TT. Two cars were entered in the 1905 event – finishing 4th and 12th – but in 1907 a 16/20 won the race 12 minutes ahead of a Humber.

In 1910 Rover re-entered the motorcycle business with a new 500cc machine.

This was the first in a line of new designs that came out over the next decade including 250cc and 350cc models. The largest machine was fitted with a 676cc JAP V-twin. However, during the early 1920s Rover's motorcycle sales fell and in 1925 the firm abandoned production.

In 1911 Rover added two new cars to its range, an 8hp single cylinder and a 12hp twin. Both these engines were sleeve valve but were not good sellers. However, the next design was far more successful. This was the Twelve, which used a four cylinder engine of 2297cc. It even had electric lights! As an example of the success of this design Rover's car sales climbed from 883 in 1911 to 1,943 in 1914. ❯

Despite this Rover's vehicles were not considered suitable for military use so during the First World War contracts were taken on to build a three-ton lorry designed by Maudslay and the Sunbeam 12/16 car. The company did, however, supply Rover motorcycles to the Russian army.

After the war Rover restarted manufacture of the Twelve, and it remained in production until 1924 with little modification over the years.

In 1920 a new Rover Eight was launched that used a 998cc flat-twin engine designed by Jack Sangster, who went on in later years to purchase Triumph Motorcycles.

This new car proved very popular and almost 18,000 were built before production ceased in 1925.

An enlarged version of the Eight appeared in 1924 in an effort to compete with the Austin Seven. This Rover used a four-cylinder overhead valve engine of 1074cc. It was offered as the 9/20 until 1927 when the engine was enlarged to 1185cc and the car renamed the 10/25. Production ran until 1933.

One Rover of note during this period was the 14/45 which was designed by Norwegian Peter Poppe who had previously been part owner of engine builder White & Poppe. Despite a very interesting engine design the car was a disappointment and very underpowered, so the 2132cc engine was enlarged to 2413cc. This version was sold as the 16/50 and production lasted for three years until 1928.

Poppe also designed a side-valve six-cylinder car of 2023cc. This went on sale in 1927 as the Two Litre but was developed into the Light Six of 1930. These were quite sporty looking cars with a fabric body made by Weyman, and later became known as the Blue Train Rovers after one had beaten the famous French express train from the south of France to Calais. However, the Weyman body was quite prone to rapidly falling apart and this earned Rover a bit of a bad name.

However, by 1928 Rover was in serious financial trouble.

The shareholders had not received a dividend for five years so called a meeting where the firm's long time chairman, Colonel W F Wyley, resigned. He was replaced with Frank Searle and Jack Starley, son of the company's founder, who would jointly run Rover. However, Starley left the following year and was replaced by a man who would turn around Rover's fortunes – Spencer Wilks.

Wilks had been born in 1891 and after school he studied law before joining the British Army in 1914. He left in 1918 having risen to the rank of Captain, and joined the car maker Hillman. He later married into the Hillman family and was then appointed joint managing director alongside his brother-in-law John Black. When Hillman was purchased by Rootes, Wilks resigned and ended up at Rover.

Initially things were still bad financially at Rover and one of its biggest shareholders, W D Sudbury, together with Frank Searle blamed Wilks – who was looking after production – for the continuing problems. However, Wilks persuaded the board to hire an outside consultant to report on Rover's problems and was fully vindicated by the results – the problems did not stem from the production side. Immediately Wilks was named managing director and the consultant, H E Graham, became the financial director.

Under this new team Rover's business turned the corner and gradually got back into the black.

This was done mainly with a change of company philosophy. Previously the company had tried to compete with the likes of Austin and Morris by producing large numbers of cars to sell at the cheap end of the market. All this had done was create massive over production. For example in 1930 Rover was making around 280 cars each week, but its dealers never sold more than 55 per week. Wilks decided to move upmarket and produce quality cars in the medium price bracket.

Wilks was soon joined at Rover by two engineers, his brother Maurice, and B H Thomas – who was immediately set to work designing a new car. This was the 1410cc Pilot and fitted nicely into the range of cars the firm was then offering. This car used a six-cylinder engine and was the first of a string of small six-cylinder cars made up until 1938.

The other new cars under the new management were the 10, 12, 14 and Speed 14, that appeared in 1934. The first two cars used new engines of 1389cc and 1496cc respectively. These engines had been designed with a common stroke so that just by increasing the number of

Right: The later P4 – Auntie. *Photo National Motor Museum.*

Below: The Rover P6 was a much more modern executive vehicle.

2200 TC

cylinders or cylinder bore diameter, the factory could turn out a whole range of different sized engines.

Towards the end of the 1930s it became increasingly obvious that war was not far away and so the government introduced the 'shadow factory' scheme. These were purchased by the government but run by private companies to produce armaments. Rover took on two such factories, the first in 1937 at Adcocks Green in Birmingham and a second at Solihull in 1940. These produced aircraft engines, including the gas turbine 'jet' engine designed by Frank Whittle (see separate chapter).

During the war the main Coventry factory had been virtually destroyed and so when the conflict ended car production resumed at the Solihull plant.

As with most other manufacturers the cars made were prewar designs, including the 10, 12, and 14. These were offered until 1948 when the P3 was launched. This could be purchased as the 60, which had a 1595cc four-cylinder engine, or the 75, which used a 2103cc six-cylinder unit. In addition there were two body styles, a six-light saloon or a four-light sports saloon (the term 'light' is an old term from coachbuilding and means a side window).

The P3 was really nothing more than a stop-gap vehicle and only around 9,000 were made before production ceased in October 1949.

By then, of course, Rover had got a real winner on its hands in the shape of the new Land Rover.

This became so important to the firm, and eventually became a brand of its own, its history is dealt with elsewhere in this book. September 1949 saw the launch of what many regard as the archetypal Rover – the P4. This used the same engine as the P3 75 but the rest was all-new.

The first of this type featured a three headlight arrangement that earned the car the nickname 'Cyclops'. However, when the car received a redesign in 1952 and the centre light was dropped the car soon gained another name, 'Auntie', which just shows the affection these cars generated in their owners. Over the years other engines were also offered, together with automatic transmission on some models. Altogether some 130,000 P4 Rovers would leave the production line before it was axed in 1964.

With sales of the P4 going along quite nicely Wilks decided that a more upmarket car was required.

This large saloon appeared in 1959 as the P5 and was fitted with a 2995cc inlet-over-exhaust six-cylinder engine that developed 115bhp. The car was up-rated in 1962 with an increase in power to 134bhp. A coupe version was also launched but this was really in name only, as it still had four doors and the only difference really was the lowered roofline and sloped rear window.

These cars were made until 1967 when the new V8 Rover engine was dropped into them. This engine design had been bought from Buick (see separate chapter) and absolutely transformed the P5 – it became a huge success, particularly with the British 'establishment'. Not only was it the car of choice for various Prime Ministers, but even the Queen had one. ❯

The interior of a Mk2 P6 – very 1970s.

> **WHEN THE CAR RECEIVED A REDESIGN IN 1952 AND THE CENTRE LIGHT WAS DROPPED THE CAR SOON GAINED ANOTHER NAME, 'AUNTIE'**

Production ended in 1973 when around 20,000 cars had been made, most of them coupes.

With the 1960s there came a need for something a bit more modern. The answer came in 1963 in the shape of the P6 2000 four-door saloon.

The car was designed by David Bache, part of a team led by Charles Spencer King who was also in charge of the Range Rover project a few years later. The car the team came up with was a complete break from the normal Rover offering. The first cars used an all-new four-cylinder, overhead cam 1978cc engine that developed 90bhp. It had an all-synchromesh gearbox, servo-assisted brakes all round and a body that was made up of a steel structure to which the non-stressed panels were bolted. The following year the P6 won the first ever European Car of the Year Award. The 2000 version of the P6 actually became the best selling Rover of all time with almost 328,000 being produced by 1972.

Other versions of the P6 were also available over the years. These included the fitment of the 3.5 litre V8 and 2.2 litre four-cylinder engine. The car was given a facelift in 1970 and the subsequent cars were sold as Mark Two versions. P6 production ceased in 1977.

If there was ever a car that deserved a better fate than it actually got it's the Rover SD1.

This car, whose designation stood for Specialist Division One, had been designed by David Bache to replace several models in the British Leyland range but not to compete with Jaguar.

Work began in 1971 but the car wasn't unveiled until June 1976 when it caused a sensation. That's not surprising really when you consider what it was competing against. For example one its main rivals was the Ford Granada which looked positively boring beside the new Rover offering, with its Ferrari Daytona design influences. Hardly surprising then that it won the

European Car of the Year Award in 1977.

Initially it was available only with the 3.5 litre V8 engine but soon two new engines developed from the Triumph Six were made available. These were of 2.3 and 2.6 litre capacity. With these engines the SD1 finally replaced the Triumph 2000/2500 as well as the P6 Rover.

However, despite the accolades and the design's obvious potential problems soon started to emerge.

The car was launched on the European market at the Geneva Motor Show in 1977. Orders soon flooded in but BL could not supply any left hand drive cars at the time due to a toolmakers' strike affecting several BL factories, together with another dispute which hit the production of bodyshells at Castle Bromwich.

Also, despite the fact the SD1 was assembled in a brand new facility at Solihull the cars started to suffer from a terrible reputation for poor quality. The new thermoplastic paint finish applied to the cars could easily chip off and corrosion problems were common. In addition the electrical system was very poor, particularly the electric windows and central locking – there were even tales of owners being trapped in their cars as they wouldn't unlock!

The first Rover 200 series was a re-badged Honda Ballade.

The Rover SD1 was European Car of the Year 1977.

The 800 saloon was another joint Rover and Honda development. This is an 820SE of 1989. *Photo National Motor Museum.*

As if those problems weren't enough, the six-cylinder engines developed a reputation for excessive oil consumption and general unreliability.

Many of these problems were caused by the cars just being badly built by a demotivated workforce that simply didn't seem to care. However, management didn't help as there are reports of quality control inspections being missed just to get more cars out of the door. However, these issues will be dealt with elsewhere.

In 1981 production of the SD1 was moved to Cowley – leaving the Solihull plant to become the home of Land Rover.

The following year the cars were given a few cosmetic tweaks and also two new engine options – the 1994cc O Series petrol aimed at fleet buyers, and a 2393cc diesel from Italian maker VM.

Production of the SD1 ceased in July 1986 when around 300,000 had been built.

By then Rover was in the 'Honda era'. This partnership with Honda to produce certain cars had started with the Triumph Acclaim, which was really a badge engineered Honda Ballade. However, when Honda launched its new Ballade, BL decided that its version should carry the Rover name, so in 1984 the 213 was born. Shortly afterwards the 216 was launched that at least had the distinction of having a British engine in the shape of the 1598cc S Series used in the Austin Maestro.

The firm also worked with Honda to design and build a new executive car. This was the 800 saloon that appeared in July 1986, although Honda's version – the Legend – had gone on sale some nine months previously. The car had two engine options, the Rover 1996cc twin-cam four or the Honda 2494cc V6. The cars would be designated 820 and 825i respectively. Later versions included the hatchback Vitesse.

In 1986 Graham Day took over control of British Leyland and immediately decided to change the name to the Rover Group, and that the cars would be made by the Austin Rover Division.

As the Rover name now refers to a whole group, we'll continue just to look at the cars here, and the group history later on in the book.

In 1989, due to Day's decision, the Austin name was dropped and the Rover name was added to the Metro, Maestro and Montego.

There was also another new 'Honda Rover' in the form of the 200 series hatchback that was basically a Honda Concerto. These cars came with either a Rover 1396cc K series or Honda 1590cc engine. A saloon version of the car, called the 400 series, became available in 1990. To fit in with this numbering system the Metro was renamed as the Rover 100 in 1994 – the same year as the Maestro and Montego were axed.

In 1991 Rover updated the 800 series and added the trademark radiator grille that was eventually used on all Rovers. Two years later the 600 saloon was launched which shared a lot of it mechanical components with the Honda Accord.

BMW acquired the Rover Group in 1995 and with that move came the last car developed with Honda – the new 400, which was based on the five-door Civic.

With Honda gone the next car was the new 'all-Rover' 200. This could be had as a three or five door hatchback with a choice of two petrol engines or a diesel.

In 1997 the 100 was dropped and the following year, thanks to an investment of £700 million by BMW, the 75 executive saloon was launched. Five different engines were offered, four petrols of 1795cc to 2947cc capacity, and a BMW diesel unit of 1951cc. It also had five-link rear suspension as on the BMW 3 Series.

In 1999 the 200 and 400 were restyled as the 25 and 45, but in 2000 BMW decided to sell the Rover Group, only keeping the Mini brand.

The firm was eventually bought by the Phoenix Consortium. Its ownership and vehicles will be covered later. ◆

In 1991 Rover introduced its trademark chrome-plated radiator grille. This is a Vitesse Sport of 1994. *Photo National Motor Museum.*

MINI

The Mini was a revolutionary design that changed small car design forever. Conceived as a car to counter a fuel shortage in the 1950s, it went on to achieve cult status and was made for over 40 years.

Left: The Mini's creator, Sir Alec Issigonis. *Photo National Motor Museum.*

Below: The Mini became the car to own in the 1960s. This Cooper S belonged to George Harrison of the Beatles. *Photo National Motor Museum.*

In the late 1950s a new type of car was to be seen in increasing numbers on Britain's roads. This was the 'bubble car', a small car fitted with a small motorcycle type engine, and most were imported from Germany such as the BMW Isetta and the Messerschmitt KR. The reason they were becoming so common was due to the fuel shortage caused by the Suez Crisis of 1956.

Despite their popularity with many members of the motoring public there was one person who couldn't stand them, BMC boss Leonard Lord. He decided that if the people wanted a small car BMC would design a proper one for them.

The job was given to engineer Alec Issigonis, the designer of the incredibly popular Morris Minor.

Issigonis was born in 1906 in Turkey. His father was Greek but had taken British citizenship and ran a local engineering works. Unfortunately during the First World War the Germans confiscated their property and interned his family. With the war over more political violence saw the family once again driven from their home. His father died soon after in Malta and Alec and his mother moved to Britain virtually penniless.

MINI VAN & PICK-UP

Alec then spent three years studying mechanical engineering before getting his first job with an engineering consultancy that at the time was designing a semi-automatic gearbox. He then moved to the car maker Humber before taking a job at Morris Motors in 1936.

He stayed at Morris throughout the Second World War and in 1948 the firm launched his first car design, the Morris Minor. This became a massive success but when Morris became part of BMC in 1952, Issigonis decided to leave.

He ended up at Alvis where he designed an advanced luxury car that was fitted with a 3.5-litre V8 engine. Unfortunately it never went into production for cost reasons although a prototype was built and tested.

Leonard Lord had long been impressed with Issigonis's work and in 1956 invited him to return to BMC to design Project ADO15, which would become the Mini.

The design brief was simple. The car would have to fit in an imaginary box 10ft x 4ft x 4ft, with the passenger space taking up 6ft of the 10ft length. In addition an existing engine had to be fitted in order to keep costs down.

The engine chosen was the BMC 'A' series four cylinder unit from the Austin A40 but enlarged to 848cc. However, in order to get the required cabin room Issigonis had to come up with some ingenious ideas. Firstly the engine was turned through 90° and was fitted transversely. The front wheels were then driven via a four-speed gearbox which was then placed directly under the engine in the sump. The gearbox was lubricated by the engine oil. The radiator was mounted on the nearside of the car so that precious space could be saved.

The suspension was also new and was designed by Dr Alex Moulton. This used rubber cones instead of steel springs and so saved even more space. This set-up gave the car its famous 'go-kart' like handling that would make it such a success in motorsport over the years.

The next problem was the wheels and tyres. In the end a 10in wheel was decided upon and Dunlop agreed to start manufacture of suitable tyres.

The intended name for this new car was the 'Newmarket' but when it was launched to world in 1959 it had become either the Morris Mini-Minor or the Austin Seven, or Se7en as it was sometimes advertised. The name Mini was used as of 1961.

Initial sales were disappointing but things soon picked up, although the profit on each car was quite low. In fact many say there was no profit in the car at all at the time. Ford famously agreed, and after taking one apart it was worked out that BMC was losing around £30 on each car.

It wasn't long before the superb handling of the Mini came to the attention of motorsport enthusiasts. However, with only an 848cc engine something needed to be done. The answer came from racing car builder John Cooper who enlarged the engine to 997cc, tuned it and fitted it with twin SU carburettors. This upped the power to 65bhp and the top speed to 85mph.

BMC authorised the Cooper conversion and in 1962 the BMC Competition Department started rallying them. Over the next few years the firm's list of rally victories was astounding. These included the 1962 German, Swedish, Tulip and Route du Nord rallies. The following year the Mini Cooper S appeared that had a 1071cc engine, quickly followed by a 1275cc version. These cars went on to win the Monte Carlo Rally in 1964, 65, 66 and 67, although the 1966 victory was disqualified due to a minor rule infringement to do with the headlight dipping system. ›

The Mini was available in many different guises, including vans and pick-ups.

The Mini Cooper became very successful in international rallying. This is Paddy Hopkirk taking part in the 1968 Monte Carlo Rally. *Photo National Motor Museum.*

Minis also took to the tracks. In 1961 a pre-Cooper Mini driven by Sir John Whitmore won the British Saloon Car Championship. The following year John Love repeated the win in a Mini Cooper.

The Mini Cooper was made until 1967 and the Cooper S until 1971. The name would however return many years later.

VARIANTS

`It wasn't long after the launch of the Mini in 1959 that variants were introduced. These included estates (the Morris Mini Traveller and Austin Mini Countryman), vans and pick-ups. There were also the Wolseley Hornet and Riley Elf versions that had reworked front and rear styling and a lot more luxury, and the Mini Moke which had been designed for military use but went on instead to be a cult fun car.

Throughout the 1960s the Mini became the car to own and was driven by all manner of celebrities. In addition it also ended up as a film star, and its best performance has got to be The Italian Job of 1969.

In 1969 British Leyland decided to introduce the Clubman to replace the Elf and Hornet variants. This had a squarer front end that made it look a bit like a small Maxi. There was also an estate and the 1275GT that was the sports model. The Mini actually became a marque of its own the following year.

To its credit BL didn't drop the original design and continued to offer it alongside the Clubman. It's quite a good job really as the Clubman never really captured people's hearts as the original car had done. As a result the Clubman only lasted until 1980 while the original design went on for much longer.

In 1976 the four millionth Mini rolled off the assembly line, which was a production record for British cars. However, 10 years later another million Minis had gone on the road.

There were a few changes of design throughout the 1970s including the fitment of 12in wheels and a heated rear window. Front disc brakes became standard on all Minis in 1984 but by 1992 the only engine available was the 1275cc which had a catalytic converter.

Later, 1999 saw the welcome return of the Mini Cooper S which had a 90bhp engine. It also had an airbag and five-speed gearbox.

Production of the Mini continued until 2000 when BMW put the name on a completely new car. It has shades of the original Mini about it but one thing it isn't is small, as anyone who's ever seen an original Mini and the BMW version side-by-side will tell you. An estate was also brought out, which revived the Clubman name and diesel engines became available, even on the Cooper models which really dosen't seem right. But that is a totally different story. ✦

End of EMPIRE

When the British Leyland Motor Corporation was founded in 1968 it was the second largest vehicle maker in Europe, just behind Volkswagen. At times the BL expansion almost made it number one. But various problems had always plagued the firm and eventually it was renamed Rover Group because British Leyland was just regarded as too much of a failure.

In 1986 a Canadian businessman named Graham Day was appointed as managing director of BL. Upon taking control he decided that the name British Leyland was now regarded with derision and so dropped it and renamed the firm the Rover Group plc. This was the Thatcher era and privatisation was now the name of the game. Jaguar had already escaped and done very well, so what about the rest of the group?

The following year, 1987, the company allowed its Leyland Truck division to merge with Dutch commercial vehicle maker DAF. This firm became Leyland DAF but unfortunately collapsed in 1993. Three firms rose from the ashes, DAF Trucks and Leyland Trucks, both of which are now part of the American giant PACCAR, who have long owned the US truck makers Kenworth and Peterbilt among others. The other survivor was Leyland DAF vans who made the Sherpa van descendents, the Convoy and Pilot (see separate chapter).

1987 saw the departure of Unipart, the vehicle spare parts business set up in 1974 by John Egan, who went on to get Jaguar privatised. I'm pleased to say Unipart still exist at the time of writing.

One year later Leyland Bus was purchased by Volvo, and again is still trading very successfully to this day. Later that year the rest of the Rover Group was purchased by British Aerospace for £150million. Graham Day became joint chairman while Kevin Morley, who previously had been the Rover Group's marketing manager became the managing director of Rover Cars.

In 1989 the company name was changed again, this time to Rover Group Holdings and in 1994 the company was purchased by the German vehicle maker BMW for the price of £800million.

Many have wondered about why Rover should be so attractive to a firm such as BMW. The answer is simple; Rover produced two vehicle types it didn't – a small compact car, the Mini and a four-wheel-drive, the Land/Range Rover. ›

Above: A 2002 Rover 25. *Photo National Motor Museum.*

Below: The Rover 75 was developed using BMW money. *Photo National Motor Museum.*

– 129 –

To give BMW its due it spent an awful lot of money on Rover trying to turn it into a successful company. Millions were spent for example on the development of the Rover 75 executive saloon, which also used some BMW components including its diesel engine.

Other big investments included the development of the Land Rover Freelander and the Series II Discovery. The Freelander was particularly important as it was the first Land Rover that was aimed specifically at the 'soft roader' market – a four-wheel-drive that was bought by people that would never dream of taking it off-road. That's not to say it couldn't go off-road, and had such innovative features as a hill descent control that used the vehicle's antilock brakes to bring the car down a slippery off-road hill safely. It was also a decent tow-car and became the best selling 4x4 in Europe for several years.

However, BMW was very disappointed with Rover and in 2000 decided to sell the company. Surprisingly it didn't hold on to Land Rover which was purchased by Ford. The company had however by then started to produce an inferior vehicle in the X5 that used a lot of Land Rover technology. Inferior? Yes – flash as it may be it just can't go where a Land Rover can go and there's no point in pretending otherwise. BMW did however decide to keep hold of the Mini brand – together with a few other names from the British motor industry's past that may or may not resurface at some point in the future.

After it looked like the buyer of the rest of the company would be the Alchemy Partners, the eventual buyers were Phoenix Venture Holdings. This firm continued production at Longbridge but planned a fantastic future for the firm. This was backed up by legislation that stated that if a firm goes bankrupt within three years, the previous owner, if there was one, is responsible for any redundancy payments. This would cost BMW some £427million, including stocks of assembled cars.

The Phoenix plan was to concentrate on the MG sports car side, particularly the MGF. Other cars were also introduced including an Anglo-American hybrid that used a Rover body fitted with a Ford Mustang V8.

Over the next few years Phoenix managed to reduce the firm's losses but unfortunately never made a profit. As well as that the company's sales between 2003 and 2004 actually fell and so in April 2005 the firm ceased trading.

The previous year MG Rover as it was then known had signed an agreement with the Shanghai Automotive Industry Corporation of China (SAIC) to jointly develop new cars. Unfortunately the deal had to be ratified by the Chinese government who concluded that if BMW couldn't save MG Rover nobody could. In addition the Indian car maker TATA, who supplied the car that was re-badged as the 'City Rover', was unsure of whether it would continue to supply cars if the deal went through.

However the killer blow came when the Labour government decided to withdraw the offer of a £120million loan in order to see the deal through. Several other potential buyers then stepped forward including Sir Richard Branson who hoped to revive the firm to make hybrid electric cars. In the end SAIC acquired the rights to several vehicles including the Rover 75. Everything else was purchased by the Nanjing Automobile Group of China.

NAG soon started stripping the machinery from Longbridge and shipping it to China where production of several models would continue.

Today MG Motor, with all cars made in China, markets itself as "a truly international car brand at the forefront of delivering a range of vehicles that lead the electric revolution."

So that's it. What a sad end to so many iconic British vehicle makers. There are survivors – Land Rover, Jaguar, Unipart, Mini, Swindon Pressings (Pressed Steel), Leyland trucks, and a few other obscure parts of BL. I'm glad they've survived but it really is a poor reflection of what might have been. ✦

BMW hung onto the Mini brand for its own version of the car. *Photo National Motor Museum.*